STURTEVANT

DRAWING DOUBLE REVERSAL

TABLE OF CONTENTS
INHALTSVERZEICHNIS

FOREWORD AND ACKNOWLEDGEMENTS

Here at the MMK Museum für Moderne Kunst Frankfurt am Main, we are delighted to join the Albertina in Vienna and the Nationalgalerie in the Hamburger Bahnhof in Berlin to present the first major museum exhibition of the drawing œuvre of the American artist Elaine Sturtevant, who last lived in Paris.

This catalog is being published in conjunction with the first large-scale exhibition ever devoted to the drawings of this artist. Born in Lakewood, Ohio, Sturtevant attained outstanding importance for the history of art of the second half of the twentieth century. Featuring more than one hundred of her drawings, the show provides in-depth insight into her graphic work over four decades, from 1964 to 2004.

The results of the research on Sturtevant's graphic work suggest that her early drawings of the 1960s are the key to understanding her uncompromising conceptual œuvre. Particularly the so-called "Composite Drawings" of 1965 and 1966 convey an impression of her artistic thought and her status in art history as a kind of "mega Pop" or "Pop surplus."

Over the past 50 years, Sturtevant developed what is perhaps the most radical œuvre of her generation, an œuvre distinguished by rigorous and unwavering conceptual thought. Concerned with more than the mere contemplation of art, she aimed for a change in attitude. She irritated and provoked art appreciators and the art world alike by replicating the original works of contemporary artists, which she used—surprisingly soon after the "original"—as a source and catalyst for "expanding and developing current aesthetic ideas, examining the concept of originality and exploring the relationship between original and originality, as well as accessing space for new thinking." (Sturtevant)

Two years ago, Sturtevant received the Golden Lion for Lifetime Achievement from the 54th Venice Biennale, and last fall she was awarded the prestigious Kurt Schwitters Prize in Hanover.

We would hereby like to extend our thanks posthumously first and foremost to Sturtevant, who accompanied this project with all of her energy and passion, and without whose untiring dedication and generosity such an exhibition never could have been realized.

We are likewise sincerely indebted to Loren Muzzey for her consistent and continual support of this undertaking. Over the past two years, Mario Kramer, the head of the MMK collection, developed an exhibition concept in close collaboration with the artist. We would like to express our heartfelt appreciation to the numerous private and institutional lenders for their willingness to part with their Sturtevant works, some of which are very fragile, for a relatively long period of time. The following individuals and institutions contributed in myriad ways to the realization of the exhibition and the catalog, and for that we owe them our very special thanks: Guillaume Benaich, Studio Sturtevant, Paris; Emilie Bannwarth, Paris; Emily Bates, New York; Lionel Bovier, JRP|Ringier Publisher, Zurich; Gavin Brown's enterprise, New York; Collection de Bruin-Heijn; Bénédicte Burrus, Paris; Lucy Chadwick, New York; Meredith Darrow, Venice, CA; Virginia Dwan, New York; Lonti Ebers, New York; Peter Eleey, New York; Detlev Gretenkort, Munich; Aladin and Maxime Guinnebault, Paris; Bruce Hainley, Los Angeles; Mark Kelman, New York; Markus Kormann, Salzburg; Anne Kovach, New York; Ingrid Langston, New York; Matthieu Lelièvre, Paris; Michael Lobel, New York; Michael Loulakis, Frankfurt am Main; Paul Maenz, Berlin; Gabriele and Tilman Osterwold, Stuttgart; Renaud Pillon, Paris; Collection Ringier, Zurich; Galerie Thaddaeus Ropac, Paris/Salzburg; Christina Ruf, Zurich; Katrin Sauerländer, Frankfurt am Main; Bridgette Toraason, Venice, CA; Gerd de Vries, Berlin; Robin Wright and Ian Reeves, and further persons who wish to remain anonymous.

Susanne Gaensheimer
Director of the MMK Museum für Moderne Kunst Frankfurt am Main

Klaus Albrecht Schröder
Director of the Albertina, Vienna

Udo Kittelmann
Director of the Nationalgalerie, Staatliche Museen zu Berlin

VORWORT UND DANK

Es ist für das MMK Museum für Moderne Kunst Frankfurt am Main eine große Freude, gemeinsam mit der Albertina in Wien und der Nationalgalerie im Hamburger Bahnhof in Berlin die erste große Museumsausstellung zum zeichnerischen Werk der zuletzt in Paris lebenden Amerikanerin Elaine Sturtevant zu präsentieren.

Der Katalog begleitet die erste große Ausstellung, die den Zeichnungen Sturtevants gewidmet ist. Sie unterstreicht die herausragende Bedeutung der in Lakewood, Ohio geborenen Künstlerin für die Kunstgeschichte der zweiten Hälfte des 20. Jahrhunderts. Die Ausstellung, die mehr als 100 von Sturtevants Zeichnungen zeigen wird, erlaubt einen konzentrierten Blick auf die grafischen Arbeiten der Künstlerin über vier Jahrzehnte, von 1964 bis 2004.

Die Forschungsergebnisse zu Sturtevants grafischem Werk legen nahe, dass ihre frühen Zeichnungen der 1960er Jahre der Schlüssel zum Verständnis des kompromisslosen konzeptuellen Werks der Künstlerin sind. Insbesondere ihre Zeichnungen von 1965 und 1966, die sogenannten „Composite Drawings", geben eine Vorstellung von Sturtevants künstlerischem Denken und ihrem Status in der Kunstgeschichte als eine Art „Mega-Pop" oder „Pop Surplus".

In den letzten 50 Jahren erarbeitete sich Sturtevant das vielleicht radikalste Werk ihrer Generation, das durch ein rigoroses und beharrliches konzeptuelles Denken bestimmt wird. Ihr geht es um mehr als um die Betrachtung von Kunst, sie zielt auf eine Veränderung der Geisteshaltung. Sie irritiert und provoziert die Kunstbetrachter und gleichermaßen den Kunstbetrieb durch die Wiederholung von Originalwerken zeitgenössischer Künstler, die sie – überraschend zeitnah zum „Original" – als Quelle und Katalysator nutzt, um unsere „gegenwärtige Vorstellung von Ästhetik zu erweitern und zu entwickeln, Originalität zu erforschen und die Beziehung von Original zu Originalität zu erkunden und Raum für neues Denken zu eröffnen". (Sturtevant)

Vor zwei Jahren erhielt Sturtevant auf der 54. Biennale in Venedig den Goldenen Löwen für ihr Lebenswerk und im letzten Herbst wurde sie in Hannover mit dem prestigeträchtigen Kurt-Schwitters-Preis ausgezeichnet.

Unser postumer Dank gilt allen voran Sturtevant, die dieses Projekt mit all ihrer Kraft und Leidenschaft begleitet hat und ohne deren Großzügigkeit und unermüdliches Engagement eine solche Ausstellung nie hätte realisiert werden können.

Herzlich danken möchten wir ebenfalls Loren Muzzey für ihre begleitende und fortwährende Unterstützung dieses Vorhabens. In den vergangenen zwei Jahren entwickelte Mario Kramer, Sammlungsleiter am MMK, das Ausstellungskonzept in enger Zusammenarbeit mit der Künstlerin. Ein herzlicher Dank geht an die zahlreichen privaten und institutionellen Leihgeber, die sich für einen verhältnismäßig langen Ausstellungszeitraum von ihren zum Teil sehr empfindlichen Werken getrennt haben. In vielfältiger Weise haben folgende Personen und Institutionen zur Verwirklichung der Ausstellung und des Kataloges beigetragen. Ihnen gilt unserer ganz besonderer Dank: Guillaume Benaich, Atelier Sturtevant, Paris; Emilie Bannwarth, Paris; Emily Bates, New York; Lionel Bovier, JRP|Ringier Kunstverlag, Zürich; Gavin Brown's enterprise, New York; Collection de Bruin-Heijn; Bénédicte Burrus, Paris; Lucy Chadwick, New York; Meredith Darrow, Venice, CA; Virginia Dwan, New York; Lonti Ebers, New York; Peter Eleey, New York; Detlev Gretenkort, München; Aladin und Maxime Guinnebault, Paris; Bruce Hainley, Los Angeles; Mark Kelman, New York; Markus Kormann, Salzburg; Anne Kovach, New York; Ingrid Langston, New York; Matthieu Lelièvre, Paris; Michael Lobel, New York; Michael Loulakis, Frankfurt am Main; Paul Maenz, Berlin; Gabriele und Tilman Osterwold, Stuttgart; Renaud Pillon, Paris; Sammlung Ringier, Zürich; Galerie Thaddaeus Ropac, Paris/Salzburg; Christina Ruf, Zürich; Katrin Sauerländer, Frankfurt am Main; Bridgette Toraason, Venice, CA; Gerd de Vries, Berlin; Robin Wright und Ian Reeves sowie weiteren Personen, die ungenannt bleiben möchten.

Susanne Gaensheimer
Direktorin MMK Museum für Moderne Kunst Frankfurt am Main

Klaus Albrecht Schröder
Direktor der Albertina, Wien

Udo Kittelmann
Direktor Nationalgalerie, Staatliche Museen zu Berlin

INTRODUCTION
STURTEVANT DRAWING DOUBLE REVERSAL

Exactly ten years have passed since the MMK Museum für Moderne Kunst Frankfurt am Main presented the first comprehensive–and, indeed, ground-breaking–Sturtevant show. On that occasion, for the first time ever, the MMK devoted the entire museum building to a single artistic œuvre. And within that context, a catalogue raisonné of the artist's paintings, sculptures, film and video works of the years 1964 to 2004 was published by the MMK. Major Sturtevant exhibitions were subsequently staged at the Musée d'Art moderne de la Ville de Paris, the Moderna Museet in Stockholm, the Kunsthalle Zürich, the Serpentine Gallery in London and, most recently, at the Julia Stoschek Collection in Düsseldorf.

The current show is the first to feature a selection of more than one hundred drawings from throughout the Sturtevant œuvre from 1964 to the present. The earliest drawings in this exhibition mark the commencement of the artist's work fifty years ago. From the beginning, Sturtevant consistently pursued the strategy of simultaneity between her own art and that of her contemporaries. In its chronology, the selection of drawings of four decades mirrors the course of Sturtevant's overall œuvre. Her works on paper are characterized by high quality, precise craftsmanship, and great artistic freedom. It took in-depth research to bring together the works from private collections in Europe and the U.S. as well as the artist's archive. Eighty of them are on exhibit for the first time.

Even her first exhibition catalog of 1971 revealed the great importance the artist attached to her drawings. The publication by the Reese Palley Gallery of New York entitled *Studies Done for Beuys' Action Objects and Drawings* contains reproductions of six drawings. The Bess Cutler Gallery in New York presented a show exclusively featuring drawings in 1988, as did the Galerie Daniel Blau in Munich in 2002; in both cases Sturtevant was involved in the planning.

Born in Lakewood, Ohio, in the 1960s the artist lived and worked in New York City. It was there that, in 1965 and 1966, she executed the so-called "Composite Drawings," which convey an impression of her radical artistic thought. In that period, Sturtevant cultivated very close and productive relationships with fellow artists such as Jasper Johns and Robert Rauschenberg. Her first solo exhibition in 1965, staged by the Bianchini Gallery in New York, amounted to a critical commentary on the art world of the time and its marketing strategies, and as such played a key role for the protagonists of American Pop art. That now legendary show and Sturtevant's first solo exhibition in Europe–*America America* at the

Galerie J in Paris in 1966—can both be referred to as "composite exhibitions" in correspondence with her drawings of the period in question. In New York, Sturtevant juxtaposed her *Warhol Flowers* (1964/65) with a *Johns Flag* (1965/66), a *Stella Benjamin Moore* (1964), etc. In Paris, her *Study for Rosenquist Spaghetti Grass* (1966) shared the space with an *Oldenburg Hamburger* (1966) and a *Wesselmann Great American Nude* (1966).

In her early drawings, such as *Study Johns 0–9 Lichtenstein Hot Dog* [p. 49], *Wesselmann Great American Nude Johns Flag* [p. 54], *Warhol Flowers Lichtenstein Pointed Hand* [p. 63] or *Johns 0–9 Rosenquist Spaghetti* [p. 67], Sturtevant devoted herself to her immediate artistic environment and thus to the prototypical American Pop art artists. Employing a collage technique, she united various motifs by various artists in a single work. *Warhol Flowers*, for example, encounters the famous Uncle Sam gesture "I want you for the U.S. Army" in *Lichtenstein Pointed Finger* [p. 62]. And when—to cite a further example—the highly stylized and identity-less female nude in *Wesselmann Great American Nude* is combined with *Lichtenstein Hot Dog* [p. 64], Sturtevant intensifies the sexual connotations by compositional means. The artist stressed: "I have nothing to do with feminism."

In 1966, Sturtevant began commuting regularly between New York and Paris, and in 1967 she consequently turned to Marcel Duchamp. All of the abovementioned artists of her generation and artistic milieu were interested in the work of Marcel Duchamp, who was still alive at the time. The choices she made in the context of her preoccupation with Duchamp are significant for her drawings. The *Duchamp Rotary Discs* series [pp. 78–89] illustrates the principle of contra-rotation as within a loop. The idea of animated drawing in the style of an optical toy already anticipates the video works of Sturtevant's late phase.

Her interest in Joseph Beuys from 1969 onward, on the other hand, comes as quite a surprise. It was a point in time at which hardly anyone in the U.S. was truly acquainted with Beuys's œuvre. Even in the German-speaking world, Beuys had not been known to a wider art-interested public until his first museum exhibition in Mönchengladbach in 1967 and the 1969/70 traveling exhibition of the Karl Ströher collection. Not only her duplication of Beuys's famous *Fat Chair* or her filmic re-enactments of his actions in her studio in New York, for which she donned the German artist's characteristic garb, but above all the drawings [pp. 96–101] are astonishing. At this early point in time, Sturtevant could have been acquainted with Beuys's work only from the few publications by the Kunstmuseum Basel (1969/70) and the Moderna Museet in Stockholm (1971). Those volumes contain illustrations of all of the Beuys pieces she "processed" in her own work. All the more amazing is the extent of her appropriation of his seismographic drawing style and her unrestrained handling of the same. Finally, in what would be her last solo exhibition for many years, mounted at the Onnasch Gallery in New York in 1974, she exhibited exclusively Beuys-related works.

Faced with increasing incomprehension, harsh criticism, distrust and misunderstandings, Sturtevant ceased her artistic production in 1974. It was not until a decade later, in 1985, that she made her fulminant reappearance in the art world, uncompromisingly picking up where her early work had left off. Perhaps it was only now that the post-modern zeitgeist was ready for a new assessment and appreciation of her work. Today, in an age in which we encounter the world increasingly in media-processed form, Sturtevant's œuvre appears more topical than ever, and of eminent significance. What, we might ask, is reality and what is fiction in our world; what is original and what is copy? In the areas of film and music, we have grown accustomed to using such terms as "sampling," "remix," "cover versions" and "remake" without batting an eyelash.

In the mid eighties, Sturtevant also resumed her work in the drawing medium. Her intuitive sense of artistic phenomena and her foresight led her to Keith Haring's chalk drawings [p. 105]. Eventually she produced extensive groups of drawings, which took her back to her own artistic beginnings: the so-called *Reversal Series*. In 1988, entering a kind of infinity loop, she once again devoted herself to Roy Lichtenstein [pp. 111–130] and in 1990 to Jasper Johns [pp. 133–165]. This development may have been inspired by the exhibitions of Roy Lichtenstein's drawings at the MoMA in 1987 and of Jasper Johns's at the National Gallery of Art in Washington in 1990. Drawings such as the *Lichtenstein Study for Two Paintings, Folded Sheets* (1988) [p. 125] represent an unbroken continuation of her early "Composite Drawings," as Roy Lichtenstein's original already combined two artworks: a motif by Jasper Johns and his own work *Sketches of Brushstrokes*.

Sturtevant's last group of works, dating from 2000 onward, is devoted to notations for her video works in storyboard style. One case in point is the *Dillinger Running Series* [p. 168], in which—taking her cue from Beuys's 1974 action—she assumes the role of the notorious American gangster John Dillinger; another is *Dark Threat of Absence Fragmented & Sliced* [pp. 169–171], in which she cites Paul McCarthy and advertising images produced by the American television industry.

Öyvind Fahlström's *Krazy Kat* figure appears again and again throughout Sturtevant's drawing œuvre from 1965 onward. In his works of the early sixties, Fahlström frequently quoted the comic strip of the same name by George Herriman. After moving to New York in 1961, the Swedish artist had been featured in a number of exhibitions in the context of the American Pop art artists, for example at the Sidney Janis Gallery. Sturtevant had a special penchant for the absurd adventures of these comic strip characters, for the subversive game of cat-and-mouse devoid of any morals whatsoever [pp. 58; 106–110; 172]. Krazy Kat can also be seen as a kind of Sturtevant alter ego and the source of what could almost be her life motto: "The *Krazy Kat* that walks by herself."

With her reproductive method, Sturtevant followed and expanded on Marcel Duchamp in the sense that she took existing artworks as her models. The results are "anti-readymades," for what she created are original "Sturtevants." The title of the MMK exhibition ten years ago was, accordingly, *The brutal truth is that it is not a copy*. "The emotional and intellectual shock of encountering a known object whose contents are then denied, even if it doesn't trigger immediate rejection, always causes erratic and bewildering trains of thought. They lead to a loss of balance which promotes thought."[1]

Sturtevant placed duplicated originals at the side of her contemporaries' artworks. In connection with the conceptual principle of her œuvre, she herself cited "the force of non-identity." After all, her "parallel connections" represent the logical continuation of the line of succession formed by Duchamp's readymades, Warhol's silkscreens and Beuys's multiples.

The exhibition STURTEVANT DRAWING DOUBLE REVERSAL is enhanced by Sturtevant's early artist's books [pp. 174–177] and the original materials, drawings, sketches and collages she employed for the draft of her artist's book *The Brutal Truth*, appearing in conjunction with her solo exhibition at the MMK in 2003/04 [p. 178]. Conceptually, this group of works culminates in the artist's book *STURTEVANT, Author of the QUIXOTE* [pp. 180–181], not published until 2009, although she produced the original manuscript in Paris in September 1970. In a virtual dialogue with the Argentine author Jorge Luis Borges, Sturtevant here expanded on his famous short story *Pierre Menard, autor del Quijote* (1939) about a fictional author who undertook to rewrite Miguel de Cervantes's *Don Quixote*. In the original text, Cervantes also has his tale recounted by a fictional narrator, Cide Hamete Benengli. In a manner consistent with her overall œuvre, Sturtevant here embarked on a large-scale thought experiment with the concepts of authorship, the original, the genuine creator role and the identity of the work. If the "Menard" case is a model of literary production, then the "Sturtevant" case is a continuing process. Every one of the works she took as a model thus assumed a kind of un-ending quality. The artist explored the relationship between original and originality and put both up for negotiation. In this context, aura, authenticity, innovativeness, individuality, uniqueness and genuineness are all synonyms of the original. Sturtevant adopted "the beauty of repetition" as her artistic strategy. Her works are the echo of their models in the present. They function like mirrors without the reversal of the image; they are perceptibility themselves and thus the quintessence of art.

A look at Sturtevant's overall œuvre with a special focus on her drawings reveals the extent to which she has concentrated on the once-formulated issues since the very beginning in 1964, and how she has insisted on the once-made selection of pictorial motifs. Hers was an exceedingly radical gesture, which vehemently resisted every flood of images. Sturtevant's art is undoubtedly one of the most interesting and exceptional contributions to contemporary art. Although her name goes unmentioned in the majority of art-historical discussions of Pop and Concept art, her work is essential for understanding both movements. The exhibition of Sturtevant's drawings sheds new light on this aspect of recent art history.

As Robert Fleck—an established authority on her œuvre—pointed out on the occasion of a symposium on the artist's work taking place at the MMK in 2004: "Sturtevant drew her conclusions from the Pop art and the Concept art of the 1960s. And with them, she carried out a pictorial revolution. Already her first work, *Johns Flag* of 1964, was consummate in the sense of her entire œuvre. There was nothing left to be developed. Like a philosopher, she thinks things through to the end with intellectual rigor and veracity."[2] And John Waters, a close artist friend of Sturtevant's, remarked the following in an interview about the artist: "Getting right down to it. Cutting out all the stuff that doesn't matter. Down to the bone. That is what I admire about Sturtevant's work: no messing around. Very brutal."[3]

The exhibition is accompanied by this publication, which was produced in close cooperation with the artist. Apart from a few non-locatable exceptions it contains a complete catalog of her drawing œuvre. In this sense, it is a catalogue raisonné—a "first draft," as Sturtevant would insist.

Mario Kramer
Curator of the exhibition and head of the collection of the MMK
Museum für Moderne Kunst Frankfurt am Main

1   Sturtevant in: Ursula Frohne, "Das Meisterwerk als Double," Uwe Fleckner (ed.) *Jenseits der Grenzen, vol 3: Dialog der Avantgarden*, DuMont, Cologne 2000, p. 271.

2   Robert Fleck, "Sturtevant und die Idee des Radikalismus in der zeitgenössischen Kunst," a lecture held at the symposium "STURTEVANT: The Beauty of Repetition," October 30, 2004, MMK Museum für Moderne Kunst Frankfurt am Main.

3   John Waters, "STURTEVANT AS STURTEVANT AS STURTEVANT IS JOHN WATERS AS JOHN WATERS AS JOHN WATERS IS," MMK Museum für Moderne Kunst Frankfurt am Main, Udo Kittelmann and Mario Kramer (ed.), *Sturtevant The Brutal Truth*, Hatje Cantz, Ostfildern 2004, p. 52.

EINFÜHRUNG
STURTEVANT DRAWING DOUBLE REVERSAL

Es liegt genau zehn Jahre zurück, dass das MMK Museum für Moderne Kunst Frankfurt am Main die erste umfangreiche und durchaus wegweisende Werkschau von Sturtevant zeigte. Das MMK widmete aus diesem Anlass erstmals das gesamte Museumsgebäude einem einzigen künstlerischen Œuvre. Hierzu erschien der vom MMK herausgegebene *Catalogue Raisonné* der Gemälde, Skulpturen, Film- und Videoarbeiten der Künstlerin von 1964 bis 2004. In der Folge hatte Sturtevant große Einzelausstellungen im Musée d'Art moderne de la Ville de Paris, im Moderna Museet Stockholm, der Kunsthalle Zürich, der Serpentine Gallery in London und zuletzt in der Julia Stoschek Collection in Düsseldorf.

Die aktuelle Ausstellung zeigt erstmals eine Auswahl von über 100 Zeichnungen aus dem gesamten künstlerischen Schaffen Sturtevants von 1964 bis zur Gegenwart. Mit den frühesten Zeichnungen in dieser Ausstellung aus der Mitte der 1960er Jahre blickt man zurück auf eine Werkgeschichte, die vor 50 Jahren ihren Anfang nahm. Die Simultanität der Werke Sturtevants zu denen ihrer Zeitgenossen blieb die kontinuierliche Strategie der Künstlerin. Die Auswahl der Zeichnungen aus vier Jahrzehnten bildet in ihrer Chronologie gleichsam den Werklauf des Gesamtwerkes Sturtevants ab. Hohe Qualität, handwerkliche Präzision und große künstlerische Freiheit zeichnen das grafische Werk der Künstlerin aus. Die Arbeiten, von denen 80 erstmalig ausgestellt werden, wurden nach aufwendiger Recherche aus Privatsammlungen in Europa, den USA und dem Archiv der Künstlerin zusammengetragen.

Welch hohen Wert die Zeichnungen für die Künstlerin hatten, macht bereits der erste Ausstellungskatalog von 1971 deutlich: in *Studies done for Beuys' Actions Objects and Drawings* der Reese Palley Gallery in New York sind sechs Zeichnungen abgebildet. 1988 fanden in der Bess Cutler Gallery in New York und 2002 in der Galerie Daniel Blau in München reine Zeichnungs-Ausstellungen statt, die Sturtevant selbst mitkonzipiert hatte.

Während der 1960er Jahre lebte und arbeitete die in Lakewood, Ohio geborene Künstlerin in New York City. Hier entstanden in den Jahren 1965 und 1966 die sogenannten „Composite Drawings", die eine Vorstellung von dem radikalen künstlerischen Denken Sturtevants vermitteln. In dieser Zeit pflegte Sturtevant eine sehr enge und produktive Beziehung zu Künstlerfreunden wie Jasper Johns und Robert Rauschenberg. Ihre erste Einzelausstellung 1965 in der Bianchini Gallery in New York spielte als kritischer Kommentar zur aktuellen Kunstszene und ihrer Vermarktung eine Schlüsselrolle für die Künstler der amerikanischen Pop Art. Sowohl diese mittlerweile legendäre Ausstellung als auch ihre erste europäische Einzelausstellung *America America* in der Galerie J in Paris 1966 könnte man in Anlehnung an die Zeichnungen dieser Zeit als „Composite Exhibitions" bezeichnen. Sturtevant kombinierte in New York u.a. ihre *Warhol Flowers* (1964/65) mit einer *Johns Flag* (1965/66) oder einem *Stella Benjamin Moore* (1964). In Paris traf ihre *Study for Rosenquist Spaghetti Grass* (1966) auf einen *Oldenburg Hamburger* (1966) und eine *Wesselmann Great American Nude* (1966).

In den frühen Zeichnungen wie *Study Johns 0–9 Lichtenstein Hot Dog* [S. 49] oder *Wesselmann Great American Nude Johns Flag* [S. 54], *Warhol Flowers Lichtenstein Pointed Hand* [S. 63] oder *Johns 0–9 Rosenquist Spaghetti* [S. 67] widmet sich Sturtevant zunächst ihrem engsten künstlerischen Umfeld und damit den Prototypen amerikanischer Pop-Art-Künstler. In einer Art Collagetechnik fügt sie unterschiedliche Motive verschiedener Künstler auf einem Blatt zusammen. So treffen *Warhol Flowers* auf die berühmte Geste Uncle Sams „I want you for the U.S. Army" in *Lichtenstein Pointed Finger* [S. 62]. Und wenn in einem weiteren Beispiel der hoch stilisierte und identitätslose Frauenakt in *Wesselmann Great American Nude* auf *Lichtenstein Hot Dog* [S. 64] trifft, erhöht Sturtevant die sexuellen Konnotationen durch die Bildkomposition. Die Künstlerin betonte: „I have nothing to do with feminism."

Seit 1966 pendelte Sturtevant regelmäßig zwischen New York und Paris und wandte sich ab 1967 konsequenterweise Marcel Duchamp zu. Alle genannten Künstler ihrer Generation und ihres künstlerischen Umfeldes rezipierten damals das Werk von Marcel Duchamp, der zu diesem Zeitpunkt noch lebte. Ihre Auswahl bei der Beschäftigung mit Duchamp ist für ihre Zeichnungen signifikant. Die Serie der *Duchamp Rotary Discs* [S. 78–89] illustriert das Prinzip der gegenläufigen Bewegung wie in einem Loop. Die Idee der animierten Zeichnungen in der Art eines optischen Spielzeugs weist bereits auf das Spätwerk der Videoarbeiten Sturtvants.

Ihre Beschäftigung mit Joseph Beuys ab 1969 überrascht dagegen sehr. Zu diesem Zeitpunkt kannte wohl kaum jemand in Amerika das Werk von Beuys wirklich. Selbst im deutschsprachigen Raum wird Beuys erst ab 1967 mit seiner ersten Museumsausstellung in Mönchengladbach und der Wanderausstellung der Sammlung von Karl Ströher 1969/70 einer größeren kunstinteressierten Öffentlichkeit bekannt. Verblüffend sind nicht nur die Verdopplung des berühmten „Fettstuhls" von Beuys oder die von ihr in ihrem New Yorker Atelier filmisch reinszenierten Aktionen, bei denen sie in das markante Künstlerhabit von Beuys schlüpfte, sondern vor allem die Zeichnungen [S. 96–101]. Sturtevant wird zu diesem frühen Zeitpunkt das Werk von Beuys lediglich aus den wenigen Publikationen des Kunstmuseums Basel (1969/70) und des Moderna Museet in Stockholm (1971) gekannt haben. Hier finden sich alle von ihr rezipierten Beuys-Werke als Abbildungen. Umso erstaunlicher ist das Maß der Aneignung von dessen seismografischem Zeichenstil und des freien Umgangs damit. Schließlich zeigte die Künstlerin in ihrer vorerst letzten Einzelausstellung in der New Yorker Onnasch Gallery 1974 ausschließlich Werke zu Beuys.

Zunehmendes Unverständnis und harsche Kritik an der Künstlerin sowie Misstrauen und Missverständnisse führten dazu, dass Sturtevant 1974 ihr künstlerisches Schaffen aufgab. Erst eine Dekade später, im Jahr 1985, gelingt ihr ein fulminanter Neubeginn, der kompromisslos an das Frühwerk anschließt. Vielleicht war der Zeitgeist der Postmoderne erst jetzt reif für eine neue Ein- und Wertschätzung ihres Werkes. Gerade in unserer Gegenwart, in der uns die Welt zunehmend medial aufbereitet entgegentritt, erscheint das Werk Sturtevants aktueller denn je und von eminenter Bedeutung. Was, so könnte man fragen, ist in unserer Lebenswelt Realität, was Fiktion, was Original, was Kopie? Wir alle sprechen wie selbstverständlich von Sampling, Remix, Coverversionen oder Remake im Bereich des Films oder der Musik.

Ab Mitte der 1980er Jahre setzt Sturtevant ihr zeichnerisches Werk fort. Ihr Gespür für künstlerische Phänomene und ihre Weitsicht führen sie zu den Kreidezeichnungen von Keith Haring [S. 105]. Schließlich entstehen umfangreiche Werkblöcke von Zeichnungen, die zu den künstlerischen Anfängen ihres Werkes zurückführen: die sogenannten *Reversal Series*. Wie in einer Endlosschleife widmet sie sich ab 1988 nochmals Roy Lichtenstein [S. 111–130] und ab 1990 Jasper Johns [S. 133–165]. Auslösender Impuls hierfür mögen die Zeichnungsausstellungen zu Roy Lichtenstein am MoMA 1987 und zu Jasper Johns an der National Gallery of Art in Washington 1990 gewesen sein. Eine Zeichnung wie *Lichtenstein Study for Two Paintings, Folded Sheets* (1988) [S. 125] knüpft unmittelbar an ihre frühen „Composite Drawings" an, denn bereits in der originalen Vorlage von Roy Lichtenstein kombiniert dieser zwei unterschiedliche Kunstwerke miteinander: ein Motiv von Jasper Johns und sein eigenes Werk *Sketches of Brushstrokes*.

Sturtevants letzte Werkgruppe widmet sich ab 2000 den Notationen zu den Videoarbeiten in der Art von Storyboards. Beispielhaft seien hier genannt *Dillinger Running Series* [S. 168], in der sie, vermittelt durch Beuys' Aktion von 1974, als der berüchtigte amerikanische Gangster John Dillinger agiert, oder *Dark Threat of Absence Fragmented & Sliced* [S. 169–171], in dem Paul McCarthy und Werbe-Images der US-amerikanischen Fernsehindustrie zitiert werden.

Durch das gesamte zeichnerische Werk Sturtevants zieht sich ab 1965 wie ein roter Faden das Motiv der Figur *Krazy Kat* nach Öyvind Fahlström, der in seinen Werken der frühen 1960er Jahre häufig den gleichnamigen Comic von George Herriman zitierte. Der schwedische Künstler hatte seit seinem Umzug nach New York 1961 mehrfach im Kontext der amerikanischen Pop-Art-Künstler u.a. in der Sidney Janis Gallery ausgestellt. Sturtevant hatte eine besondere Vorliebe für die absurden Erlebnisse dieser Comic-Figuren, für das subversive Katz-und-Maus-Spiel ohne jegliche Moral [S. 58; 106–110; 172]. Einem Alter Ego vergleichbar könnte man auch Sturtevants Lebensdevise dieser Figur entlehnen: „The *Krazy Kat* that walks by herself."

Sturtevant folgt und erweitert mit ihrer reproduktiven Methode in gewissem Sinne Marcel Duchamp, indem sie bereits existierende Kunstwerke als reales Modell nimmt. Es sind Anti-Readymades, da die Künstlerin originale „Sturtevants" schafft. *The Brutal Truth is that it is not a Copy* lautete dementsprechend der Titel der MMK-Ausstellung vor zehn Jahren. „Der emotionale und intellektuelle Schock, auf ein bekanntes Objekt zu stoßen, dem dann sein Inhalt abgesprochen wird, hat, wenn nicht unmittelbare Ablehnung, unstete und verstörende Gedankengänge zur Folge. Sie führen zu einem Gleichgewichtsverlust, der das Denken immer weiter vorantreibt."[1]

Sturtevant stellt den Kunst-Produktionen ihrer Zeitgenossen ein dupliziertes Original zur Seite. Sie selbst spricht bezüglich der konzeptuellen Grundlagen ihres Werkes von der Kraft der Nicht-Identität („the force of non-identity"). Schließlich finden Duchamps Readymades, Warhols Siebdrucke und Beuys' Multiples in Sturtevants „Parallelschaltungen" ihre konsequente Fortführung.

Die Ausstellung STURTEVANT DRAWING DOUBLE REVERSAL wird ergänzt durch Sturtevants frühe Künstlerbücher [S. 174–177] und die originalen Materialien, Zeichnungen, Skizzen und Collagen, die sie für den Entwurf ihres Künstlerbuches *The Brutal Truth* anlässlich ihrer Einzelausstellung im MMK 2003/2004 verwendete [S. 178]. Ihr erst im Jahr 2009 publiziertes Künstlerbuch *STURTEVANT, Author of the QUIXOTE* bildet hierbei einen konzeptuellen Höhepunkt [S. 180–181]. Das originale Manuskript entstand bereits im September 1970 in Paris. Sturtevant erweiterte hier quasi in einem Dialog mit dem argentinischen Schriftsteller Jorge Luis Borges dessen berühmte Erzählung *Pierre Menard, autor del Quijote* (1939) über einen fiktiven Autor, der sich vorgenommen hat, den *Don Quijote* des Miguel de Cervantes noch einmal zu schreiben. Bereits im Originaltext von Cervantes lässt dieser die Geschichte ebenfalls von einem fiktiven Erzähler, dem Cide Hamete Benengli, berichten. Sturtevant spielt hier, beispielhaft für ihr Gesamtwerk, in einem groß angelegten Gedankenexperiment mit den Konzepten der Autorschaft, des Originals, der genuinen Schöpferrolle und der Identität des Werkes. Wenn der Fall Menard ein Modell literarischer Produktion ist, dann ist der Fall Sturtevant ein fortführender Prozess. Jedes rezipierte Werk hat damit etwas Un-Endliches. Die Künstlerin erkundet dabei auf reflektierte Weise die Beziehung von Original und Originalität und stellt beides zur Disposition. Aura, Authentizität, Innovationszwang, Individualität, Unikat und Echtheitsdefinition sind dabei Synonyme des Originals. Die Ästhetik der Wiederholung, „The Beauty of Repetition", wurde für Sturtevant zur künstlerischen Strategie. Sturtevants produktiv rezipierte Werke sind das Echo ihrer

Vorlagen in unserer Gegenwart. Sie funktionieren wie Spiegel ohne Spiegelverkehrung, sie sind die Wahrnehmbarkeit selbst und damit der Inbegriff von Kunst.

Der Blick auf das Gesamtwerk mit besonderem Fokus auf Sturtevants Zeichnungen macht deutlich, wie sehr sich Sturtevant von Anbeginn im Jahr 1964 auf die einmal formulierten Fragestellungen konzentrierte und wie sie regelrecht auf die einmal getroffene Auswahl von Bildmotiven insistierte. Eine überaus radikale Geste, die sich gegen jegliche Art von Bilderflut vehement wehrte. Sturtevants Kunst zählt zweifellos zu den interessantesten und außergewöhnlichsten Beiträgen der Gegenwartskunst. Obwohl sie in den meisten kunsthistorischen Diskursen über Pop Art und Konzeptkunst nicht genannt wird, ist ihr Werk essenziell für das Verständnis beider Kunstbewegungen. Die Ausstellung der Zeichnungen Sturtevants wird ein neues Licht auf diesen Aspekt der jüngeren Kunstgeschichte werfen.

Robert Fleck, langjähriger Kenner des Werkes, betonte anlässlich eines Symposiums zum Werk der Künstlerin im MMK 2004: „Sturtevant hat ihre Konsequenzen aus der Pop-Art und der Concept-Art der 1960er Jahre gezogen. Und sie schafft damit eine Bildrevolution. Bereits ihr erstes Werk *Johns Flag* von 1964 war im Sinne des Gesamtwerkes bereits vollendet. Es musste nichts mehr entwickelt werden. Sie denkt wie ein Philosoph die Dinge zu Ende mit intellektueller Rigorosität und Aufrichtigkeit."[2] Und John Waters, ein enger Künstlerfreund Sturtevants, äußerte sich in einem Interview über die Künstlerin: „Zum Kern vordringen. Es wird alles weggeschnitten, was keine Rolle spielt. Bis auf die Knochen. Das bewundere ich an Sturtevants Arbeit: kein Herumpfuschen. Sehr brutal."[3]

Die Ausstellung wird von der vorliegenden Publikation begleitet, die in enger Zusammenarbeit mit der Künstlerin konzipiert wurde. Sie umfasst bis auf wenige Ausnahmen, die nicht auffindbar waren, eine vollständige Katalogisierung ihres zeichnerischen Œuvre. Die Publikation ist in dem Sinne ein *Catalogue Raisonné* – „First Draft", worauf Sturtevant insistieren würde.

Mario Kramer
Kurator der Ausstellung und Sammlungsleiter MMK
Museum für Moderne Kunst Frankfurt am Main

1   Sturtevant in: Ursula Frohne, „Das Meisterwerk als Double", in: Uwe Fleckner (Hg.), *Jenseits der Gren-
     zen. Band 3: Dialog der Avantgarden*, Köln 2000, S. 271.

2   Robert Fleck, „Sturtevant und die Idee des Radikalismus in der zeitgenössischen Kunst", Symposium
     „STURTEVANT The Beauty of Repetition", 30. Oktober 2004, MMK Museum für Moderne Kunst
     Frankfurt am Main

3   John Waters, „STURTEVANT ALS STURTEVANT ALS STURTEVANT IST JOHN WATERS ALS JOHN
     WATERS ALS JOHN WATERS IST", in: MMK Museum für Moderne Kunst Frankfurt am Main, Udo
     Kittelmann und Mario Kramer (Hg.): *Sturtevant The Brutal Truth*, Ostfildern 2004, S. 48.

DRAWING AND THE ROOTS
OF STURTEVANT'S ART

Sturtevant's drawings of the 1960s supply some of the earliest records of her approach as it developed in that decade, and as such offer substantial insight into the underpinnings of her mature practice as an artist. They reveal the strategic thinking behind her work as she fashioned an artistic project around the repetition of existing works by well-known contemporaries. A study of these drawings, then, illuminates the roots of Sturtevant's art, and in so doing helps construct a longer historical lineage for the wide-spread embrace of reproduction, repetition, and appropriation in the field of contemporary art.

As is frequently the case with the discourse surrounding Sturtevant, even the seemingly straightforward task of simple description can grow complicated when her work is subjected to sustained attention. One might begin by noting that Sturtevant's drawings from the mid-1960s are often characterized by the juxtaposition on a single sheet of several images borrowed from different artists. A Tom Wesselmann Great American Nude will be combined with a Jasper Johns Flag, or an Andy Warhol Flowers with a Roy Lichtenstein Pointing Hand. This involved no small degree of stylistic mimicry, as the rendering in each component element differs depending upon the artist from which it was borrowed. Sturtevant did a good job, for example, of imitating Johns' animated hatching marks, which are differentiated from the more regularized application characteristic of the surface of Lichtenstein's drawings. (In the case of Warhol, she reportedly went so far as to borrow the silkscreen used in his Flowers painting series, hence sidestepping the handwork that was necessary to recreate the individual styles of other artists.)

But already, within the context of such seemingly straightforward description, complications arise. About a decade ago, I wrote a piece for Parkett magazine in which I challenged the "appropriation" label that had been anachronistically affixed to Sturtevant, since her work predated that critical term, and the strategies aligned with it, by more than a decade.[1] I also drew attention to the substantive changes she had made in the process of borrowing, as exemplified by the works in her 1966 Galerie J exhibit in Paris: that, for instance, she modified a round Wesselmann Great American Nude and turned it into a rectangular composition, and that she transformed a Crying Girl by Roy Lichtenstein, which had originally appeared as a print, into a large painting (which was, in addition, shown on its side and propped rather than hung on the wall).[2] That is to say, she made significant changes in medium, size, shape, orientation, and mode of exhibition, ones that undermine any claims that she was "merely" copying or repeating existing works.

Similar observations can be made about Sturtevant's drawings of the 1960s, which look to have served as a sort of warm-up exercise for the works exhibited in the Galerie J show. A 1966 sheet, *Study Wesselmann Great American Nude Johns Target* [p. 66], indicates that Sturtevant well knew that Wesselmann's painting was a tondo, that is to say a circular picture—which, as noted, she transformed into a rectangular composition for the Galerie J exhibition. In fact, in the drawing she emphasized the image's circular shape by relating it to that of a target, one of Johns's frequent subjects. The drawings also provide further evidence that Sturtevant viewed existing works by other artists not as images to be copied—which underscores her strong contention, over the years, that the motivation behind her work is not related to the logic of the copy—but rather as prior models that could be modified and transformed in various ways.[3] For example, in some of her drawings that include Lichtenstein's *Pointing Hand*, the dot screen covers the hand itself, while in others the hand is devoid of dots, which are instead used to fill the field around it. (In Lichtenstein's version, the hand is covered by the dots.) Similarly, if several of her drawings include the image of a nude borrowed from Wesselmann—juxtaposed with, in different instances, a Johns *Flag* and a Lichtenstein *Hot Dog*, Sturtevant took some liberties in rendering that feminine figure. In *Working Drawing Wesselmann Great American Nude Lichtenstein Hot Dog* (1966) [p. 64] the nude has been outfitted with a collaged pair of lips, in accord with Wesselmann's original; in two other drawings, combined in different configurations with a Johns *Flag*, the figure lacks that collage element.

Other aspects of Sturtevant's reuse of Wesselmann's *Great American Nude* images confirm her inclination to depart, sometimes significantly, from the original, particularly in her treatment of its surroundings. In his *Great American Nude #51* of 1963,[4] Wesselmann had set his nude against a series of painted and collaged elements: two white stars on a red field; a bowl of fruit; a vase of flowers; and a verdant forest by a lake. In her drawings, Sturtevant included selected elements from Wesselmann's painting—some flowers here, a star there—but substantially altered its setting. Whatever the changes she made to the image, there is something that links her various treatments: in all the recorded instances of her reuse of Wesselmann's reclining nude, she relocated the figure from its aforementioned sylvan environment to an urban one. More specifically, these all look to be views of New York City: in one the monumental arch of Greenwich Village's Washington Square Park is visible behind the nude's elbow [p. 65], while another includes the billboards of Times Square, including the sign for the famed Horn & Hardart Automat (the latter appears at the upper right of *Working Drawing Wesselmann Great American Nude Lichtenstein Hot Dog*, 1966) [p. 64]. What might have motivated Sturtevant's relocation of the figure from country to city? It is not merely that New York was the principal locale where she lived and worked at the time, for it was also, in a sense, one of the primary subjects of her art. Sturtevant's focus in her work of the mid-1960s was on those artists who had helped make that city the center of the postwar art world. The then-dominance of New York (and, more generally, of American art) was perhaps most memorably signaled in 1964 when Robert Rauschenberg—whom, as Bruce Hainley has documented, Sturtevant knew well—was awarded the grand prize for painting at the 1964 Venice Biennale.[5]

Sturtevant's drawings signal a broader interest in Americanness as an artistic subject, and perhaps also as an object of critique. In my *Parkett* essay, I called attention to the title—*America, America*—of Sturtevant's 1966 Galerie J solo show. That phrasing sparked several observations, including that its employment of verbal repetition underscored the duplication inherent in Sturtevant's practice. I also noted that the title emphasized the connection between Pop art and national identity at the same time that the siting of the exhibit in Paris implied a distancing from its chosen subject. A concomitant exploration of Americanness can be detected in Sturtevant's drawings from that same period, in both the images she selected and how she chose to combine them. It is there, for instance, in the two instances in which she juxtaposed Wesselmann's American-themed nude with an American flag à la Jasper Johns. It is there in her repeated borrowing of the Lichtenstein hot dog, a symbol of American popular taste if there ever was one. And it is there, finally, in the lower section of *Lichtenstein Hot Dog Magnifying Glass Oldenburg Charms Hamburger* (1965–66), where a pair of glaring eyes from Lichtenstein's 1965 painting *Image Duplicator* is situated above a pointing hand borrowed from the same artist [p. 53]. The resulting configuration echoes an indelibly American popular image (and one that conveys the strength of the nation's military might, no less)—that of Uncle Sam in James Montgomery Flagg's 1917 "I Want You" U.S. Army recruiting poster.[6]

One wants to pause here and point out that this play of associations is not only one of the effects but also one of the very subjects of Sturtevant's combinatory drawings. That is to say, she looks to have been methodically exploring how the placement of two or more images in close proximity inevitably prompts multiple and divergent meanings. So, for instance, while the combination of elements in *Working Drawing Wesselmann Great American Nude Lichtenstein Hot Dog* could be taken to signify "Americanness," the juxtaposition of the nude female figure with the blatantly phallic hot dog generates sexual meanings as well (of course, these two significations often go hand in hand). It is clear that Sturtevant was conducting this investigation in a systematic way, as evidenced by her execution of *Wesselmann Great American Nude Johns Flag* (1965) and *Johns Graphite Flag Wesselmann Great American Nude* (1966) [pp. 54 and 65]. The two drawings are differentiated primarily by a shift in the positioning of the component images with respect to one another, above and below. Why create two such closely related works if not to put the image combinations through their paces, to gauge the impact of differing organization and placement on the meanings of the resulting juxtapositions?

If, as noted, the combination of face and pointing hand in *Lichtenstein Hot Dog Magnifying Glass Oldenburg Charms Hamburger* evokes a memorable propaganda image, that is not the only connection to print culture and publicity evident in Sturtevant's drawings. At the time she made *Study Wesselmann Great American Nude Johns Target*, the Wesselmann painting on which it was based had not been publicly exhibited for several years. However, that painting had been featured prominently on the first page of a 1963 *Time* magazine article that surveyed the Pop movement (*Pop Art–Cult of the Commonplace*).[7] In fact, many of the images she incorporated into her drawings can be linked to the publicity Pop had generated. This is certainly true of the Lichtenstein motifs to which she gravitated, including the two–the hot dog and the pointing hand–that appear most frequently in her drawings of the 1960s. The former appeared on the cover of John Rublowsky's 1965 book *Pop Art*,[8] one of the first full-length publications about the Pop movement. The latter came to life not as a painting or drawing but rather as a screen-printed poster for a 1964 exhibition,[9] *Amerikansk Pop-konst*, at the Moderna Museet in Sweden–although the cropping of the cuff in Sturtevant's rendition suggests she may have taken the image not from the poster but from the more tightly-cropped version on the exhibition catalog's cover (which is of interest considering that the hot dog seems to have been drawn from a book cover as well).[10]

Of course, Pop art was firmly rooted in the worlds of advertising and publicity, a condition on which Sturtevant may very well have been commenting. Not to mention that, as Hainley has pointed out, the artist's husband worked in the advertising field.[11] Her artistic investigations were in part predicated on the fact that, through the efforts of figures like the legendary art dealer Leo Castelli, who was given a great deal of credit for Rauschenberg's 1964 Venice Biennale win, artists' signature styles had become so readily identifiable that substantial alterations could be made to the configuration of existing works by them without voiding their recognizability. In other words, by the 1960s an astute observer would no doubt have recognized that certain artists had come to be defined as brand names. Tellingly, Sturtevant announced the first major manifestation of her new artistic approach through a drawing that functioned as an advertisement: the invitation to her solo exhibition at the Bianchini Gallery in New York, in 1965 [p. 57]. That sheet, with "Sturtevant/October 2–23" emblazoned across it, is divided into six sections, each of which contains a separate image. Some are more readily identified in their connection to what was included in the Bianchini show: for instance, the figure pulling a garment rack in the upper right of the invitation corresponds to the work titled *7th Avenue Garment Rack with Warhol Flowers* (1965), which appears in the one extant installation photograph of the exhibition.[12] Some of the motifs on the invitation correspond to the objects that Sturtevant hung on the garment rack, including the Johnsian American flag and the inset squares that mimic a Frank Stella geometric painting. Other elements have gone hitherto unidentified, including the grouping of forms at lower center, which closer inspection reveals to be articles of clothing–dresses, men's suit jackets, and the like.

Those garments look to have been derived from a work by the Swedish artist Öyvind Fahlström, who was then active on the New York art scene.[13] Fahlström's *Planetarium*, a piece with moveable vinyl elements, was reproduced in the April 25, 1964 issue of *Art International*, on a page that followed an image of Tom Wesselmann's *Great American Nude #51*– which, as we've seen, had also caught Sturtevant's attention. Writing in the article–a series of linked reviews–that those images accompanied, the critic Max Kozloff described Fahlström's *Planetarium* in this way: "… 188 vinyl 'elements,' meticulously hand crafted to copy clothing worn by personages in science fiction comic books of the fifties, are attachable by magnets to blank figures whose sex can thereby be identified, or even contradicted. In addition, each of the garments is numbered to correspond to words in an adjacent 'control' chart, which, in turn, have been picked at random from Nathalie Sarraute's novel, *The Planetarium*."[14] In the context of Sturtevant's borrowing of these motifs from Fahlström, there is a great deal of note in Kozloff's account, including the observation that Fahlström had himself arrived at those shapes through the act of copying. Of particular interest is Kozloff's mention of blank figures "whose sex can thereby be identified, or even contradicted." He is referring to the major conceit of Fahlström's piece, in which the viewer was invited to place articles of clothing onto figures represented by outlined silhouettes.

If, as Kozloff observed, Fahlström's piece invoked the assignment of gendered roles and the possibility of contradicting them, Sturtevant's strategy of borrowing (primarily) from the work of male artists functioned in a similar way.[15] And the evidence suggests that she was already taking note of how attire, and its use in fashioning identity, might play a role in her work. Once those elements borrowed from Fahlström have been identified, they can be connected to the motif of the garment rack, also on the Bianchini invitation, in that both make reference to clothing. While Sturtevant's rendering of a figure with a garment rack suggests the image of a worker in the apparel industry, it also evokes an assortment of costumes backstage at a theater, ready to be used by actors in assuming their roles; or, alternatively, a spy's collection of disguises. Indeed, in the years that followed the Bianchini exhibition, Sturtevant not only continued to mimic a diverse range of artistic styles in her work but also began to adopt the personas of selected artists by (cross-)dressing as them. She masqueraded as figures like Marcel Duchamp and Joseph Beuys in recreations of well-known photographs and films in which they had appeared. In short, she was exploring the ways in which the figure of the artist is fashioned through the particularities of style, persona, branding, and attire—and in so doing demonstrating how those ostensibly unique signs of identity could be studiously imitated, coopted, and undone.

For the critic and curator Lawrence Alloway, who was considering the importance of drawing in this very period, one of the primary features of the medium was its autographic nature. While I have been focusing on the properties of drawing internal to Sturtevant's practice in the 1960s, her use of that medium as a basis for her artistic investigations coincided with a growing interest in its significance to the wider field of contemporary art. In that same year—1964—to which Sturtevant's earliest identified mature drawings have been dated, Alloway, then working at the Guggenheim Museum in New York, organized an exhibition that provided a snapshot of the current state of the medium. Titled *American Drawings*, the show was on view at the museum from September 17 to October 25 of that year.[16] It included work by artists on whom Sturtevant would train her gaze in the coming years—Johns, Rauschenberg, Lichtenstein, Claes Oldenburg— as well as others familiar to audiences in New York, among them Jackson Pollock, Lee Krasner, Robert Motherwell, Agnes Martin, Ed Ruscha, Cy Twombly, Jules Olitski, and Ellsworth Kelly. The exhibition was the third in a series, the first two having been devoted to nineteenth-century and twentieth-century drawings, respectively.

Rejecting the contention of other observers that contemporary drawing was characterized by artists calling attention to the medium (which he saw as a mere ventriloquizing of critic Clement Greenberg's diagnosis of modernism as a search for medium-specific purity and self-definition), Alloway asserted instead that "the historical functions of drawing seem not to have changed much since the sixteenth century."[17] Arguing, thus, for a continuity between past and present, Alloway envisioned drawing as defined over a longer historical arc by two main, interrelated characteristics, which he labeled as the systematic (or diagrammatic) and the autographic. He connected the former to the Renaissance notion of *disegno*, which emphasized the intellectual content of the artistic act, and the latter with gestural immediacy, with its promise of revealing the artist's personality. Alloway did not view these two functions as contradictory but, rather, in dialogue with one another.[18]

Sturtevant's approach to drawing accords with Alloway's observations and, at the same time, points beyond them. Her drawing practice, particularly as it emerged in the mid- to late-sixties, demonstrates the medium's potential for intellectual reflection, inasmuch as her drawings lay out image combinations and permutations in a methodical and considered way. The systematic underpinnings of her approach are under-scored by the term "working drawing," that she used to identify some of these sheets, which is more readily identified with the types of techni-cal studies or plans produced in fields like architecture and engineering. Nevertheless, although her titles–some of which use the related term "study"–imply a systematic intent, it is not clear to what extent these drawings functioned as preparatory steps toward finished works in other mediums. As Alloway noted in his catalog essay, "one of the functions of drawings is to serve as intermediate steps towards some other work by the artist…." However, Sturtevant's use of the medium does not reveal a clear path from beginning (conception) to end (execution), since there are no extant paintings by her from this period that juxtapose images by two– or more–artists, as her drawings often do.[19] What then, one might ask, are these "studies" for? It seems more apt to take them as indicative of the artist's interest in developing a lexicon of imagery, a means to exploring how borrowing, juxtaposition, recombination, and related strategies could provide the basis for an extended artistic project.

Alloway, whose theoretical leanings prompted him to place art within a broader framework of sign systems and communication channels, offered the following reflections toward the end of his essay: "Content, the message, is expressed by the organization of form, the development of which in a single work, the regularity of which in a group of works, identifies authorship with semantic function. The artist is present in such works not as a signature but as a construction."[20] This description of the constructed nature of artistic identity accords closely with what one takes to be the intended aims of Sturtevant's drawings, which were to reveal the nature of the artist's mark not as an indisputable expression of personality but rather as an iterable sign. Nevertheless, Alloway, who as I've already noted voiced his belief in the continuity of the medium, maintained that "there is a persistent tradition, *which has not yet been broken*, that drawing is the least conventional and most authentic act of the artist, more intimate, often, than the finished works."[21]

If, in 1964, Alloway could assert the unbrokenness of the tradition of drawing as the most direct and authentic of pictorial mediums, that is because he hadn't yet seen–or didn't foresee–the very type of intervention Sturtevant had begun to make that same year. It was precisely such claims to originality and expressiveness that her drawings sought to undermine. Her adoption of strategies of imitation, repetition, and recombination in her work would directly challenge the tradition Alloway was describing, with new avenues opened up in the process.

Michael Lobel

1   Michael Lobel, "Sturtevant: Inappropriate Appropriation," *Parkett*, no. 75, December 2005, pp. 142–147.

2   Sturtevant exhibition at Galerie J, Paris, 1966. Reproduced in MMK Museum für Moderne Kunst Frankfurt am Main, Lena Maculan, *Sturtevant, Catalogue Raisonné 1964–2004, Painting Sculpture Film and Video*, Hatje Cantz, Ostfildern-Ruit 2004, pp. 106/107.

3   "There's a big difference in repeating in the sense of Deleuze, and copying. […] a copy must be absolutely of the same intention as the original, whereas my work deals with an interior movement, and repetition as difference." Sturtevant in conversation with Hans Ulrich Obrist (Winter 2008/2009), *032c*, no. 16, http://032c.com/2008/elaine-sturtevant, retrieved March 28, 2014.

4   Tom Wesselmann, *Great American Nude #51*, 1963, oil and collage on canvas (in three sections), 304.8 × 365.76 cm, Private Collection. Reproduced in *Art International*, vol. 8, no. 3, April 25, 1964.

5   Bruce Hainley, *Under the Sign of [sic]: Sturtevant's Volte-Face*, Semiotext(e), Los Angeles 2013.

6   James Montgomery Flagg, *I Want You for the U.S. Army*, 1917, Lithograph, 102.1 × 74.8 cm, Museum of Modern Art, New York. Reproduced in *Library of Congress prints and photographs: an illustrated guide*, Library of Congress, Washington, D.C. 1995, p. 43.

7   Information about the exhibition history of Wesselmann's painting is derived from the author's e-mails and discussions with Jeffrey Sturges of the Tom Wesselmann Estate, February, 2014. "Pop Art — Cult of the Commonplace," *Time* magazine, May 3, 1963.

8   Cover of John Rublowsky, *Pop Art*, Basic Books, New York 1965.

9   Poster for *Amerikansk Pop-konst* at Moderna Museet, 1964. Reproduced in Mary Lee Corlette, *The Prints of Roy Lichtenstein: A Catalogue Raisonné 1948–1993*, New York 1994, p. 299.

10   Cover of *Amerikansk Pop-konst* catalog, 1964. Moderna Museet, *Amerikansk pop-konst, 106 former av kärlek och förtvivlan: Jim Dine, Roy Lichtenstein, Claes Oldenburg, James Rosenquist, George Segal, Andy Warhol, Tom Wesselmann*, Stockholm 1964.

11   Hainley, *Under the Sign of [sic]*, p. 78.

12   Ibid., p. 84.

13   Öyvind Fahlström, *Planetarium*, 1963, Large panel: painting on canvas and metal plates on the back, 94 magnetic elements: painting on vinyl, 197 × 234 cm. Small panel: ink and tempera on paper mounted on wood, 94 magnetic elements: ink on paper, 57 × 57 cm. Centre Pompidou, Paris. Reproduced in *Art International*, vol. 8, no. 3, April 25, 1964.

14   Max Kozloff, "New York Letter," *Art International*, vol. 8, no. 3, April 25 1964, p. 61.

15   While it was long claimed that Sturtevant only borrowed from male artists, Hainley's diligent archival research uncovered an important episode in which she remade a dance piece by Yvonne Rainer. See: Hainley, *Under the Sign of [sic]*, pp. 117–151.

16   A detailed record of Alloway's *American Drawings* show is contained in the Guggenheim Museum Archives, Exhibition Records (Collection A0003), Box 1074.

17   Lawrence Alloway, (1964) "Introduction," *American Drawings*, Exh. cat., Solomon R. Guggenheim Museum, New York 1964. Alloway was responding not only to Greenberg but also to a review by Max Kozloff of the *Twentieth-Century Master Drawings* show that had preceded *American Drawings* at the Guggenheim. See: Max Kozloff, "Notes on the Psychology of Modern Draftsmanship," *Arts Magazine*, vol. 38, no. 5, February 1964, pp. 58–63.

18   "Drawing has been persistently connected with brain-work, an idea rooted in the incisive nature of the medium. This tradition does not contradict the autographic definition of drawing but, rather, enlarges it: the reductive techniques of drawing are as conducive to intellectual summary as to spontaneity. The diagram and the autographic are not opposed modes in drawing. Line has been regarded as a grid, matrix, skeleton, scaffolding, or core; it is the artist's intelligence embodied in undiscursive form and concise space. The technical simplicity which makes gestural directness possible in drawing, therefore, symbolizes art's capacity for order." Alloway, "Introduction," n.p.

19   Although the *7th Avenue Garment Rack with Warhol Flowers* does extend this combinatory approach in its bringing together of a selection of borrowed works in close proximity.

20   Alloway, "Introduction," n.p.

21   Ibid. [emphasis added]

DIE ZEICHNUNG UND DIE WURZELN
VON STURTEVANTS WERK

Sturtevants in den 1960er Jahren entstandene Zeichnungen liefern einige der frühesten Belege für ihre in jenem Jahrzehnt entwickelte Vorgehensweise und bieten insofern einen fundierten Einblick in die Grundlagen ihrer zur Reife gelangten künstlerischen Praxis. Sie offenbaren die strategischen Überlegungen, mit deren Hilfe sie ein künstlerisches Projekt entwickelte, das um die Wiederholung bestehender Werke bekannter zeitgenössischer Künstler kreiste. Eine Untersuchung dieser Zeichnungen wirft daher ein Licht auf die Wurzeln von Sturtevants Werk und ermöglicht damit die historische Linie der weit verbreiteten Beschäftigung mit Reproduktion, Repetition und Appropriation in der zeitgenössischen Kunst weiter zurückzuverfolgen.

Wie so häufig bei der Auseinandersetzung mit Sturtevant kann sich, betrachtet man ihr Werk insgesamt, die scheinbar einfache Aufgabe der Beschreibung als kompliziert erweisen. Zunächst könnte man feststellen, dass sich Sturtevants Mitte der 1960er Jahre entstandene Zeichnungen häufig durch ein Nebeneinander mehrerer, von verschiedenen Künstlern entlehnter Bilder auszeichnen. So wurde beispielsweise eine der *Great American Nudes* von Tom Wesselmann mit einer *Flag* von Jasper Johns oder ein *Flowers*-Bild von Andy Warhol mit einer *Pointing Hand* von Roy Lichtenstein kombiniert. Dies erforderte ein Höchstmaß an stilistischer Mimikry, da die zeichnerische Umsetzung jeder einzelnen Komponente stark von dem jeweiligen Künstler abhing, von dem sie übernommen wurde. Sturtevant gelang es beispielsweise ausgezeichnet, Jasper Johns' lebhafte Schraffuren nachzuahmen, die sich stark von der regelmäßigeren Umsetzung einer Lichtenstein-Zeichnung unterscheiden. (Bei Warhol ging Sturtevant Berichten zufolge so weit, sich bei ihm die für seine *Flowers*-Serie verwendeten Original-Siebdruckvorlagen auszuleihen, um so das handwerkliche Problem zu umgehen, das sich bei der Nachahmung der individuellen Handschriften unterschiedlichster Künstler stellte.)

Bereits im Kontext einer scheinbar simplen Beschreibung stellen sich also Schwierigkeiten ein. Vor etwa einem Jahrzehnt verfasste ich einen Aufsatz für die Zeitschrift *Parkett*, in welchem ich mich kritisch mit dem Etikett „Appropriation" auseinandersetzte, das man Sturtevant anachronistischerweise anheftete, ging doch ihr Werk diesem Terminus und den damit verbundenen Strategien um mehr als ein Jahrzehnt voraus.[1] Zudem wies ich auf die entscheidenden Veränderungen hin, die Sturtevant bei der Aneignung fremder Werke an diesen vornahm. Als Beispiel führte ich Arbeiten aus ihrer Ausstellung an, die 1966 in der Pariser Galerie J zu sehen war: Hier modifizierte Sturtevant etwa eine von Tom Wesselmanns *Great American Nudes*, ursprünglich ein Tondo, indem sie es in ein Rechteckformat überführte, so wie sie Roy Lichtensteins *Crying Girl*, im Original eine Lithografie, in ein großformatiges Gemälde transformierte (welches außerdem nicht an der Wand hing, sondern – um 90 Grad gegen den Uhrzeigersinn gedreht – gegen die Wand gelehnt präsentiert wurde).[2] Sturtevant veränderte also sowohl das Medium als auch den Maßstab, das Format, die Ausrichtung und die Art der Präsentation, was der gängigen These widerspricht, bei ihren Arbeiten handele es sich „lediglich" um Kopien oder Wiederholungen bereits existierender Werke.

Ähnliches lässt sich auch in Sturtevants Zeichnungen aus den 1960er Jahren beobachten, die als eine Art Fingerübung für die in der Galerie J gezeigten Arbeiten gedient zu haben scheinen. Das Blatt *Study Wesselmann Great American Nude Johns Target* von 1966 [S. 66] deutet darauf hin, dass Sturtevant sich sehr wohl darüber im Klaren war, dass es sich bei Wesselmanns Gemälde um ein Tondo, das heißt ein kreisförmiges Bildformat handelte – das sie, wie gesagt, anlässlich der Ausstellung in der Galerie J in ein Rechteckformat verwandelte. Tatsächlich hob sie in der Zeichnung die Kreisform des Bildes noch hervor, indem sie es zu einer Zielscheibe, einem häufigen Motiv von Jasper Johns, in Beziehung setzte. Insofern liefern die Zeichnungen weitere Belege dafür, dass Sturtevant die Arbeiten anderer Künstler nicht als bloße Kopiervorlagen betrachtete (was ihre Beteuerung stützt, die Motivation zu ihrer Arbeit basiere nicht auf der Logik der Kopie), sondern vielmehr als Vormodelle, die sich auf verschiedene Art und Weise modifizieren und transformieren ließen.[3] So erstreckt sich in einigen ihrer Zeichnungen, zu denen auch Lichtensteins *Pointing Hand* zählt, das Punkteraster über die Hand der Figur, in anderen wiederum nicht. Dafür ist der die Hand umgebende Bereich mit einem Raster versehen (in Lichtensteins Fassung ist die Handfläche gerastert). Obgleich sich in einigen ihrer Zeichnungen das Motiv eines von Wesselmann entlehnten weiblichen Aktes findet – beispielsweise neben einer Jasper-Johns-*Flag* oder einem Lichtenstein-*Hot Dog* –, erlaubte sich Sturtevant bei der Wiedergabe der weiblichen Figur einige Freiheiten. Im Falle von *Working Drawing Wesselmann Great American Nude Lichtenstein Hot Dog* (1966) [S. 64] stattete Sturtevant den Akt entsprechend Wesselmanns Original mit einem collagierten Frauenmund aus, während dieses Collage-Element in zwei anderen Zeichnungen, die auf jeweils unterschiedliche Weise mit einer Johns-*Flag* kombiniert wurden, fehlt.

Andere Aspekte der Aneignung von Wesselmanns *Great American Nudes* durch Sturtevant bestätigen die Neigung der Künstlerin, zuweilen, insbesondere was die Behandlung der Hintergründe betrifft, erheblich vom Original abzuweichen. In seiner *Great American Nude #51*[4] aus dem Jahr 1963 setzt Wesselmann den Akt vor einen Hintergrund aus verschiedenen collagierten und gemalten Elementen: zwei weiße Sterne auf rotem

Grund, eine Schale mit Obst, eine Vase mit Blumen und ein dichter Wald am Rande eines Sees. Sturtevant ließ in ihre Zeichnungen einige ausgewählte Elemente aus Wesselmanns Gemälden einfließen – hier ein paar Blumen, dort ein Stern –, während sie die Kulisse des Bildes entscheidend modifizierte. Aber unabhängig von den am Bildmotiv vorgenommenen Veränderungen gibt es stets ein verbindendes Element, was die verschiedenen Arten des Umgangs mit dem Original angeht: In sämtlichen Wiederholungen von Wesselmanns liegendem Akt platzierte Sturtevant die Figur statt in der genannten Waldkulisse in einer Stadtlandschaft. Konkret handelt es sich hierbei offenbar um Ansichten von New York: In einer von ihnen erkennt man hinter dem Ellbogen der Figur den monumentalen Triumphbogen des Washington Square Park in Greenwich Village [S. 65], ein andermal die Reklametafeln am Times Square, darunter auch ein Hinweisschild für das bekannte Automatenrestaurant Horn & Hardart (letzteres ist im rechten oberen Bildbereich von *Working Drawing Wesselmann Great American Nude Lichtenstein Hot Dog*, 1966, zu erkennen) [S. 64]. Was mag Sturtevant dazu veranlasst haben, jene weibliche Figur sozusagen vom Land in die Stadt umzusiedeln? New York war nicht nur der Ort, an dem die Künstlerin damals hauptsächlich lebte und arbeitete, die Stadt war außerdem eines ihrer zentralen künstlerischen Motive. Sturtevant legte in ihren Mitte der 1960er Jahre entstandenen Arbeiten den Fokus auf jene Künstler, die dazu beigetragen hatten, dass sich New York während der Nachkriegszeit zum Zentrum des internationalen Kunstbetriebs entwickeln konnte. Die damalige Vormachtstellung New Yorks (und ganz allgemein der amerikanischen Kunst) kündigte sich vielleicht am eindringlichsten im Jahr 1964 an, als Robert Rauschenberg – mit dem Sturtevant, wie Bruce Hainley dokumentiert hat, gut bekannt war – mit dem Großen Preis für Malerei der Biennale von Venedig ausgezeichnet wurde.[5]

Sturtevants Zeichnungen weisen auf ein größeres Interesse am Amerikanischen als künstlerischem Thema und möglicherweise auch als Gegenstand der Kritik hin. In meinem Beitrag für *Parkett* habe ich auf den Titel von Sturtevants Ausstellung 1966 in der Galerie J hingewiesen: *America, America*. Dieser Titel bewog mich zu der Feststellung, dass das Mittel der wörtlichen Wiederholung die der Praxis der Künstlerin inhärente Duplikation zusätzlich verstärkte. Daneben habe ich aber auch darauf hingewiesen, dass der Ausstellungstitel die Verbindung zwischen Pop Art und nationaler Identität hervorhob, während der Ausstellungsort Paris eine gewisse Distanz zum eigentlichen Thema der Ausstellung implizierte. Gleichzeitig erkundete Sturtevant auch in Zeichnungen aus dieser Zeit die amerikanische Identität, und zwar sowohl was die von ihr ausgewählten Motive als auch die Art ihrer Kombination betrifft. Sturtevant verband beispielsweise in zwei Fällen einen „amerikanischen" Akt von Wesselmann mit einer amerikanischen Flagge à la Jasper Johns. Dasselbe gilt auch für ihre wiederholte Entlehnung der Lichtenstein-Darstellung eines Hot Dogs, eines Symbols für den amerikanischen Massengeschmack schlechthin. Und schließlich findet sich ein weiteres Beispiel in der unteren Bildhälfte des Blattes *Lichtenstein Hot Dog Magnifying Glass Oldenburg Charms Hamburger* (1965–66), wo Sturtevant ein Paar stechender Augen aus dem Lichtenstein-Bild *Image Duplicator* von 1965 oberhalb einer zeigenden Hand desselben Künstlers platzierte [S. 53]. Die so entstandene Gestalt spiegelt ein typisches Motiv der amerikanischen Populärkultur wider (das nichts weniger als die Stärke des nationalen Militärs ausdrückt) – nämlich die Figur des Uncle Sam aus James Montgomery Flaggs Rekrutierungsplakat *I Want You* von 1917.[6]

Es sollte hier darauf hingewiesen werden, dass es sich bei diesem Spiel mit Assoziationen nicht nur um Wirkung, sondern auch um ein zentrales Thema von Sturtevants kombinatorischen Zeichnungen handelt. Die Künstlerin scheint also methodisch untersucht zu haben, wie das Nebeneinander zweier oder mehrerer Bilder zwangsläufig mehrere voneinander abweichende Bedeutungen generiert. Während man beispielsweise die Verbindung der Komponenten in *Working Drawing Wesselmann Great American Nude Lichtenstein Hot Dog* als Ausdruck des „Amerikanischen" verstehen könnte, erzeugt die Kombination aus nackter weiblicher Figur und unverhohlen phallischem Hot Dog auch eine sexuelle Bedeutung (freilich gehen diese beiden Bedeutungen häufig Hand in Hand). Offenkundig betrieb Sturtevant ihre Motiv-Recherche auf systematische Weise, wie die Arbeiten *Wesselmann Great American Nude Johns Flag* (1965) und *Johns Graphite Flag Wesselmann Great American Nude* (1966) belegen [S. 54 und 65]. Die beiden Zeichnungen unterscheiden sich in erster Linie durch eine Verschiebung der Position der einzelnen Bildkomponenten zueinander nach oben oder unten. Warum aber sollte man überhaupt zwei so eng miteinander verwandte Arbeiten produzieren, wenn nicht um mögliche Bildkombinationen zu prüfen und die Auswirkungen unterschiedlicher Anordnungen und Platzierungen auf die Bedeutung der daraus resultierenden Kombinationen zu untersuchen?

Wenn, wie dargestellt, die Verbindung aus Gesicht und zeigender Hand in *Lichtenstein Hot Dog Magnifying Glass Oldenburg Charms Hamburger* ein unverkennbares Propagandamotiv evoziert, so liegt darin nicht der einzige Bezug zur grafischen Kultur und zur Werbung innerhalb von Sturtevants zeichnerischem Werk. Zur Zeit der Entstehung von *Study Wesselmann Great American Nude Johns Target* war das Wesselmann-Bild, auf das sich Sturtevants Arbeit bezog, jahrelang nicht öffentlich ausgestellt worden. Allerdings zierte es 1963 die erste Seite eines Artikels über die Pop-Bewegung im *Time*-Magazin (*Pop Art – Cult of the Commonplace*).[7] Tatsächlich lassen sich zahlreiche der von Sturtevant in ihre Zeichnungen integrierten Motive in eine enge Beziehung zu jener öffentlichen Aufmerksamkeit setzen, welche die Pop Art erzeugt hatte. Dies gilt zweifellos auch für die Lichtenstein-Motive, von denen sie sich angezogen fühlte, einschließlich der beiden – Hot Dog und zeigende Hand –, die am häufigsten in ihren Zeichnungen der 1960er Jahre auftauchen. Während der Hot Dog sich auf dem Cover von John Rublowskys Buch *Pop Art*[8] von 1965, einer der ersten Einzeldarstellungen der Pop-Bewegung, wiederfindet, geht die zeigende Hand nicht auf ein Gemälde oder eine Grafik zurück, sondern auf das Siebdruckplakat[9] zur Ausstellung *Amerikansk Pop-konst*, die 1964 im schwedischen Moderna Museet stattfand – auch wenn die Beschneidung der Manschette in Sturtevants Fassung darauf hindeutet, dass als Vorlage für das Motiv nicht das Plakat, sondern der engere Bildausschnitt auf dem Umschlag des Ausstellungskatalogs[10] gedient haben dürfte (was insofern interessant ist, als auch die Abbildung des Hot Dog auf einen Buchumschlag zurückzugehen scheint).

Die Pop Art war ihrem Wesen nach tief in der Welt der Werbung und Reklame verwurzelt, ein Umstand, den Sturtevant wohl durchaus kommentiert haben mag, ganz abgesehen davon, dass ihr Ehemann, wie Hainley anmerkt, selbst in der Werbebranche tätig war.[11] Sturtevants künstlerische Untersuchungen fußten zum Teil darauf, dass dank des Wirkens von Personen wie dem legendären Kunsthändler Leo Castelli, der für Rauschenbergs Preis im Rahmen der Biennale in Venedig 1964 selbst hohe Anerkennung erntete, die Handschrift einiger Künstler plötzlich über einen derartigen Wiedererkennungswert verfügte, dass man wesentliche Änderungen an der Gestalt vorhandener Arbeiten vornehmen konnte, ohne diesen Wiedererkennungswert zu gefährden. Man könnte auch sagen, ein aufmerksamer Beobachter um die 1960er Jahre herum hätte zweifellos wahrgenommen, dass bestimmte Künstler inzwischen regelrecht als Markennamen gehandelt wurden. Eindrucksvollerweise kündigte Sturtevant die erste umfangreichere Manifestation ihres neuartigen künstlerischen Ansatzes in Form einer Zeichnung an, die wie eine Werbeanzeige funktionierte: die Einladungskarte zu ihrer Einzelausstellung 1965 in der New Yorker Bianchini Gallery [S. 57]. Dieses Blatt, das die Worte „Sturtevant/ October 2–23" zieren, ist in sechs Abschnitte unterteilt, die jeweils ein Einzelmotiv zeigen. Manche von ihnen sind leichter als andere im Hinblick auf ihre Verbindung zu den Exponaten der Bianchini-Ausstellung identifizierbar: So entspricht beispielsweise die einen rollbaren Kleiderständer hinter sich herziehende Figur in der oberen rechten Ecke der Einladungskarte einer Arbeit mit dem Titel *7th Avenue Garment Rack with Warhol Flowers* (1965), die auf dem offenbar einzig existierenden Installationsfoto zur Ausstellung zu sehen ist.[12] Andere Motive auf der Einladungskarte decken sich mit den Objekten, die Sturtevant anlässlich ihrer Ausstellung an den Kleiderständer gehängt hatte, darunter eine Jasper-Johns-Flagge und jene ineinandergefügten Quadrate, die ein geometrisches Bild von Frank Stella nachzuahmen scheinen. Wieder andere Komponenten konnten bisher nicht identifiziert werden, darunter eine Reihe von Formen in der unteren Bildmitte, die sich bei genauerer Betrachtung als Kleidungsstücke herausstellen – Damenkleider, Herrensakkos und dergleichen.

Diese Kleidungsstücke scheinen auf ein Werk des schwedischen Künstlers Öyvind Fahlström zurückzugehen, der Teil der damaligen New Yorker Kunstszene war.[13] Eine Abbildung von Fahlströms Arbeit *Planetarium* mit ihren beweglichen Vinyl-Elementen erschien am 25. April 1964 in einer Ausgabe von *Art International*, nur eine Seite hinter der Reproduktion von Tom Wesselmanns *Great American Nude #51* – ein Werk, das, wie wir gesehen haben, ebenfalls Sturtevants Aufmerksamkeit geweckt hatte. Der Kunstkritiker Max Kozloff beschrieb in seinem Artikel – eine Reihe miteinander verbundener Rezensionen –, der auch die genannten Abbildungen beinhaltete, Fahlströms *Planetarium* folgendermaßen: „[…] 188 Vinyl-‚Komponenten‘, akribisch von Hand gefertigte Nachbildungen von Kleidungsstücken, wie sie in Science-Fiction-Comics aus den 1950er Jahren getragen wurden, können mithilfe von Magneten unbekleideten Figuren angeheftet werden, deren Geschlecht sich auf diese Weise bestimmen oder auch konterkarieren lässt. Zusätzlich ist jedes einzelne Kleidungsstück nummeriert, entsprechend der Wörter auf einer beiliegenden ‚Kontrollkarte‘, die ihrerseits willkürlich Nathalie Sarrautes Roman *Das Planetarium* entnommen wurden."[14] Kozloffs Darstellung ist im Kontext von Sturtevants Entlehnung dieser Motive bei Fahlström außerordentlich aufschlussreich, nicht zuletzt auch aufgrund der Feststellung, dass Fahlström selbst über den Weg des Kopierens zu jenen Formen gelangt war. Von besonderer Bedeutung ist hierbei jedoch Kozloffs Erwähnung der unbekleideten Figuren, „deren Geschlecht sich so bestimmen oder auch konterkarieren lässt". Konkret geht es hierbei um das zentrale Konzept hinter Fahlströms Arbeit, die den Betrachter dazu aufforderte, lediglich durch Umrisslinien dargestellte Figuren mit Kleidungsstücken zu versehen.

Wenn sich Fahlströhms Arbeit, wie wir Kozloffs Schilderung entnehmen können, auf die Zuweisung von Geschlechterrollen sowie auf die Möglichkeit ihrer Unterminierung berief, so fungierte Sturtevants Strategie der Aneignung von Werken (vorzugsweise) männlicher Künstlerkollegen in ganz ähnlicher Weise.[15] Offensichtlich war Sturtevant bereits bewusst, welche Rolle Kleidung und ihre Verwendung zum Zweck der Identitätsbildung innerhalb ihres Werkes spielte. Da nun die von Fahlström übernommenen Elemente identifiziert sind, lassen sie sich mit dem Motiv des ebenfalls auf der Bianchini-Einladung dargestellten Kleiderständers in Verbindung setzen, da beide Elemente auf Kleidung verweisen. Während Sturtevants Version einer Figur mit Kleiderständer das Bild eines Arbeiters in der Bekleidungsindustrie suggeriert, könnte sie ebenso gut eine Ansammlung von Kostümen hinter einer Theaterbühne evozieren, bereit dazu, von den ihre Rollen spielenden Schauspielern genutzt zu werden – oder aber ein Sammelsurium von Verkleidungen eines Spions. Tatsächlich ahmte Sturtevant in den auf die Bianchini-Ausstellung folgenden Jahren nicht nur verschiedene weitere künstlerische Stile nach, sie begann darüber hinaus auch damit, in die Rollen ausgewählter (männlicher) Künstler zu schlüpfen, indem sie sich als diese verkleidete – so trat sie beispielsweise in Wiederholungen bekannter Fotografien und Filme als Marcel Duchamp und Joseph Beuys auf. Kurzum, sie erforschte, inwieweit die Figur des Künstlers (beziehungsweise der Künstlerin) durch Besonderheiten ihres Stils, ihres Auftretens, ihres Markenzeichens und ihrer Kleidung geprägt wird – und demonstrierte dabei, wie sich diese scheinbar einzigartigen Zeichen der Identität minuziös nachahmen, kooptieren und aufheben ließen.

Für den Kunstkritiker und Kurator Lawrence Alloway, der die Bedeutung der Zeichnung für diese Zeit untersuchte, bestand eines der wesentlichen Merkmale des Mediums in dessen autografer Qualität. Ich habe mich hier auf die für Sturtevants Methode der 1960er Jahre wesentlichen Charakteristika der Zeichnung konzentriert, doch fiel ihre Nutzung dieses Mediums als Grundlage ihrer künstlerischen Untersuchungen mit einem wachsenden Interesse an dessen Bedeutung für den weiter gefassten Bereich der zeitgenössischen Kunst zusammen. 1964, also in dem Jahr, auf das sich die frühesten der ausgereiften Zeichnungen Sturtevants zurückdatieren lassen, konzipierte Alloway, der damals am New Yorker Guggenheim Museum arbeitete, eine Ausstellung, die eine Momentaufnahme des gerade aktuellen Zustands des Mediums lieferte. Die vom 17. September bis zum 25. Oktober desselben Jahres laufende Schau trug den Titel *American Drawings*.[16] Sie versammelte verschiedene Werke von Künstlern, an denen Sturtevant in den darauffolgenden Jahren ihren Blick schulen sollte – Johns, Rauschenberg, Lichtenstein, Claes Oldenburg – ebenso wie dem New Yorker Publikum vertraute Namen wie Jackson Pollock, Lee Krasner, Robert Motherwell, Agnes Martin, Ed Ruscha, Cy Twombly, Jules Olitski und Ellsworth Kelly. Die Ausstellung bildete den dritten Teil einer Reihe, deren erste beide sich der Zeichnung des 19. und des 20. Jahrhunderts gewidmet hatten.

Alloway wies die Behauptung anderer Beobachter zurück, die zeitgenössische Zeichnung sei davon geprägt, dass Künstler die Aufmerksamkeit auf die Bedeutung dieses Mediums an sich lenken wollten (worin er ein bloßes Nachplappern von Clement Greenbergs Diagnose der Moderne im Sinne eines Strebens nach medienspezifischer Reinheit und Selbstbestimmung sah), und erklärte stattdessen: „Die historischen Funktionen der Zeichnung scheinen sich seit dem 16. Jahrhundert nicht grundlegend gewandelt zu haben."[17] Alloway setzte also eine Kontinuität von Vergangenheit und Gegenwart voraus und begriff die Zeichnung als über einen längeren historischen Zeitraum gespannten Bogen von zwei wesentlichen, in Wechselbeziehung zueinander stehenden Merkmalen, die er als das Systematische (oder Diagrammatische) und das Autografe definierte. Er verwies mit dem ersten Begriff auf die Renaissance-Vorstellung des *disegno*, welche den intellektuellen Gehalt des künstlerischen Aktes betonte, während er den Terminus des Autografen mit der gestischen Unmittelbarkeit und der Verheißung auf eine Enthüllung der Künstler-persönlichkeit in Verbindung setzte. Für Alloway standen diese beiden Funktionen nicht im Gegensatz zueinander, sondern in einem gegenseitigen Dialog.[18]

Sturtevants Umgang mit der Zeichnung steht im Einklang mit Alloways Betrachtungen, zugleich allerdings weist er über diese hinaus. Die zeichnerische Methode Sturtevants, insbesondere in ihrer Ausprägung Mitte bis Ende der 1960er Jahre, offenbart das intellektuelle Potenzial dieses Mediums, und zwar insofern, als ihre Zeichnungen auf methodische und reflektierte Art Bildkombinationen und -permutationen vor Augen führen. Die systematischen Grundlagen dieser Praxis werden durch den Begriff der „Arbeitszeichnung" zusätzlich hervorgehoben, mit dem Sturtevant einige dieser Blätter beschrieb und der normalerweise eher jene technischen Studien oder Pläne bezeichnet, wie man sie in der Architektur oder im Maschinenbau antrifft. Aber obwohl ihre Titel – von denen einige die verwandte Bezeichnung „Study" tragen – eine systematische Absicht implizieren, bleibt unklar, inwieweit diese Zeichnungen im Sinne vorbereitender Schritte für in anderen Medien vollendete Werke fungierten. Wie Alloway in seinem Katalogbeitrag schreibt, besteht „eine der Funktionen von Zeichnungen darin, als Zwischenschritte auf dem Weg zu einem neuen Werk des Künstlers zu dienen [...]". Sturtevants Umgang mit diesem Medium hingegen offenbart keinen klaren Weg vom Anfang (Konzeption) bis zum Ende (Ausführung), da keine eigenständigen Gemälde aus jener Zeit vorliegen, in denen Sturtevant Motive zweier – oder mehrerer – Künstler einander gegenüberstellte, wie es in ihren Zeichnungen häufig der Fall ist.[19] Worin, könnte man also fragen, besteht dann überhaupt der Sinn dieser „Studien"? Es scheint angebrachter, sie als Indizien für das Interesse der Künstlerin an der Entwicklung eines Bildlexikons zu betrachten, als Instrument zur Erforschung der Frage, inwiefern Entlehnung, Nebeneinanderstellung, Neukombinierung und verwandte Strategien die Grundlage für ein umfassenderes künstlerisches Projekt liefern können.

Alloway, dessen theoretische Orientierung ihn dazu veranlasste, die Kunst innerhalb eines weiter gefassten Gefüges aus Zeichensystemen und Kommunikationskanälen zu verorten, kam am Ende seines Aufsatzes zu folgender Überlegung: „Der Inhalt, die Aussage drückt sich in der formalen Organisation aus, deren Entwicklung innerhalb eines Einzelwerks, deren Gesetzmäßigkeit innerhalb einer Gruppe von Werken Urheberschaft mit semantischer Funktion gleichsetzt. Der Künstler ist in derartigen Werken nicht im Sinne einer Signatur, sondern einer Konstruktion anwesend."[20] Diese These von der Konstruiertheit der künstlerischen Identität stimmt eng mit dem überein, was gemeinhin als angestrebtes Ziel von Sturtevants Zeichnungen gilt, welche das Wesen der Handschrift des Künstlers nicht als unstrittigen Ausdruck seiner Persönlichkeit, sondern als wiederholbares Zeichen enthüllen sollten. Nichtsdestotrotz behauptete Alloway, indem er, wie bereits angeführt, seine Überzeugung von der Kontinuität des Mediums zum Ausdruck brachte: „[Es] existiert eine kontinuierliche, *bislang ungebrochene* Tradition, die besagt, dass es sich bei der Zeichnung um den am wenigsten konventionellen und den am stärksten authentischen Akt des Künstlers handelt, der häufig intimer wirkt als das vollendete Werk."[21]

Wenn Alloway im Jahr 1964 die Ungebrochenheit der zeichnerischen Tradition als unmittelbarstes und authentischstes bildnerisches Medium postulieren konnte, so deshalb, weil er bis dahin ebenjene Art der Intervention, wie sie Sturtevant im selben Jahr vorzunehmen begonnen hatte, noch nicht gesehen – beziehungsweise vorhergesehen – hatte. In ihren Zeichnungen wollte sie vor allem derartige Originalitäts- und Expressivitätsansprüche unterminieren. Sturtevants Übernahme von Nachahmungs-, Wiederholungs- und Rekombinationsstrategien fordert die von Alloway beschriebenen Traditionen heraus und erschließt auf diese Weise neue Wege.

Michael Lobel

1   Michael Lobel, „Sturtevant: Inappropriate Appropriation", in: Parkett, Nr. 75, Dezember 2005, S. 142–147.

2   Sturtevant-Ausstellung in der Galerie J Paris, 1966. Reproduziert in: MMK Museum für Moderne Kunst Frankfurt am Main / Lena Maculan, *Sturtevant. Catalogue Raisonné 1964–2004. Gemälde Skulptur Film und Video*, Ostfildern-Ruit 2004, S. 106–107.

3   „Es besteht ein großer Unterschied zwischen dem Wiederholen im Deleuze'schen Sinne und dem Kopieren. Zunächst muss eine Kopie dieselbe Absicht haben wie das Original, wohingegen sich meine Arbeiten mit einer inneren Bewegung sowie der Wiederholung als Differenz befassen." Sturtevant im Gespräch mit Hans Ulrich Obrist (Winter 2008/2009), 032c, Nr. 16. http://032c.com/2008/elaine-sturtevant (abgerufen: 28. März 2014).

4   Tom Wesselmann, *Great American Nude #51*, 1963, Öl und Collage auf Leinwand (in drei Teilen), 304,8 × 365,76 cm, Privatsammlung. Reproduziert in: *Art International*, Vol. 8, Nr. 3, 25. April 1964.

5   Bruce Hainley, *Under the Sign of [sic]: Sturtevant's Volte-Face*, Los Angeles 2013.

6   James Montgomery Flagg, *I Want You for the U.S. Army*, 1917, Lithografie, 102,1 × 74,8 cm, Museum of Modern Art, New York. Reproduziert in: *Library of Congress prints and photographs: an illustrated guide*, Library of Congress, Washington, D.C. 1995, S. 43.

7   Die Angaben zur Ausstellungshistorie von Wesselmanns Gemälde stammen aus der E-Mail-Korrespondenz und verschiedenen Diskussionen des Verfassers mit Jeffrey Sturges, Tom Wesselmann Estate, Februar 2014. „Pop Art – Cult of the Commonplace", *Time*-Magazin, 3. Mai 1963.

8   Buchumschlag von John Rublowsky, *Pop Art,* New York 1965.

9   Poster für *Amerikansk Pop-konst*, Moderna Museet, 1964. Reproduziert in: Mary Lee Corlett, *The Prints of Roy Lichtenstein. A Catalogue Raisonné 1948–1993*, New York 1994, S. 299.

10 Buchumschlag des Kataloges für *Amerikansk Pop-konst*, 1964. Moderna Museet, *Amerikansk pop-konst, 106 former av kärlek och förtvivlan: Jim Dine, Roy Lichtenstein, Claes Oldenburg, James Rosenquist, George Segal, Andy Warhol, Tom Wesselmann*, Stockholm 1964.

11 Hainley, *Under the Sign of [sic]*, S. 78 (wie Anm. 2).

12 Ebd., S. 84.

13 Öyvind Fahlström, *Planetarium*, 1963, Große Tafel: Gemälde auf Leinwand und Metallplatten auf der Rückseite, 94 magnetische Elemente: Gemälde auf Vinylplatte, 197 × 234 cm. Kleine Tafel: Tusche und Tempera auf Papier, auf Holz aufgezogen, 94 magnetische Elemente: Tusche auf Papier, 57 × 57 cm, Centre Pompidou, Paris. Reproduziert in: *Art International*, Vol. 8, Nr. 3, 25. April 1964.

14 Max Kozloff, „New York Letter", *Art International*, Vol. 8, Nr. 3, 25. April 1964, S. 61.

15 Während es lange Zeit hieß, Sturtevant habe sich ausschließlich der Werke männlicher Künstler bedient, förderte Hainley bei seiner sorgfältigen Archivrecherche einen entscheidenden Fall zutage, in dem die Künstlerin ein Tanzstück von Yvonne Rainer wiederholte. Vgl. hierzu Hainley: *Under the Sign of [sic]*, S. 117–151 (wie Anm. 2).

16 Ausführliche Informationen zu Alloways *American Drawings*-Ausstellung finden sich in The Guggenheim Museum Archives, Exhibition Records (Collection A0003), Box 1074.

17 Lawrence Alloway, „Introduction", in: *American Drawings*. Ausst.-Kat., Solomon R. Guggenheim Museum, New York 1964. Alloway reagierte nicht nur auf Greenberg, sondern gleichzeitig auf eine Besprechung Max Kozloffs zu der den *American Drawings* im Guggenheim vorangegangenen Ausstellung, *Twentieth-Century Master Drawings*. Vgl. Max Kozloff, *Notes on the Psychology of Modern Draftsmanship,* in: *Arts Magazine,* 38, 5, Februar 1964, S. 58–63.

18 „Man verbindet die Zeichnung stets mit geistiger Arbeit, eine Vorstellung, die in der Prägnanz des Mediums begründet liegt. Diese Tradition widerspricht nicht der autografen Definition der Zeichnung, sondern erweitert diese vielmehr: Die reduktiven Mittel der Zeichnung dienen ebenso der intellektuellen Zusammenfassung wie der Spontaneität. Das Diagramm und das Autografe stellen in der Zeichnung keine Gegensätze dar. Die Linie wird als Raster, Matrix, Skelett, Gerüst beziehungsweise Kern begriffen; es handelt sich bei ihr um die Verkörperung des Geistes des Künstlers in nicht-diskursiver Form und auf verdichtetem Raum. Die technische Schlichtheit, welche eine gestische Unmittelbarkeit der Zeichnung erlaubt, symbolisiert daher das Ordnungspotenzial der Kunst." Alloway, „Introduction", in: *American Drawings*, o. S. (wie Anm. 17)

19 Auch wenn die in der Bianchini-Ausstellung gezeigte Arbeit *7th Avenue Garment Rack with Warhol Flowers* diesen kombinatorischen Ansatz dadurch erweiterte, dass hier mehrere entlehnte Kunstwerke in einen engen räumlichen Zusammenhang gebracht wurden.

20 Alloway: „Introduction", in: *American Drawings*, o. S. (wie Anm. 17)

21 Ebd. (Hervorhebung durch den Autor)

SIXTIES

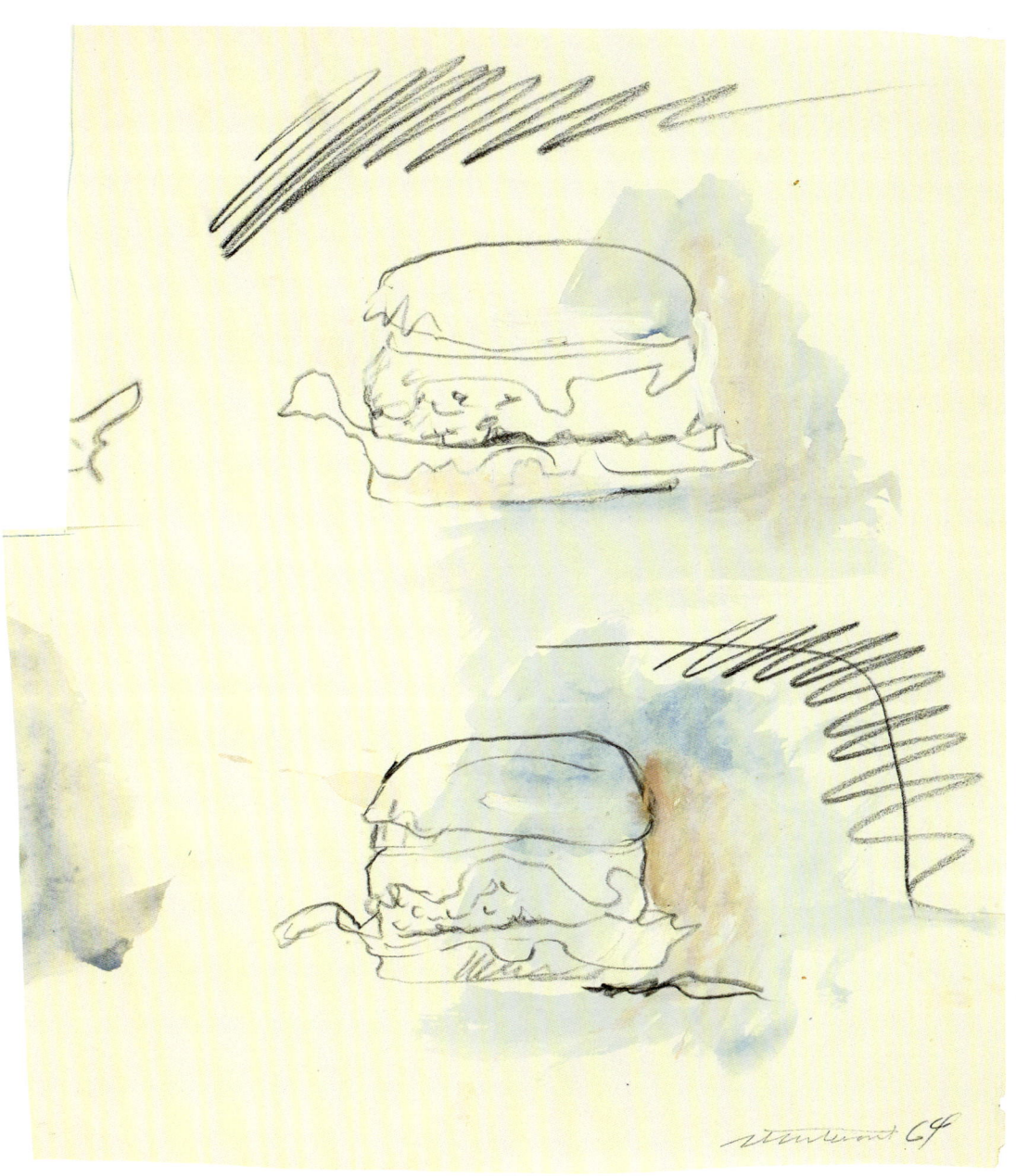

Untitled (Oldenburg), 1964   **41**

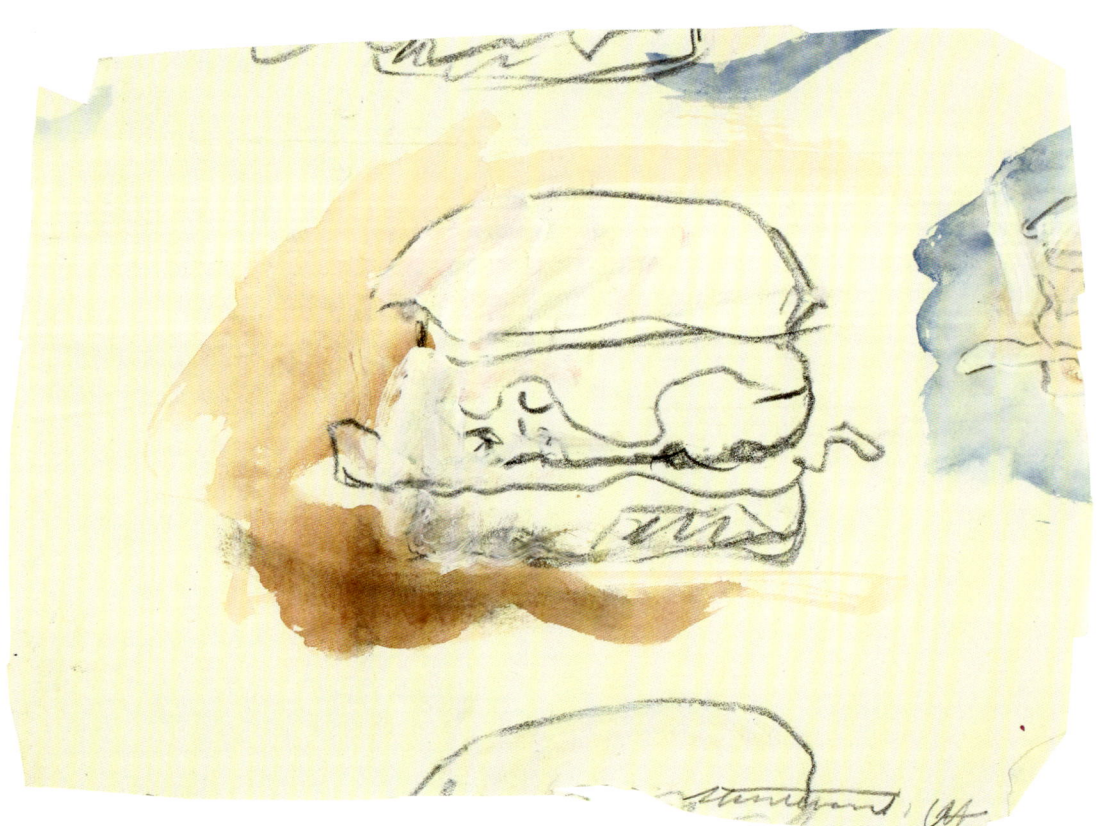

42   Untitled (Oldenburg), 1964

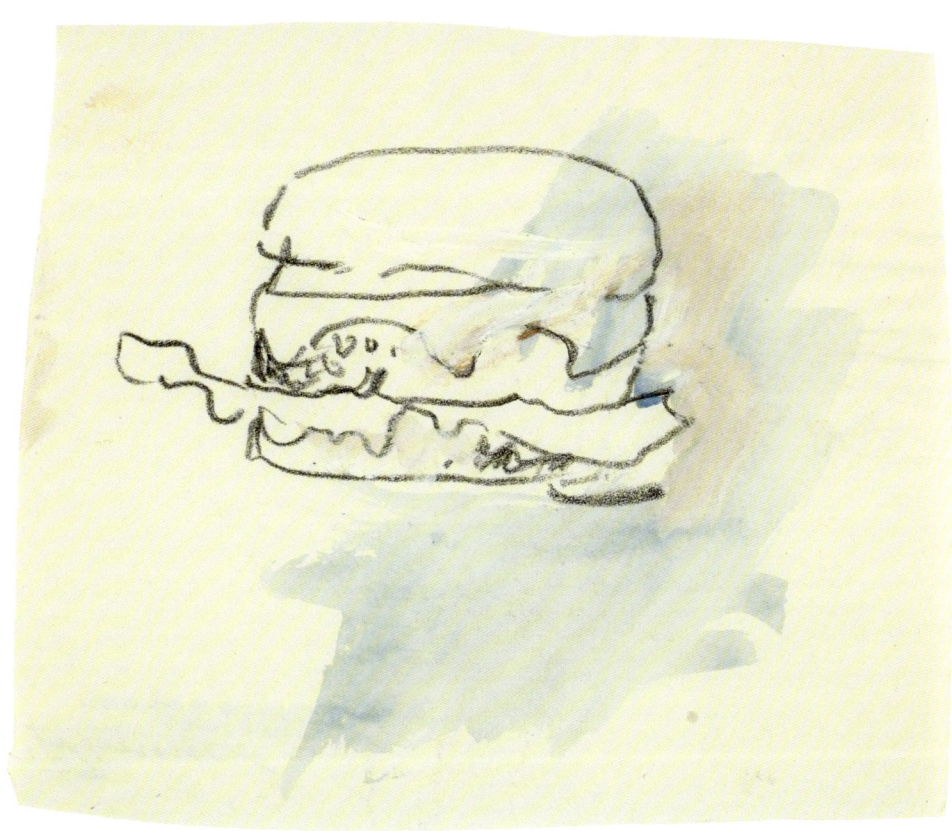

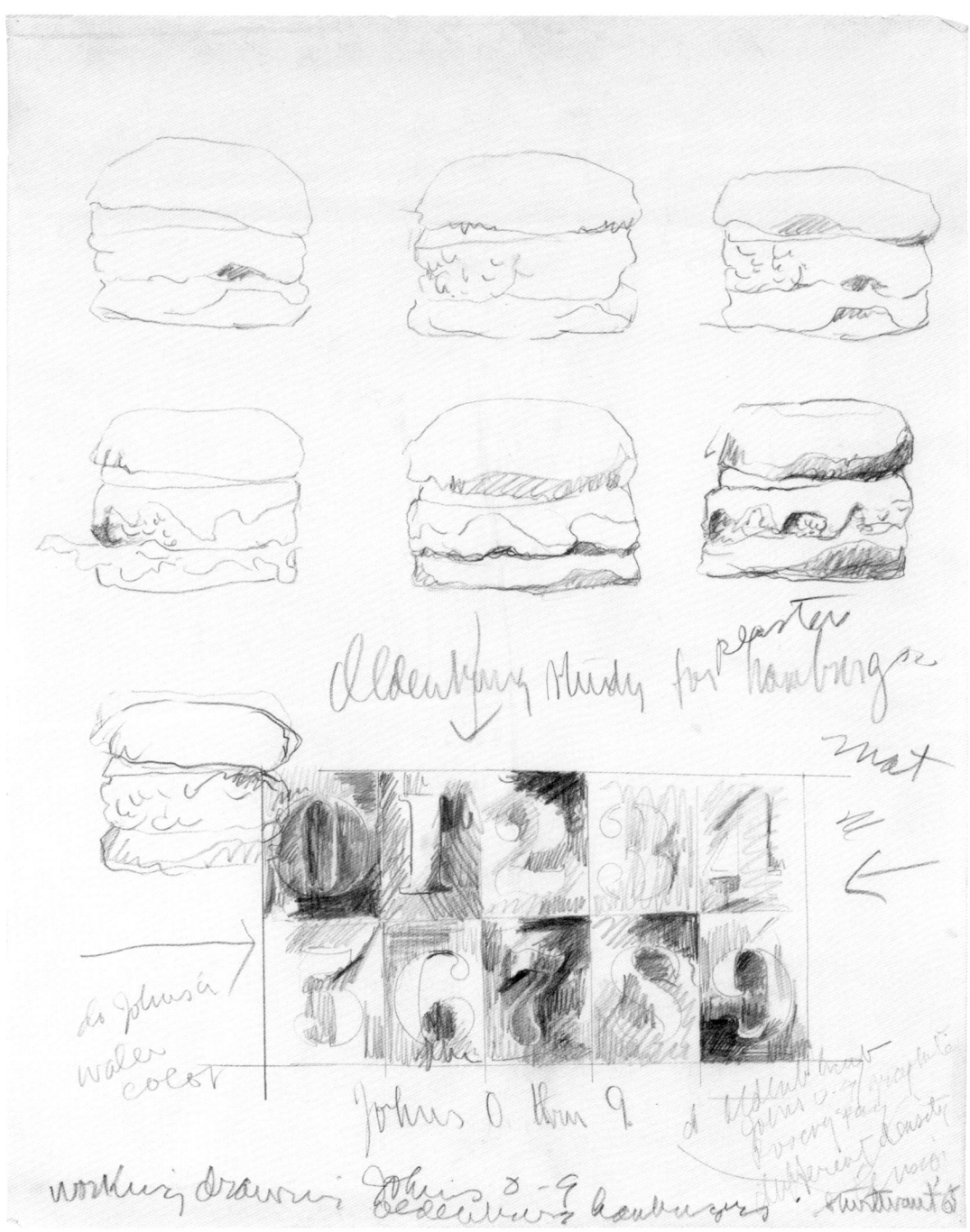

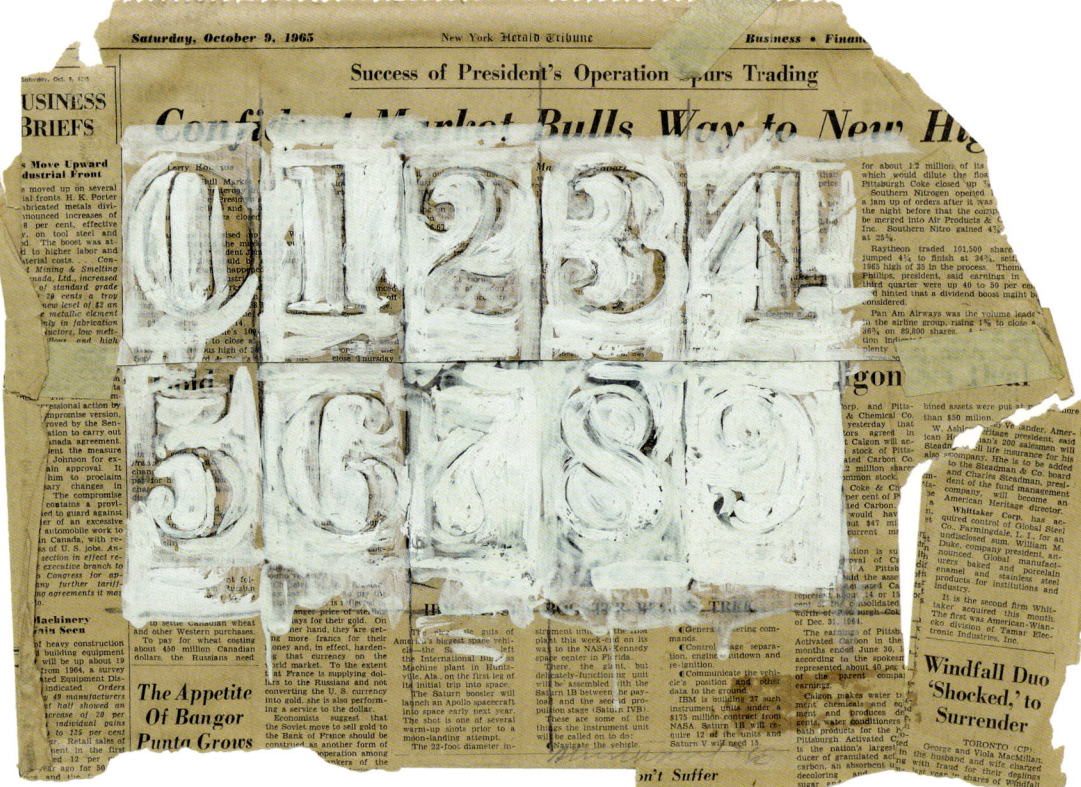

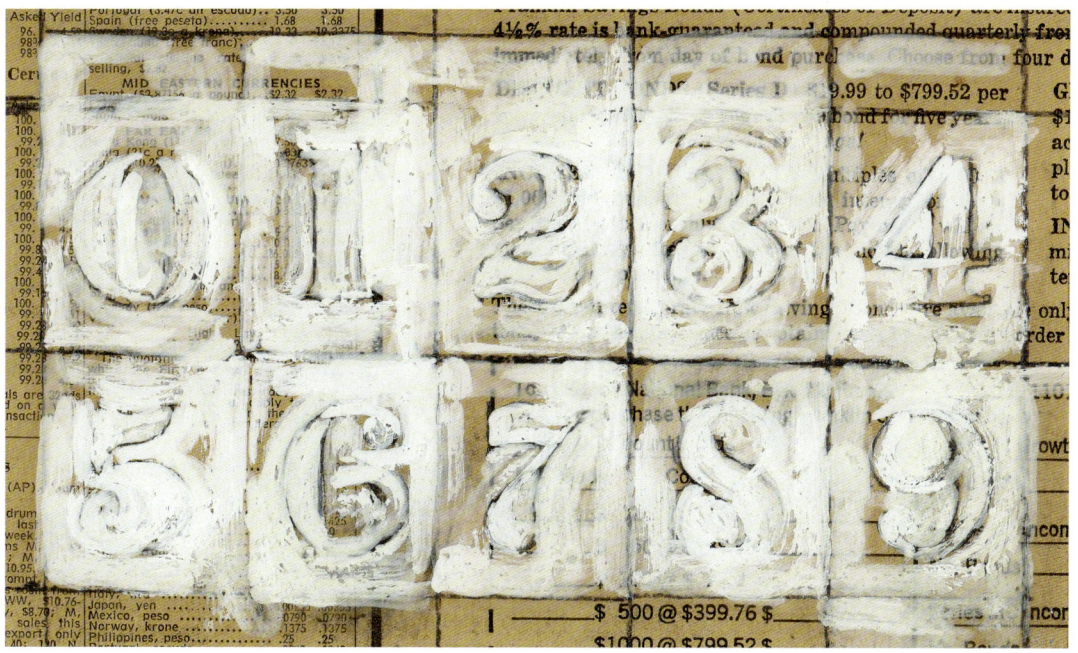

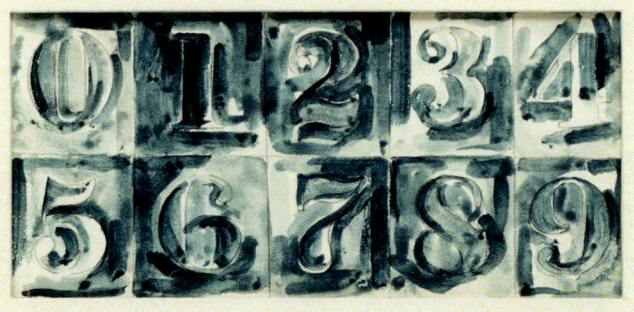

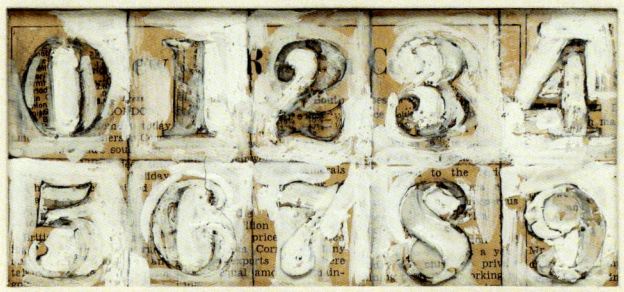

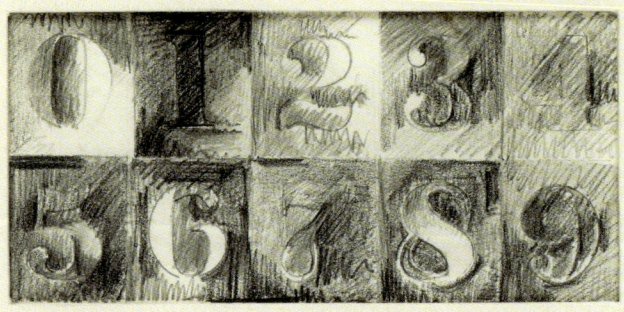

Study Johns 0–9, 1965

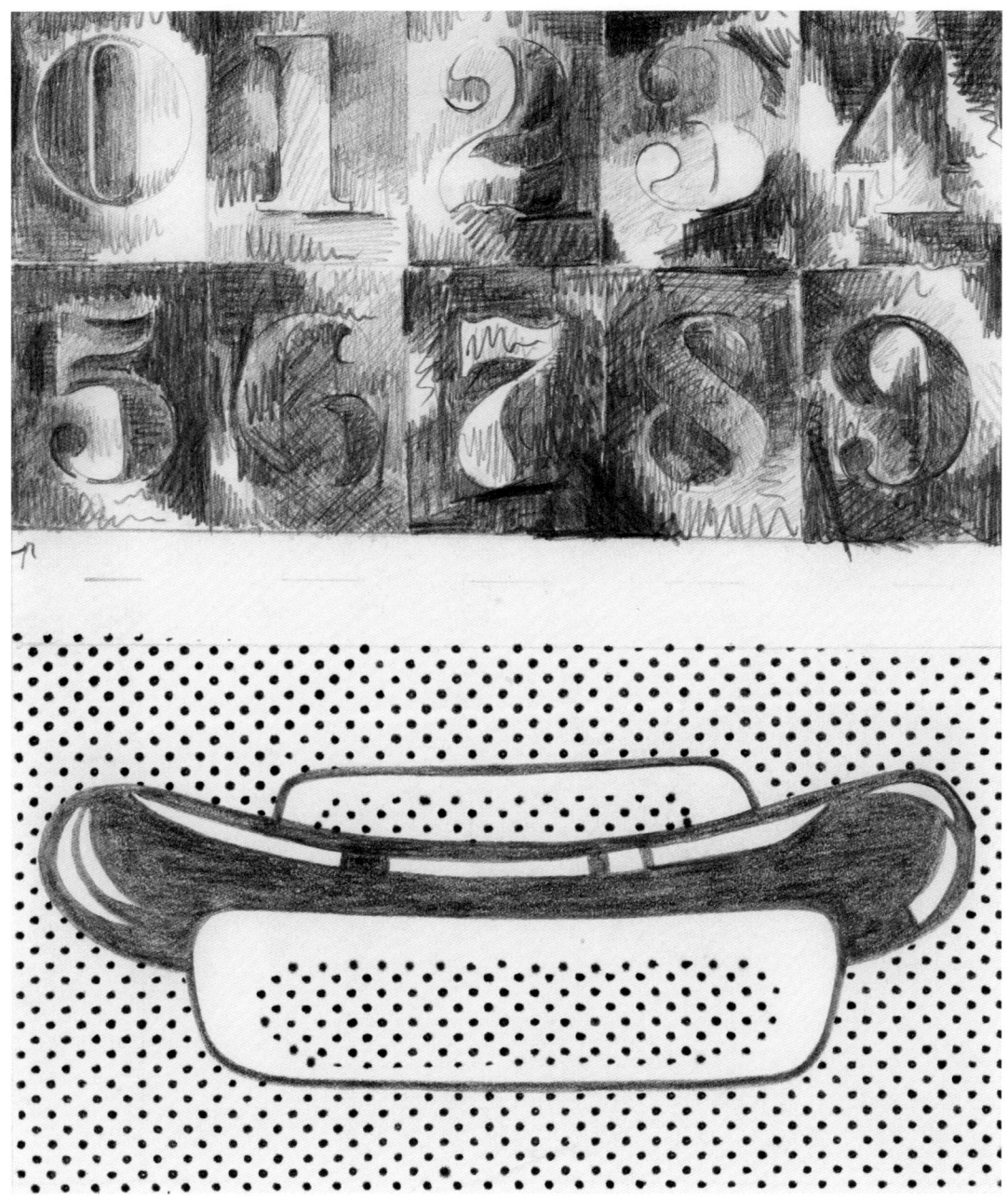

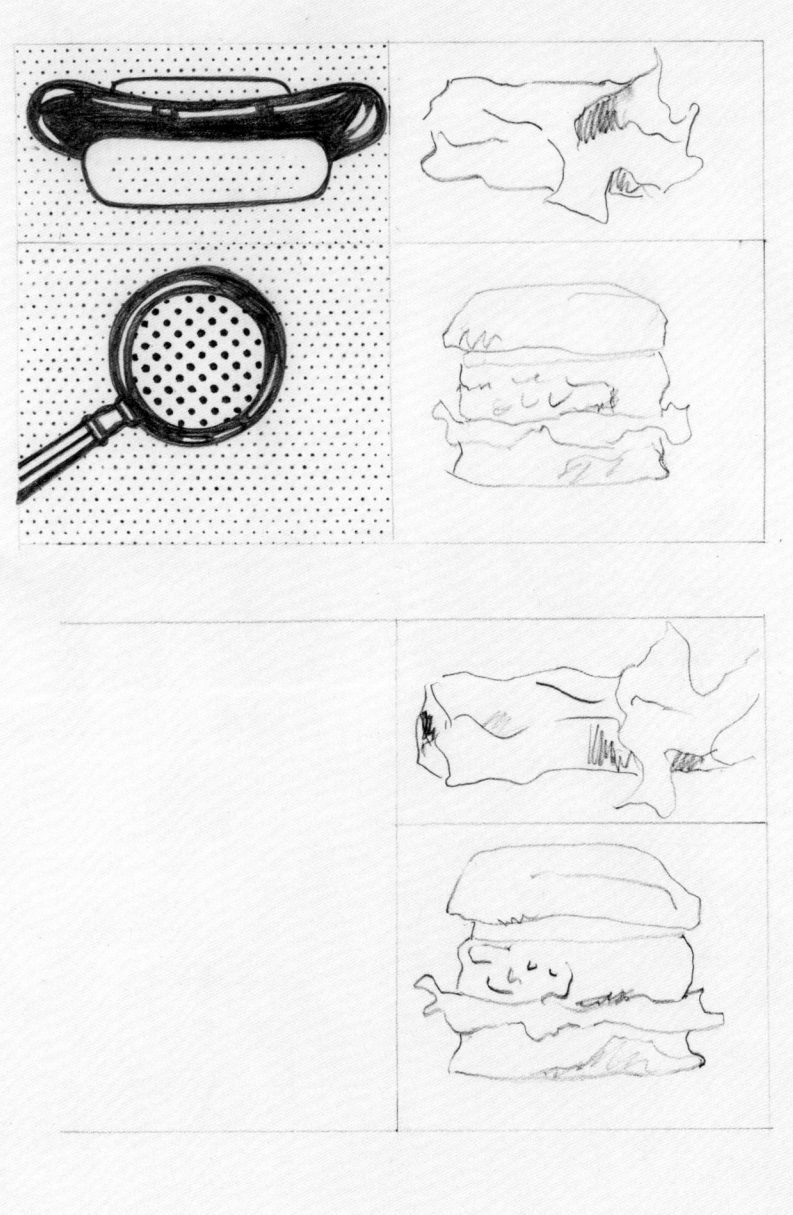

Lichtenstein Hot Dog Magnifying Glass Oldenburg Charms Hamburger, 1965 **51**

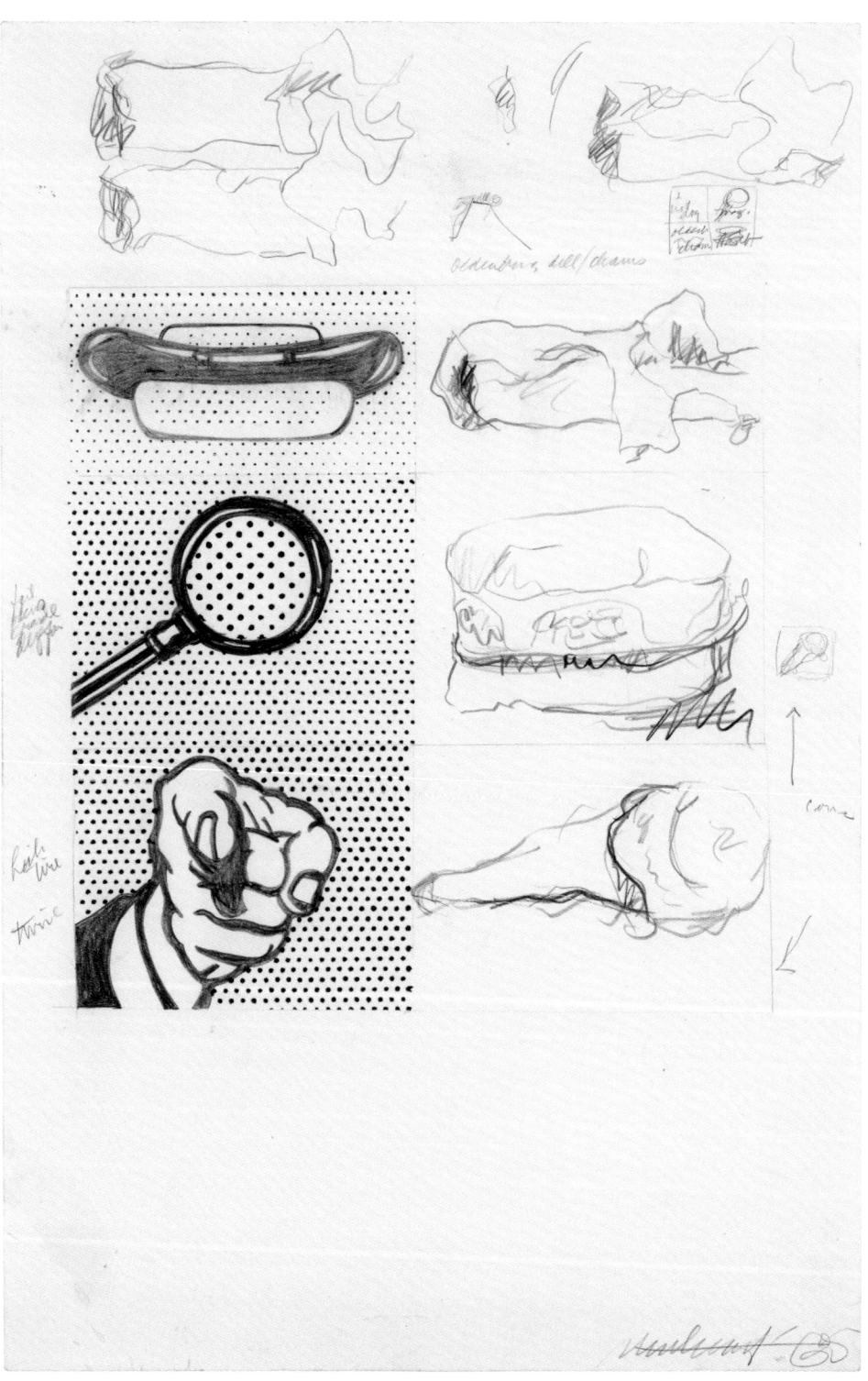

Lichtenstein Hot Dog Magnifying Glass Pointing Finger Oldenburg Charms Hamburger Ice Cream, 1965

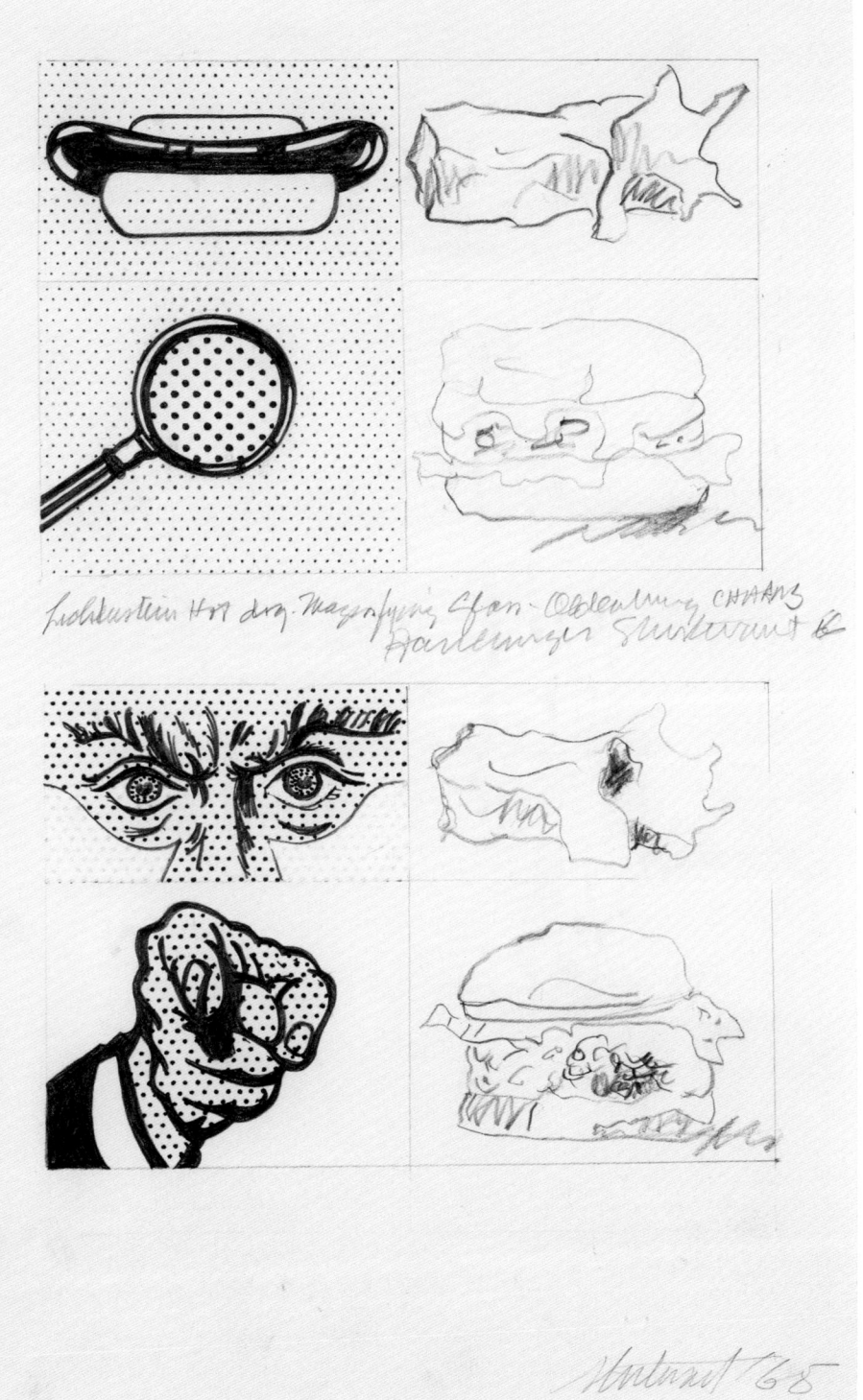

Lichtenstein Hot Dog Magnifying Glass Oldenburg Charms Hamburger, 1965 **53**

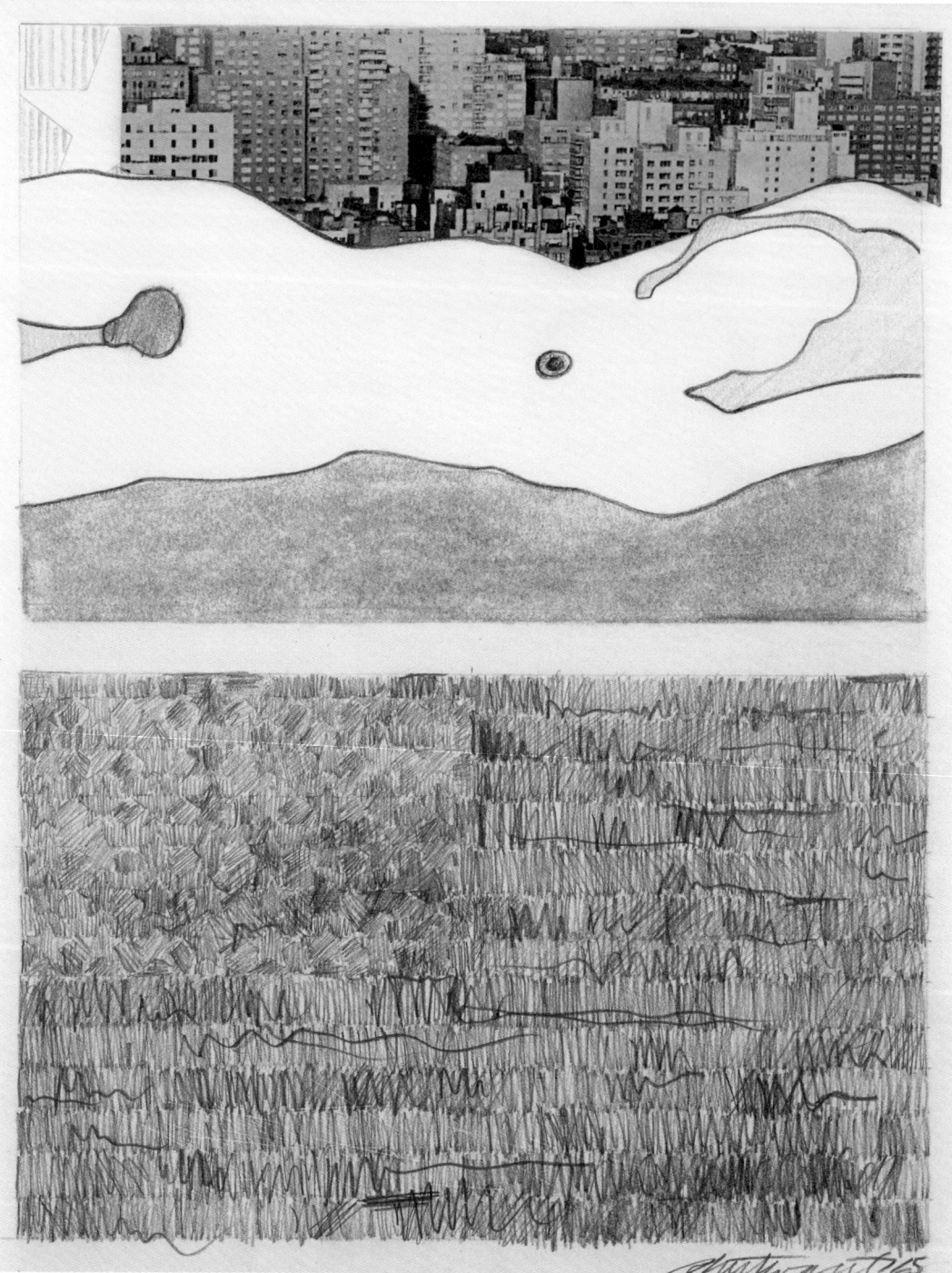

54 *Wesselmann Great American Nude Johns Flag*, 1965

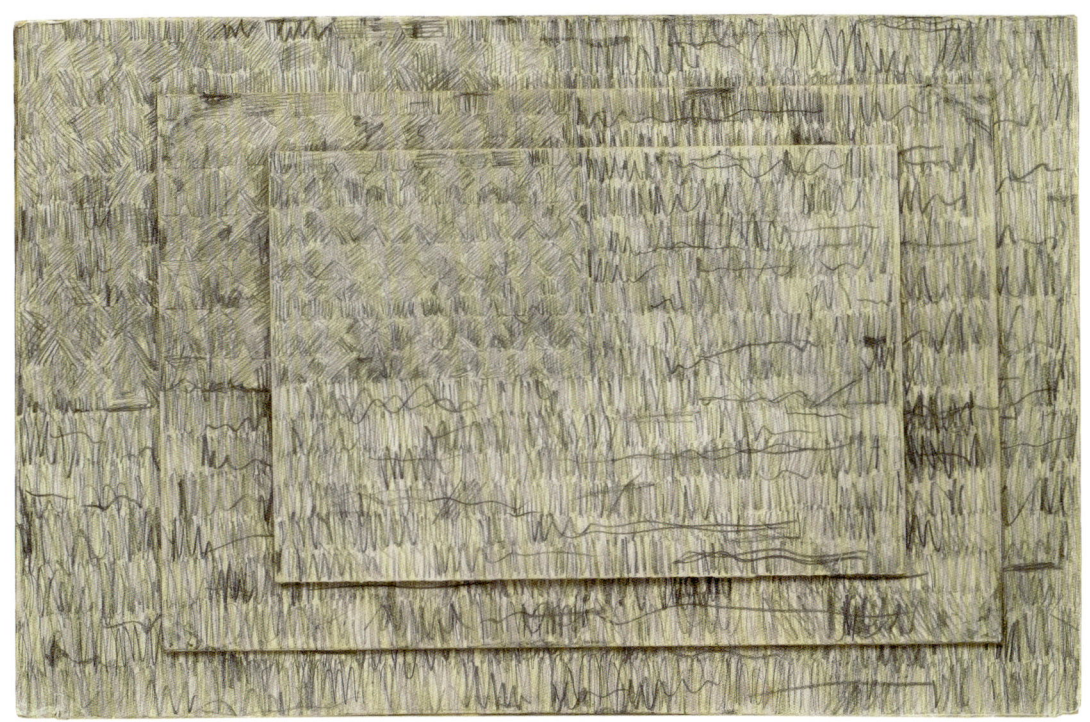

Study for Johns Three Flags, 1965   **55**

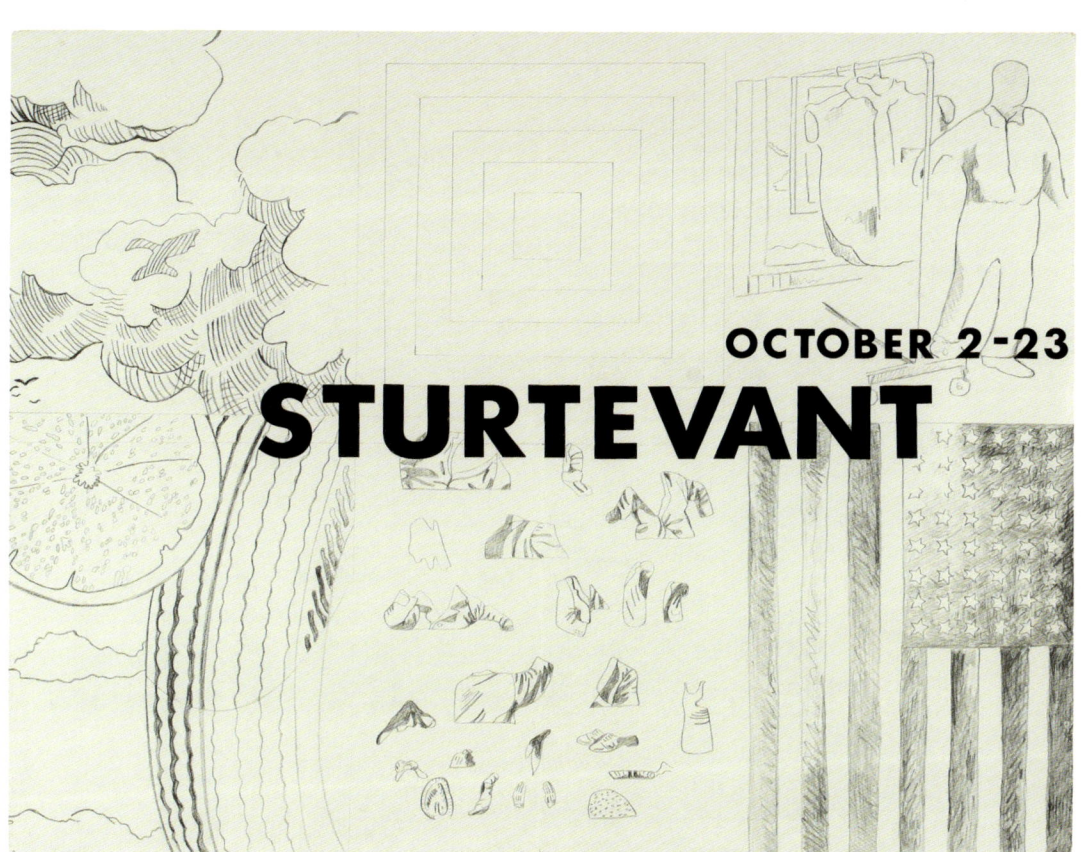

OCTOBER 2-23

STURTEVANT

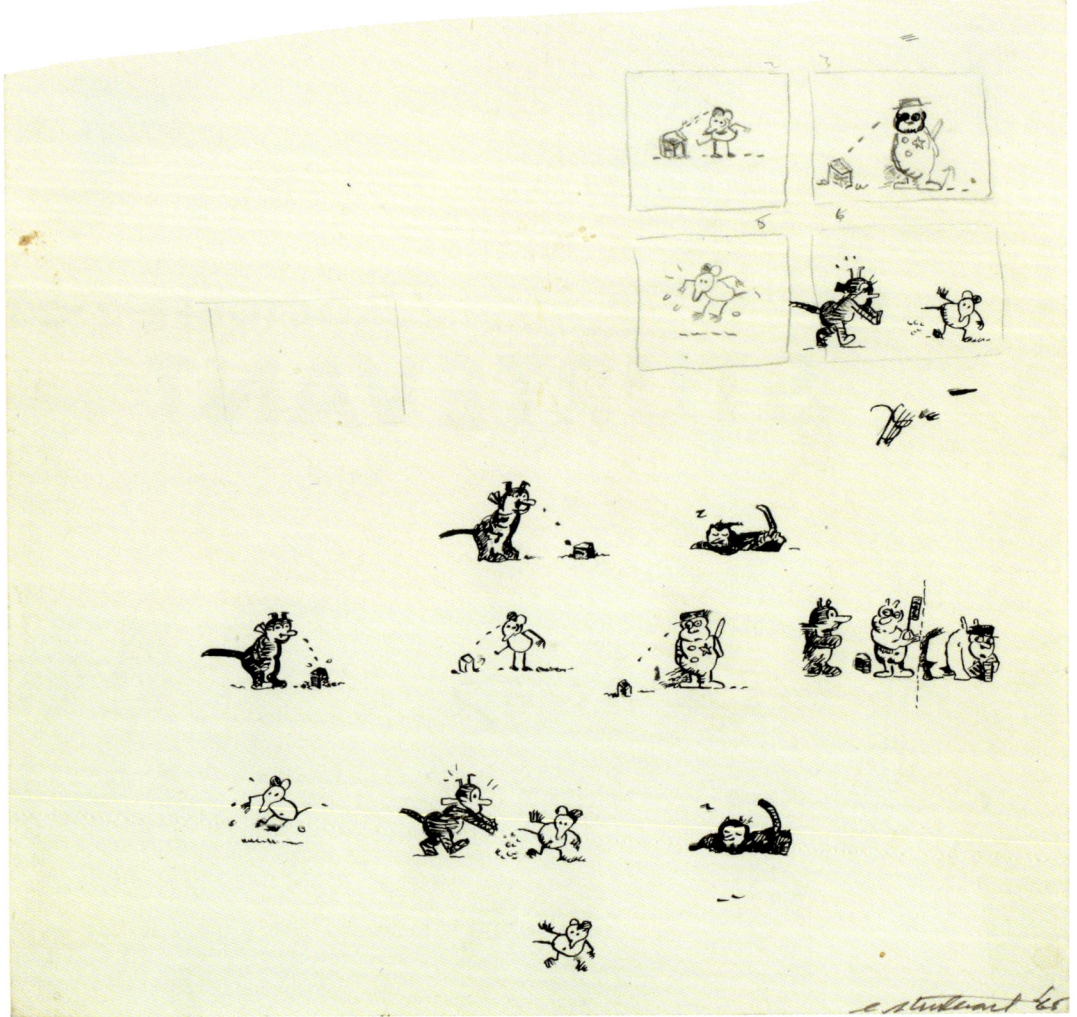

Study for Fahlström Krazy Kat, 1965

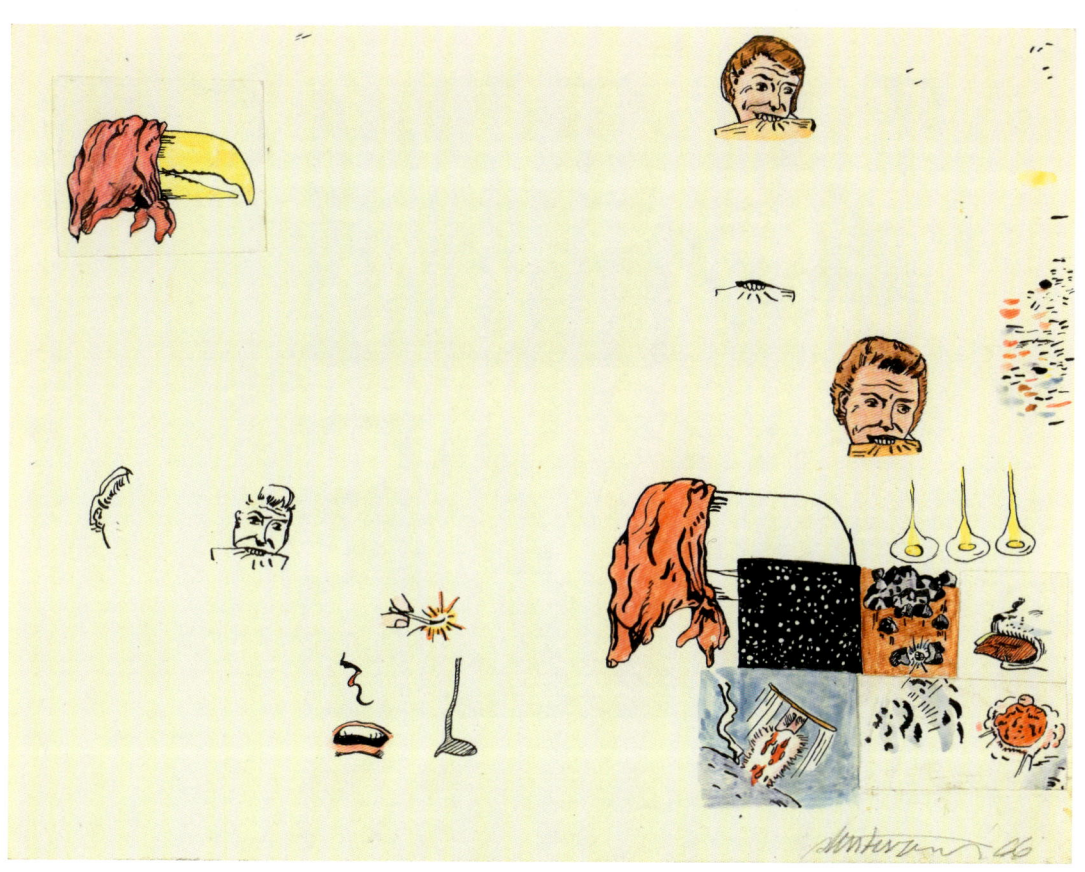

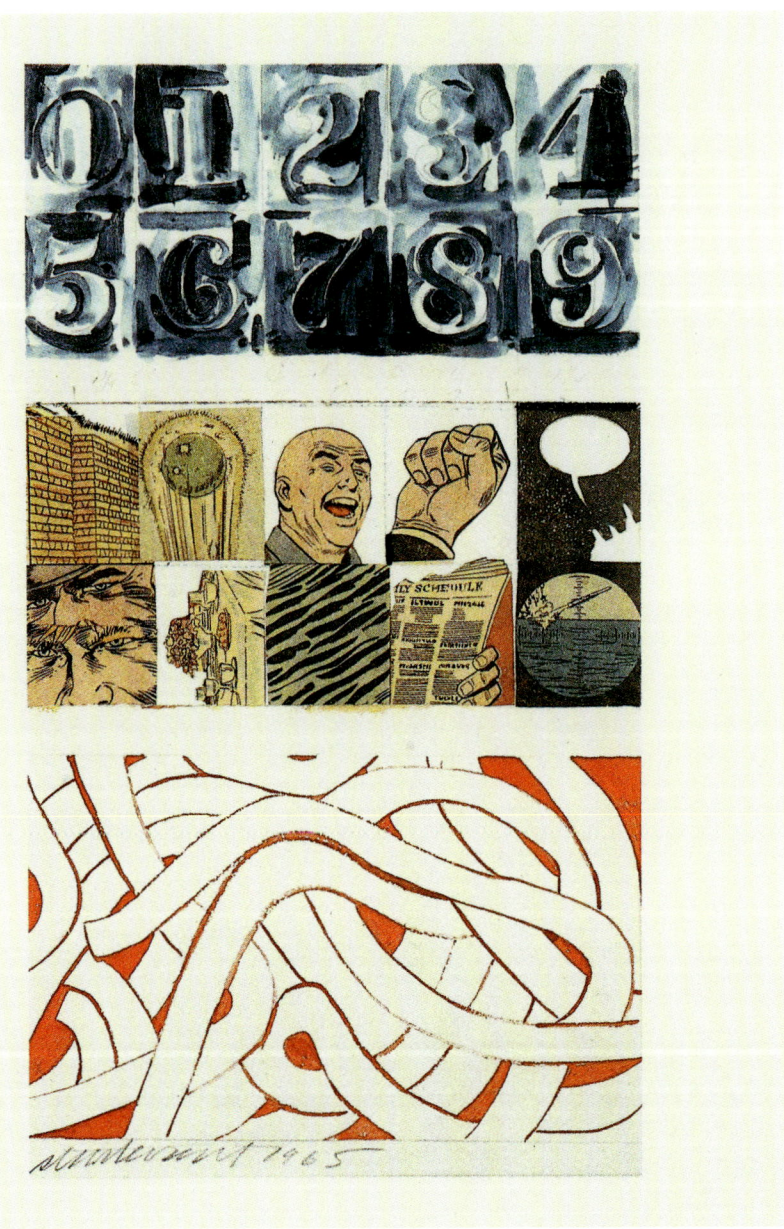

Working Drawing for Johns 0 Through 9 Fahlström Elements Rosenquist Spaghetti, 1965

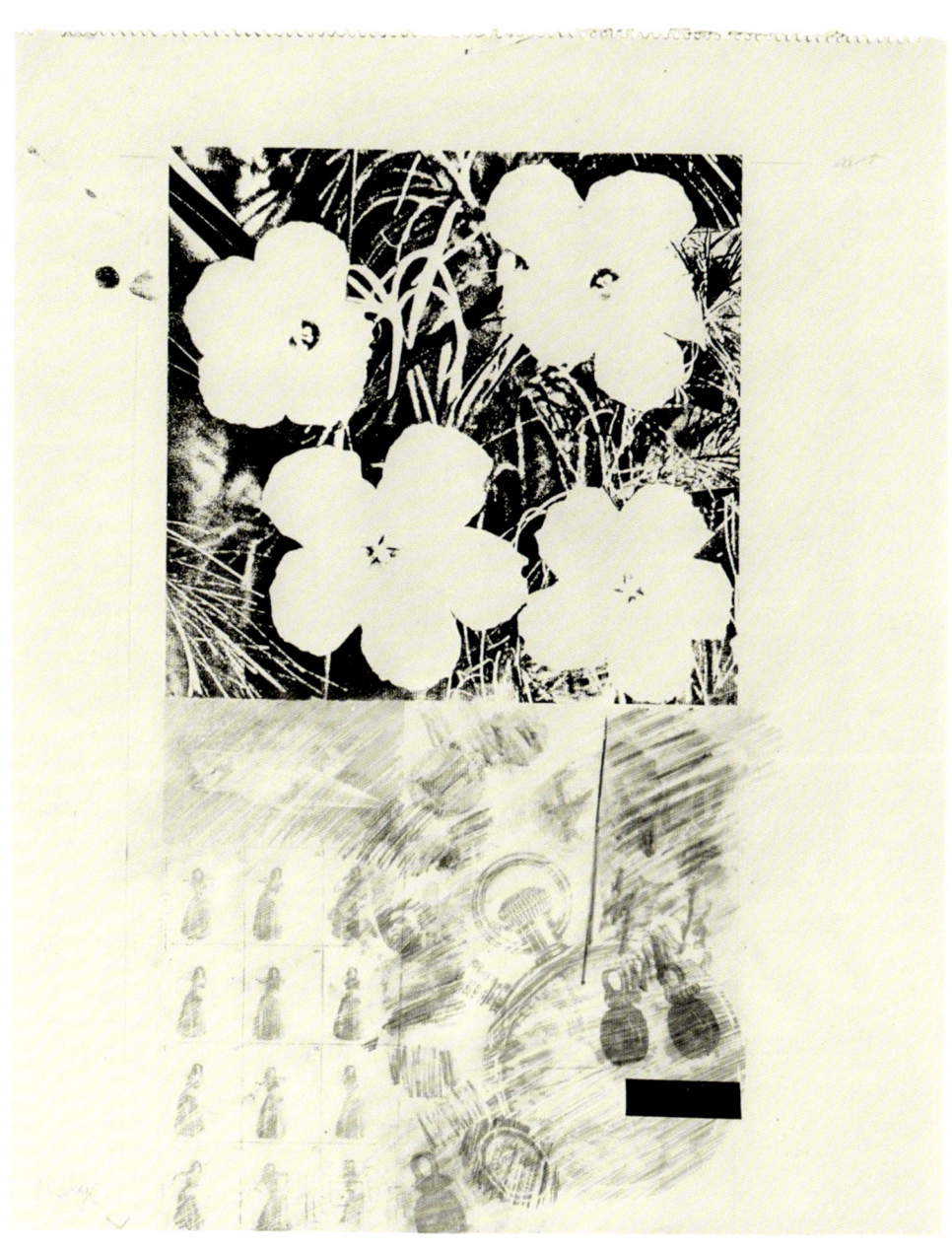

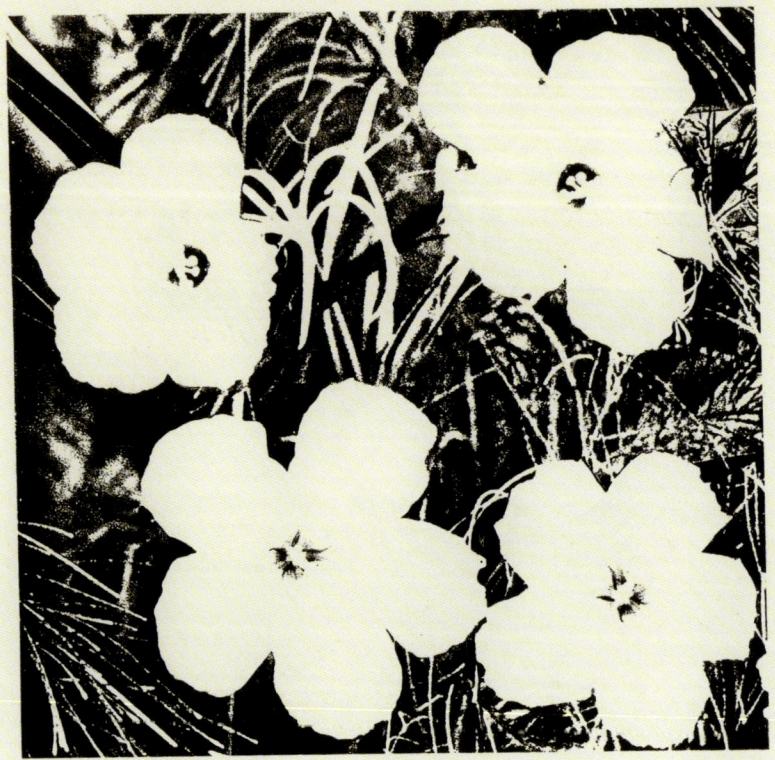

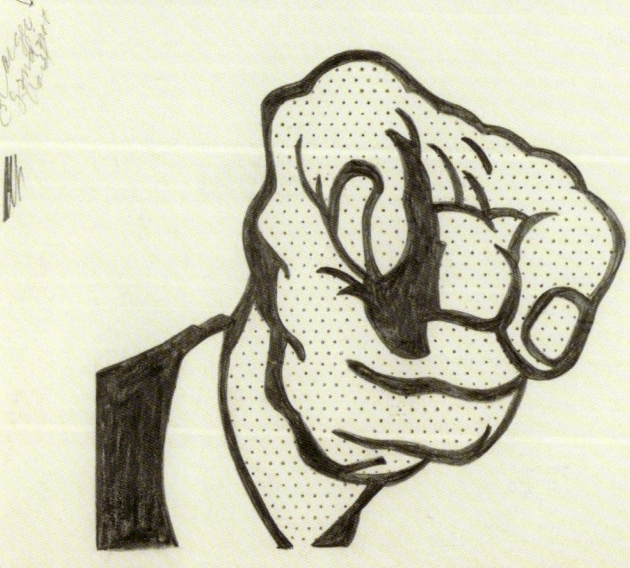

62   *Working Drawing Warhol Flowers Lichtenstein Pointed Finger*, 1966

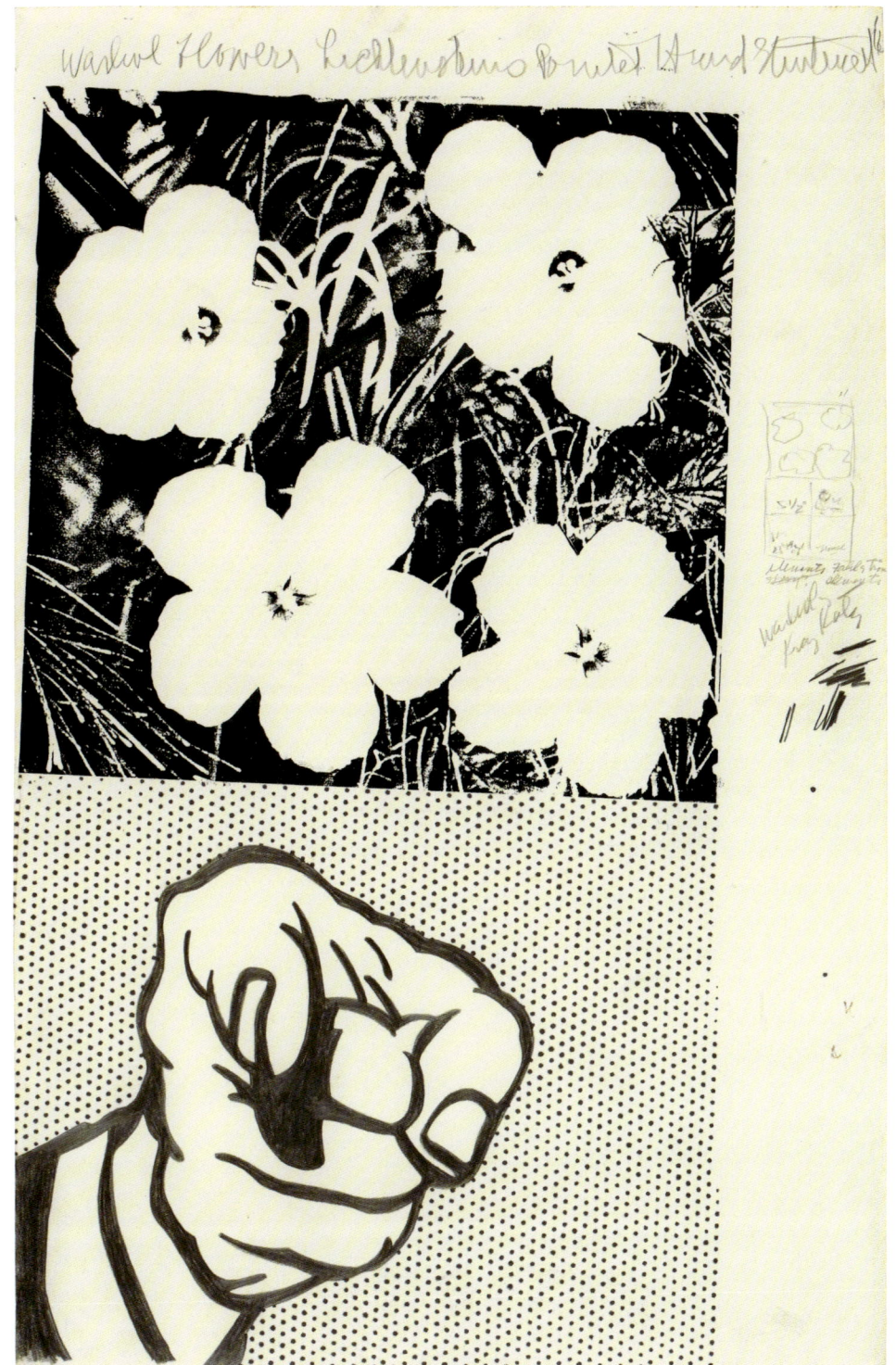

Warhol Flowers Lichtenstein Pointed Hand, 1966　**63**

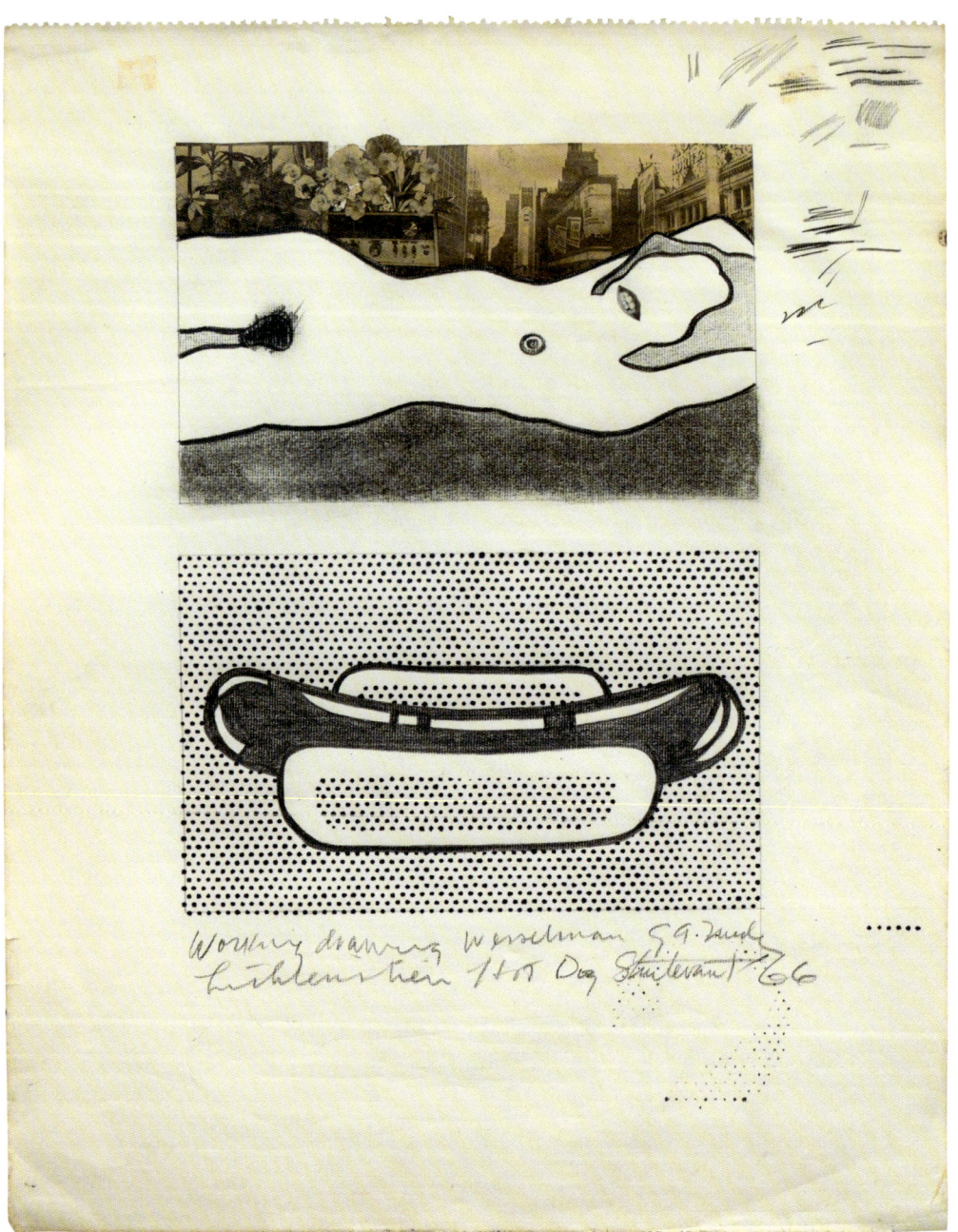

64 *Working Drawing Wesselmann Great American Nude Lichtenstein Hot Dog*, 1966

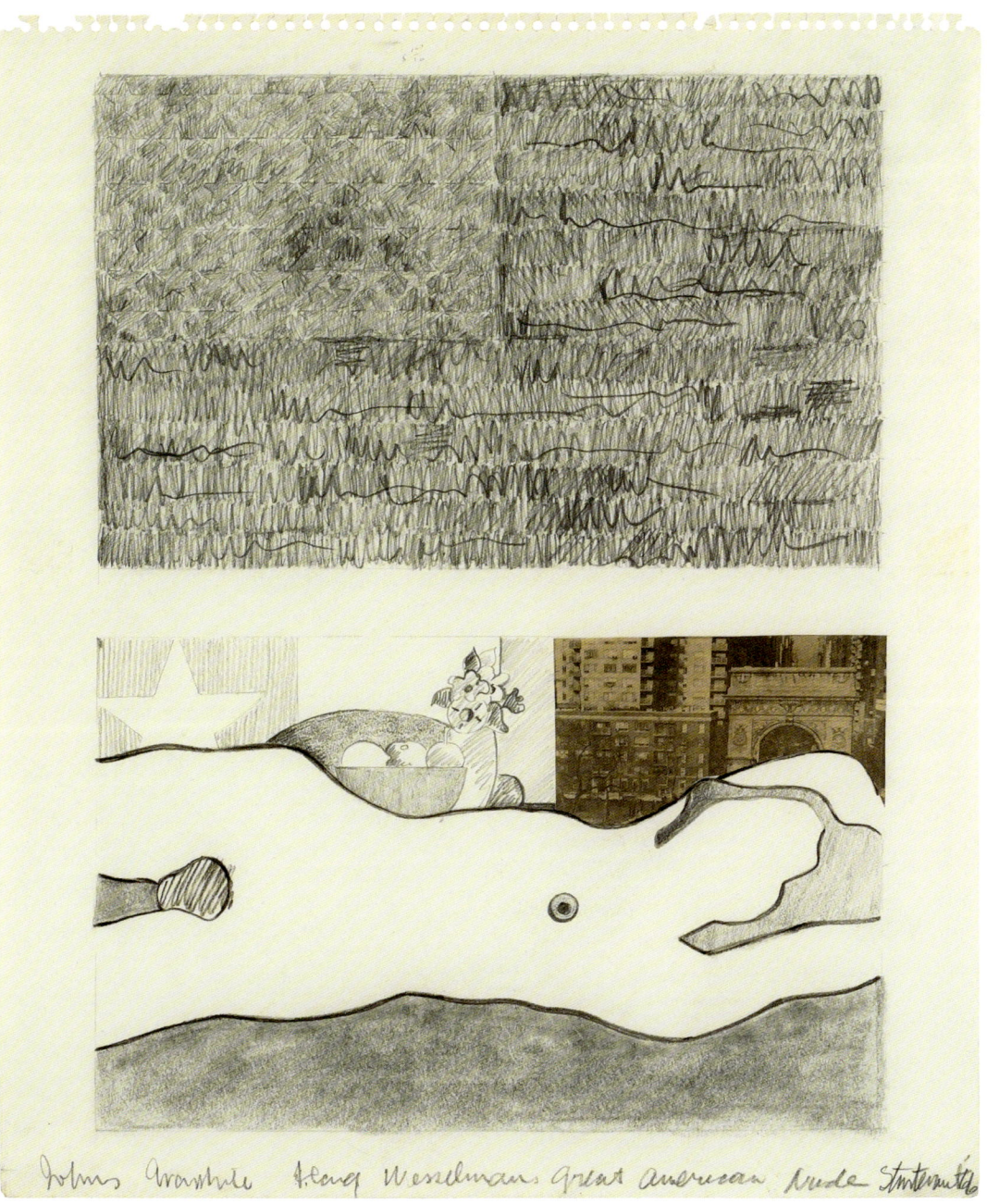

Johns Graphite Flag Wesselmann Great American Nude *handwritten*

Johns Graphite Flag Wesselmann Great American Nude, 1966 **65**

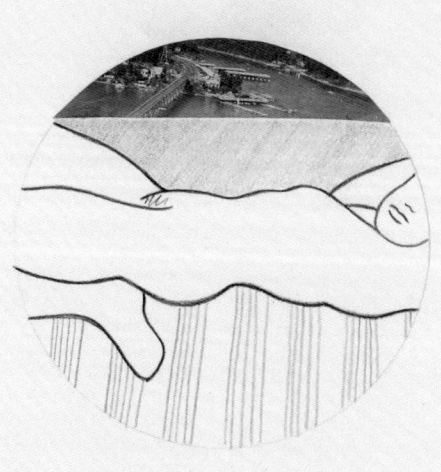

Study Wesselman graf american Nude Johns Target Shirtwaitt

Study Wesselmann Great American Nude Johns Target, 1966

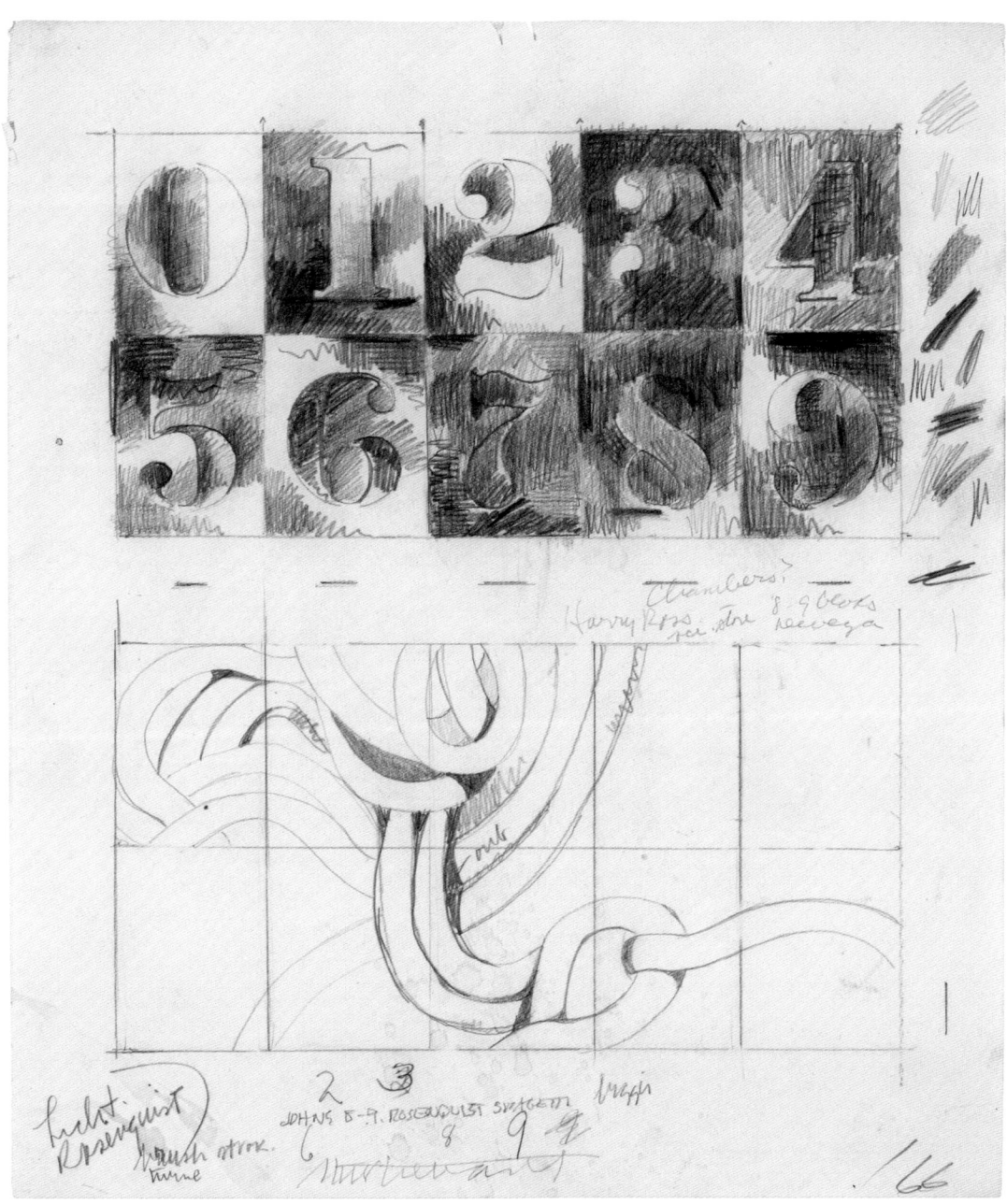

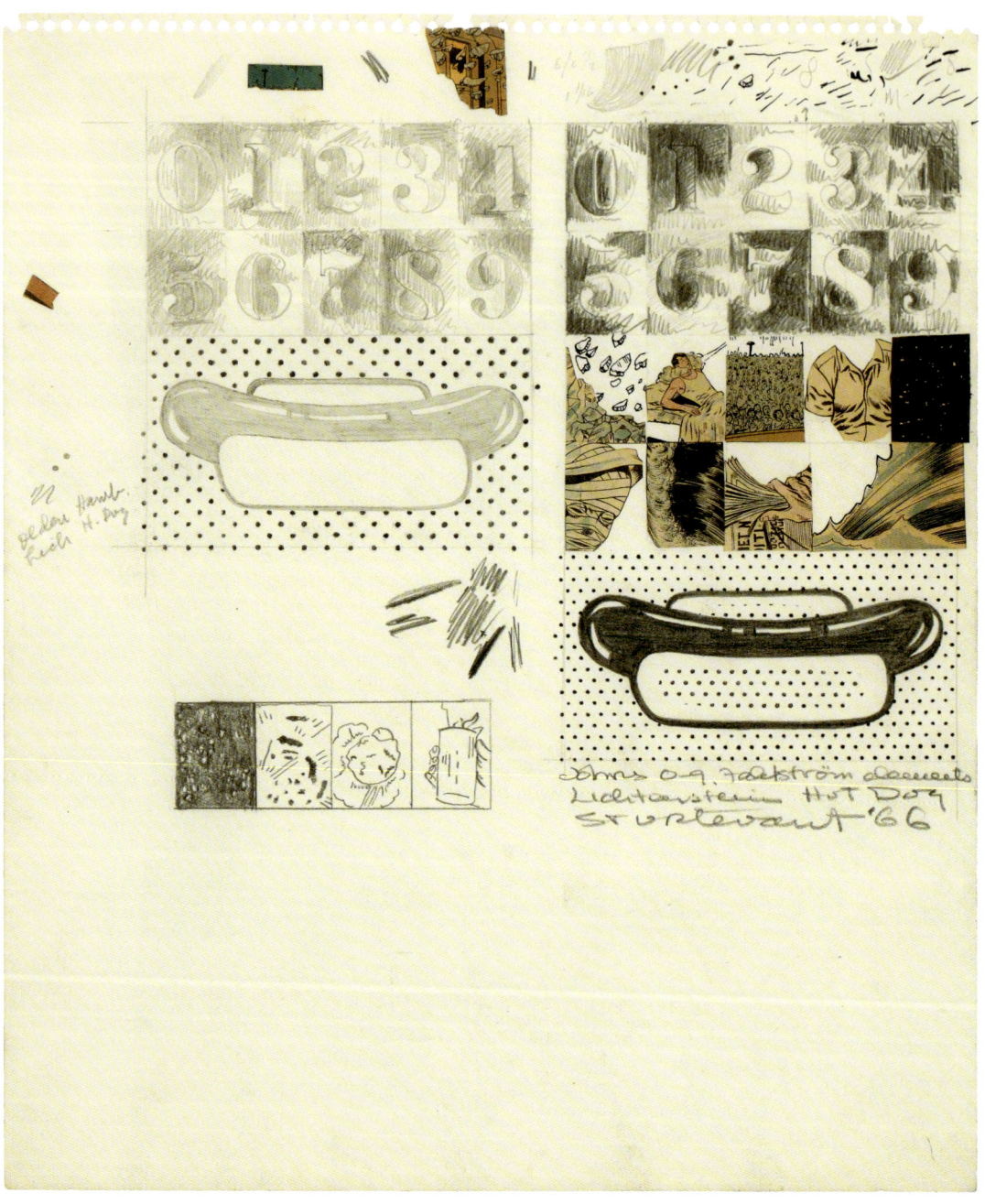

Johns 0–9 Fahlström Elements Lichtenstein Hot Dog, 1966

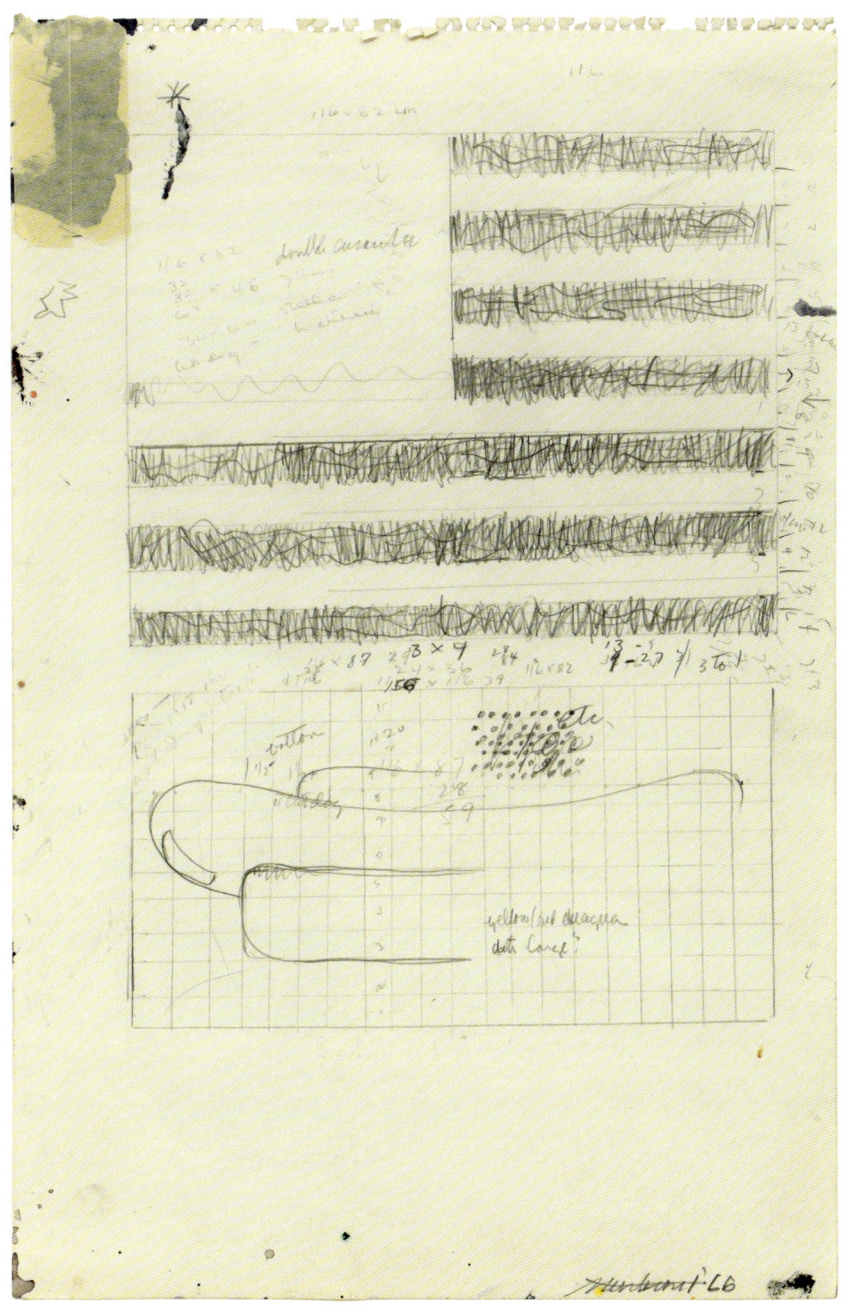

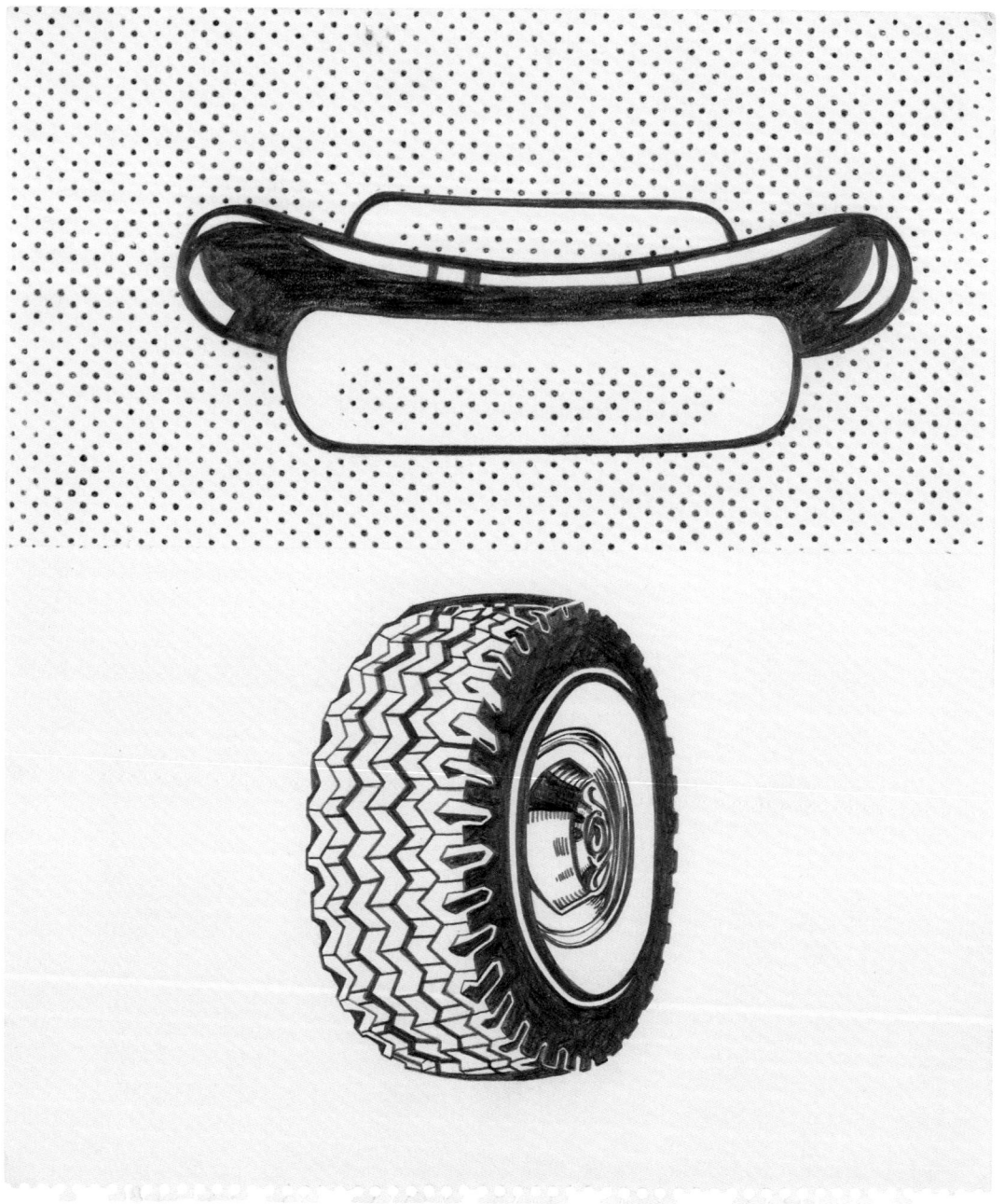

Lichtenstein Hot Dog Graphite Tire, 1966

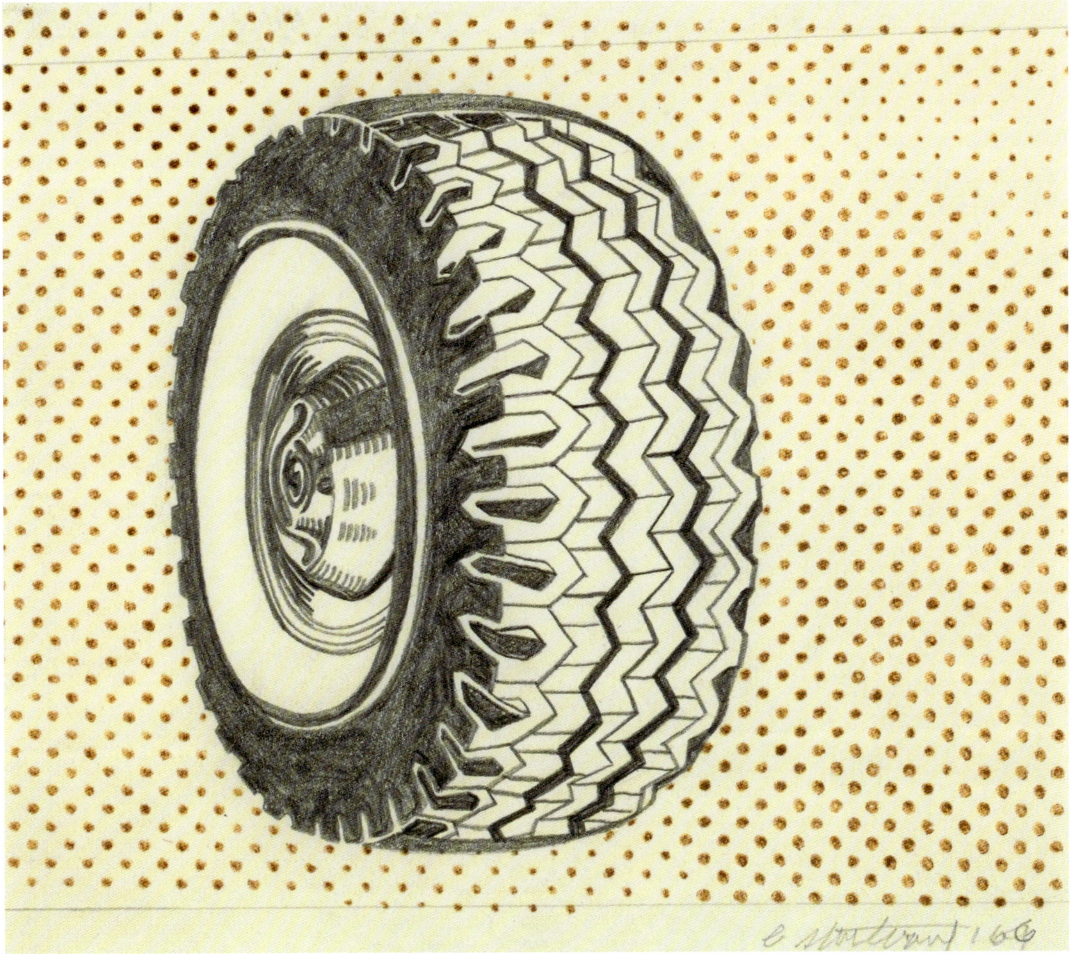

Lichtenstein Tire, 1966

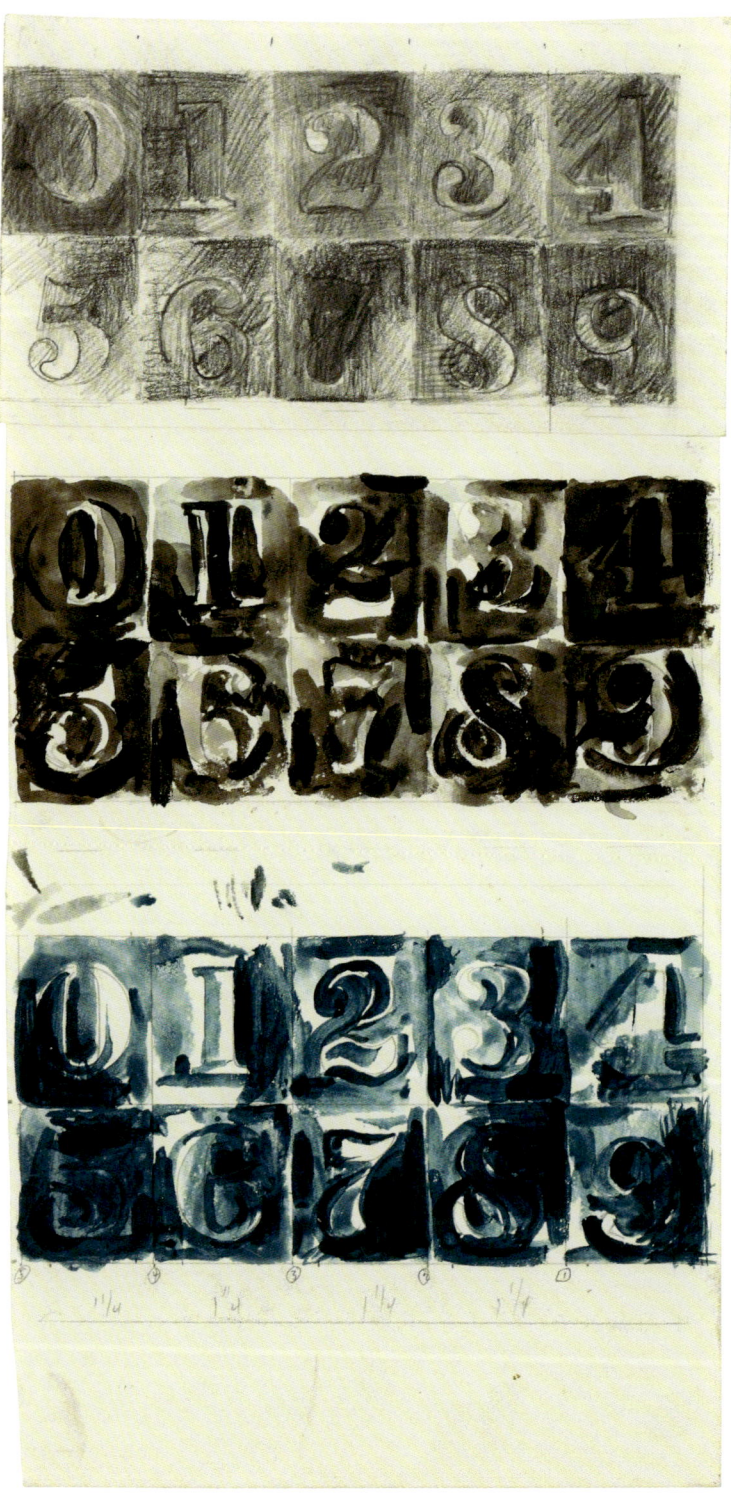

Study for Johns 0 through 9, 1966/67

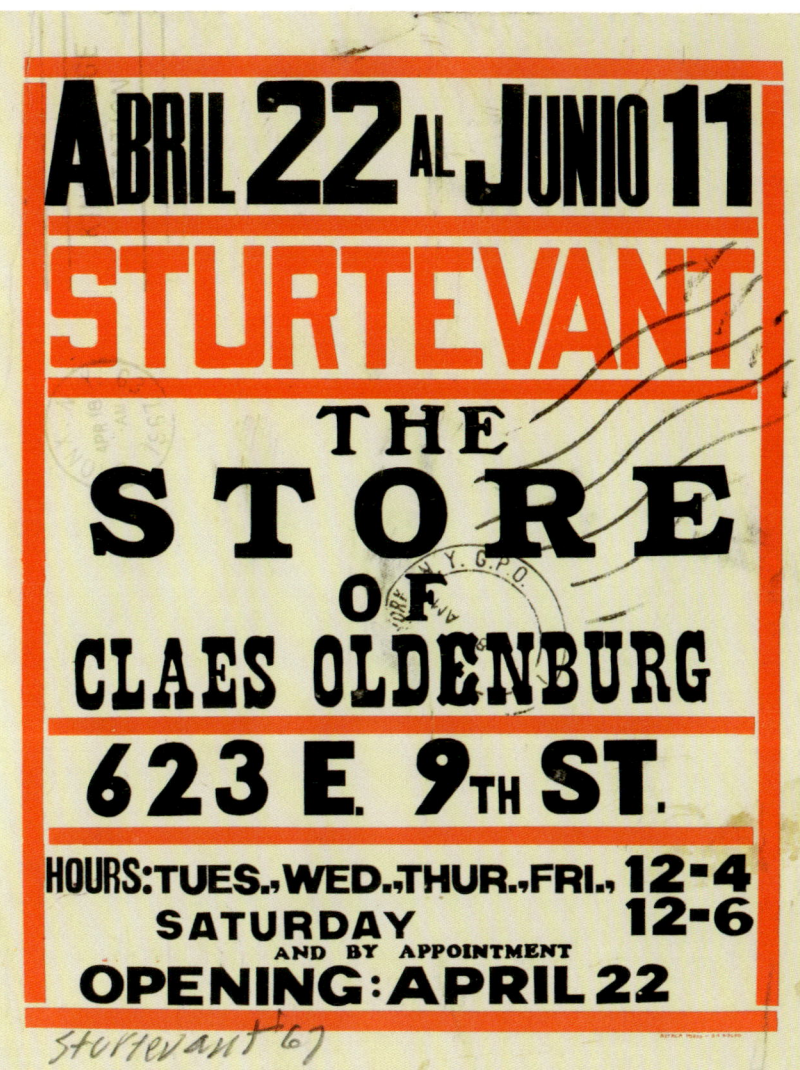

Sturtevant '67

74   Musical Score (Duchamp Erratum Musical), 1967

Musical Score (Duchamp Erratum Musical), 1967 **75**

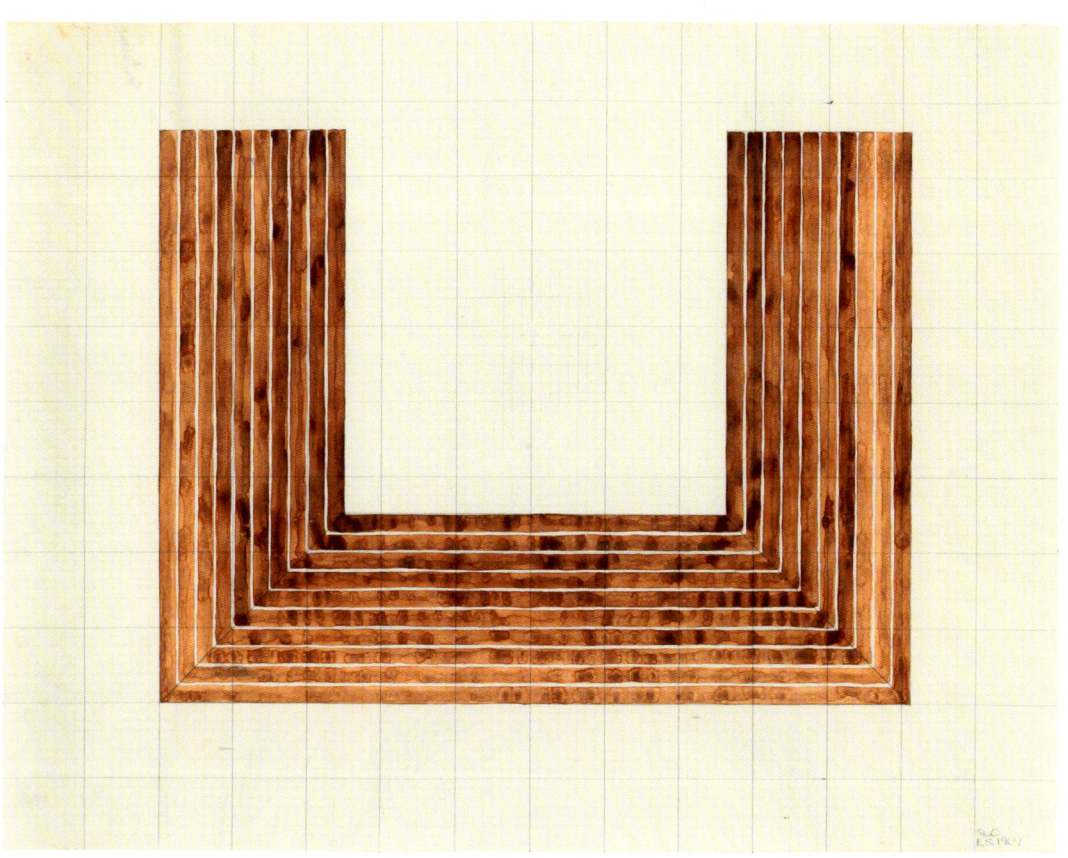

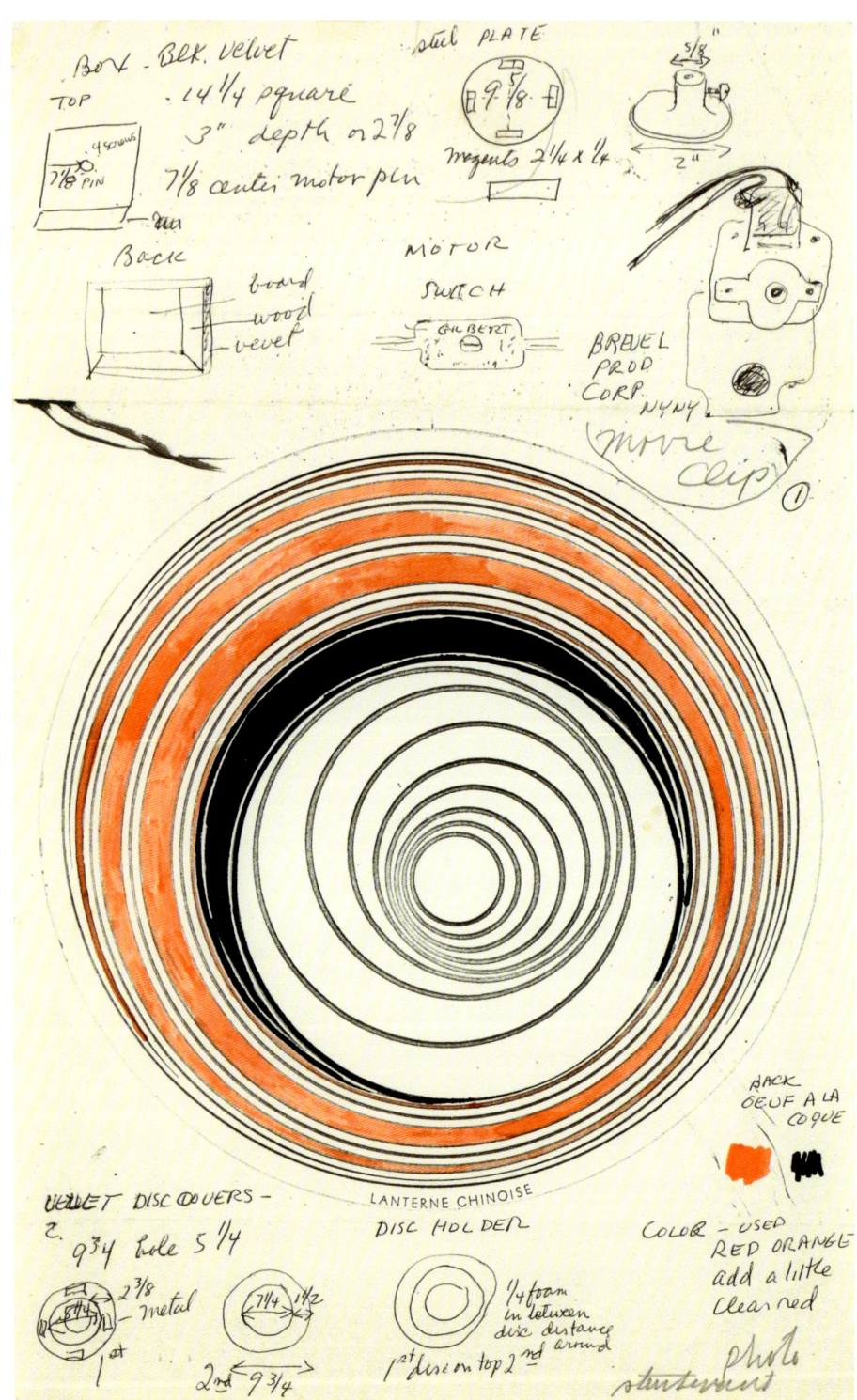

Box - Blk. velvet
TOP   .14 1/4 square
            3" depth or 2 7/8
            7/8 center motor pin

4 screws
7/8 pin

Back
            board
            wood
            velvet

steel PLATE
9 5/8
magents 2 1/4 x 1/4

MOTOR
SWITCH
GILBERT

BREVEL
PROD.
CORP. NYNY
movie clip ①

BACK
OEUF A LA
COQUE

LANTERNE CHINOISE
DISC HOLDER

VELVET DISC COVERS -
2.   9 3/4 hole 5 1/4

2 3/8
metal
1 st

7 1/4   1 1/2
2 nd   9 3/4

1/4 foam
in between
disc distance
around
1 st disc on top 2 nd

COLOR - USED
RED ORANGE
add a little
clear red

photo
sturtevant

78   *Duchamp Rotary Disc* (LANTERNE CHINOISE), 1969

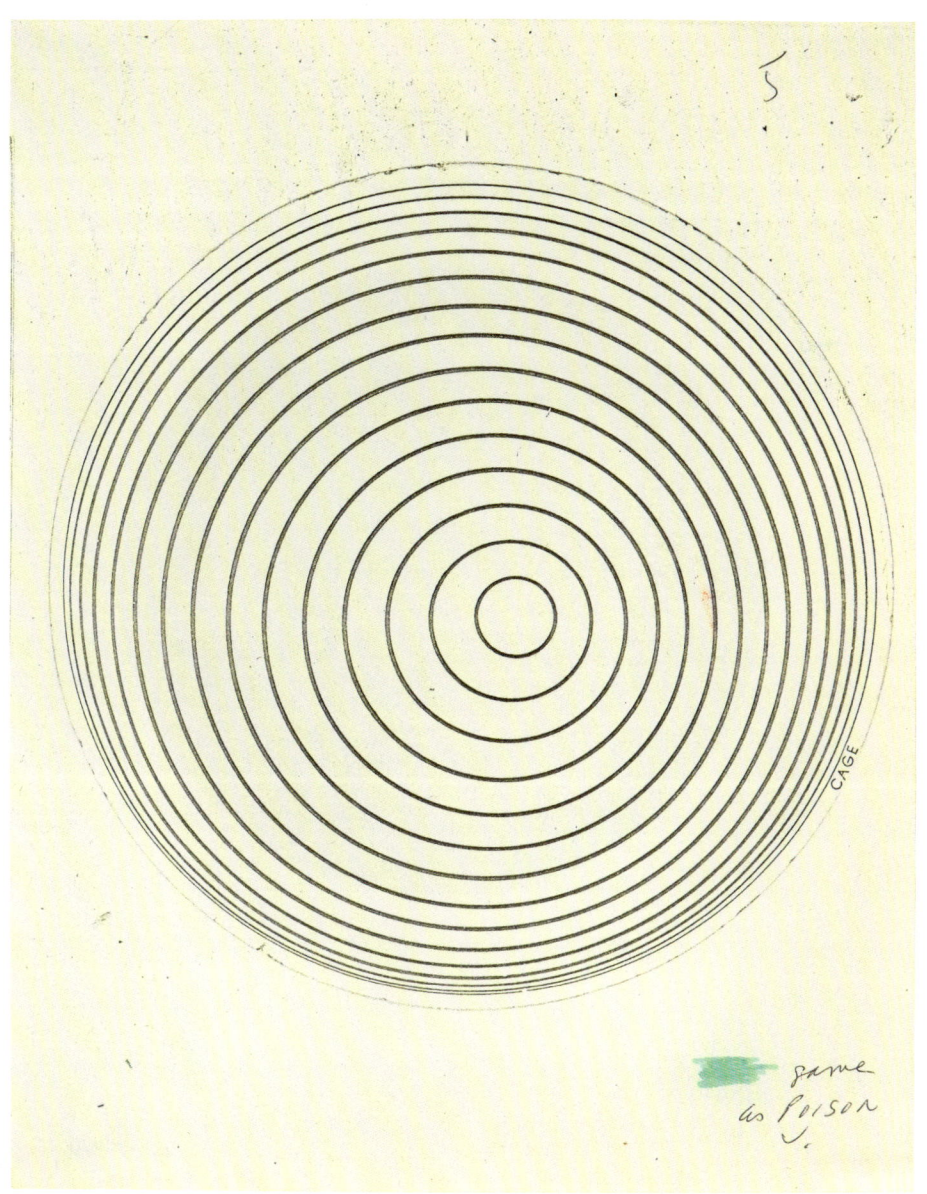

5

CAGE

same as Poison

Duchamp Rotary Disc (CAGE), 1969   **79**

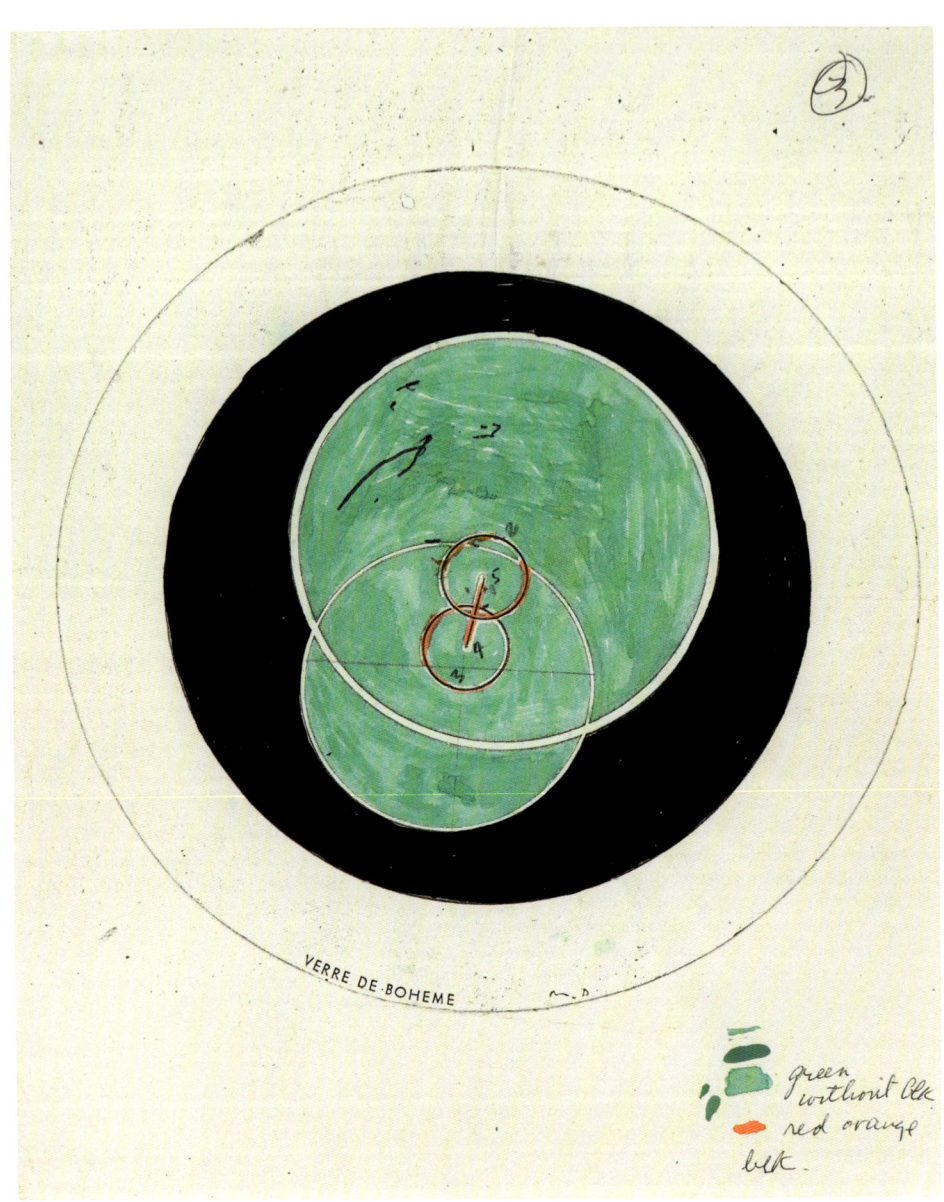

green
without blk.
red orange
blk.

VERRE DE BOHEME

80   *Duchamp Rotary Disc* (VERRE DE BOHEME), 1969

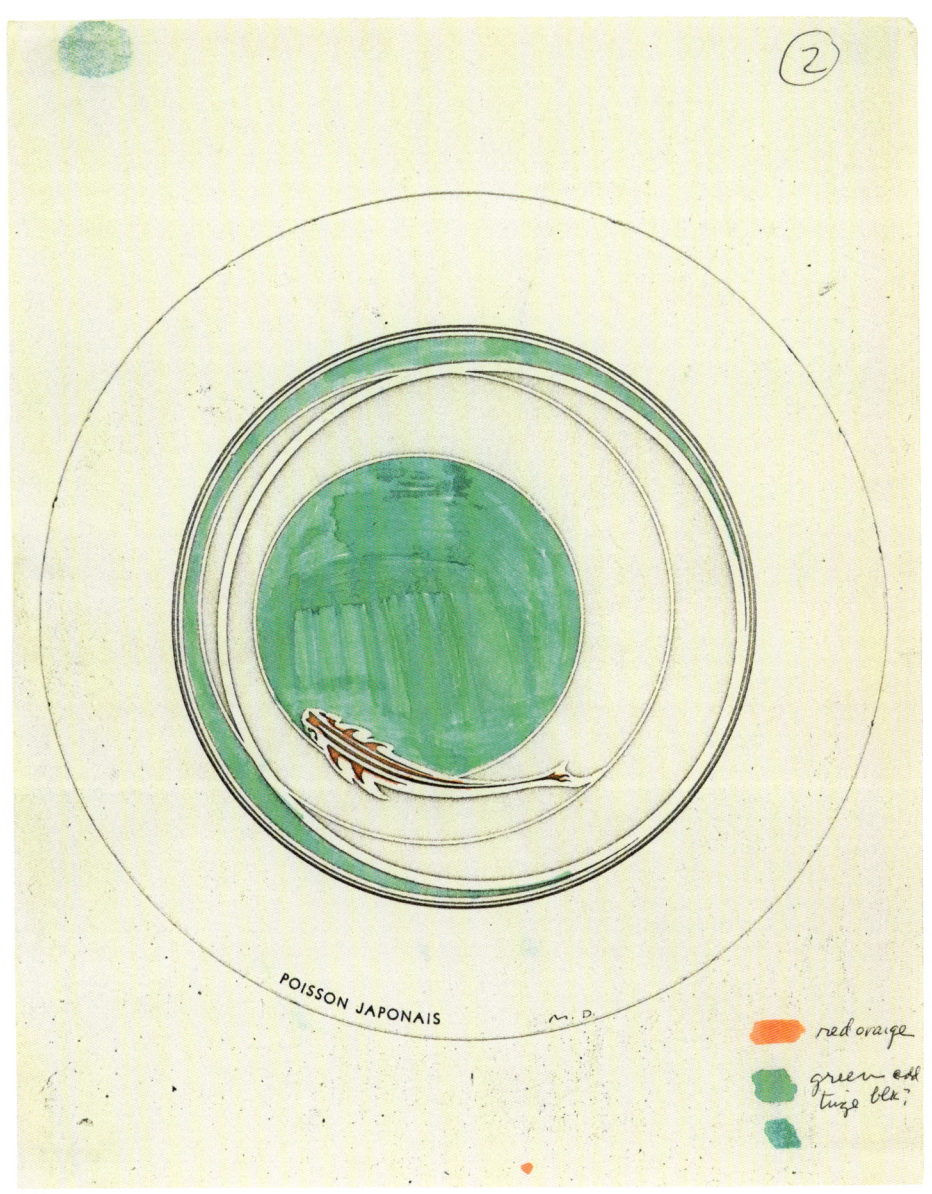

POISSON JAPONAIS

m. D.

red orange

green add tinge blk;

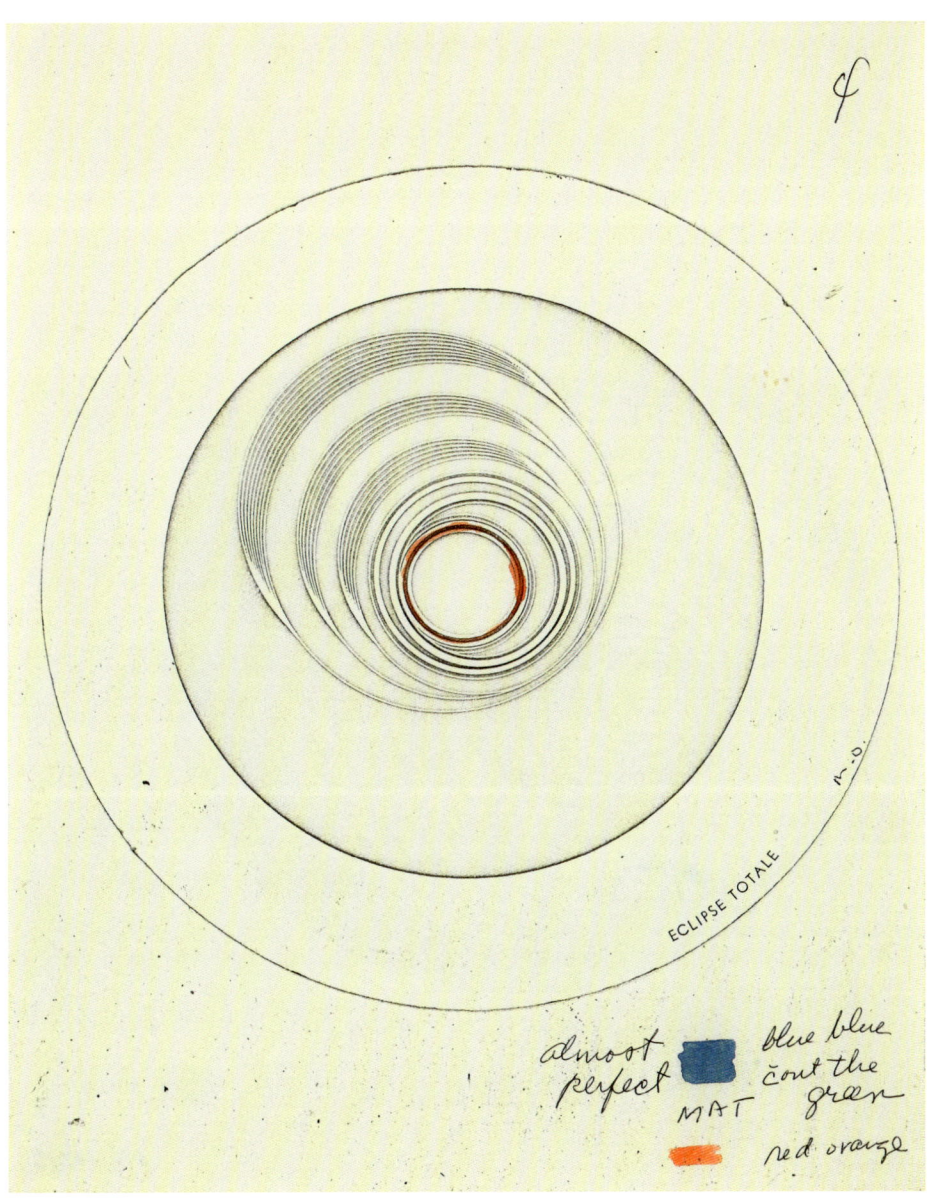

Duchamp Rotary Disc (ECLIPSE TOTALE), 1969 **83**

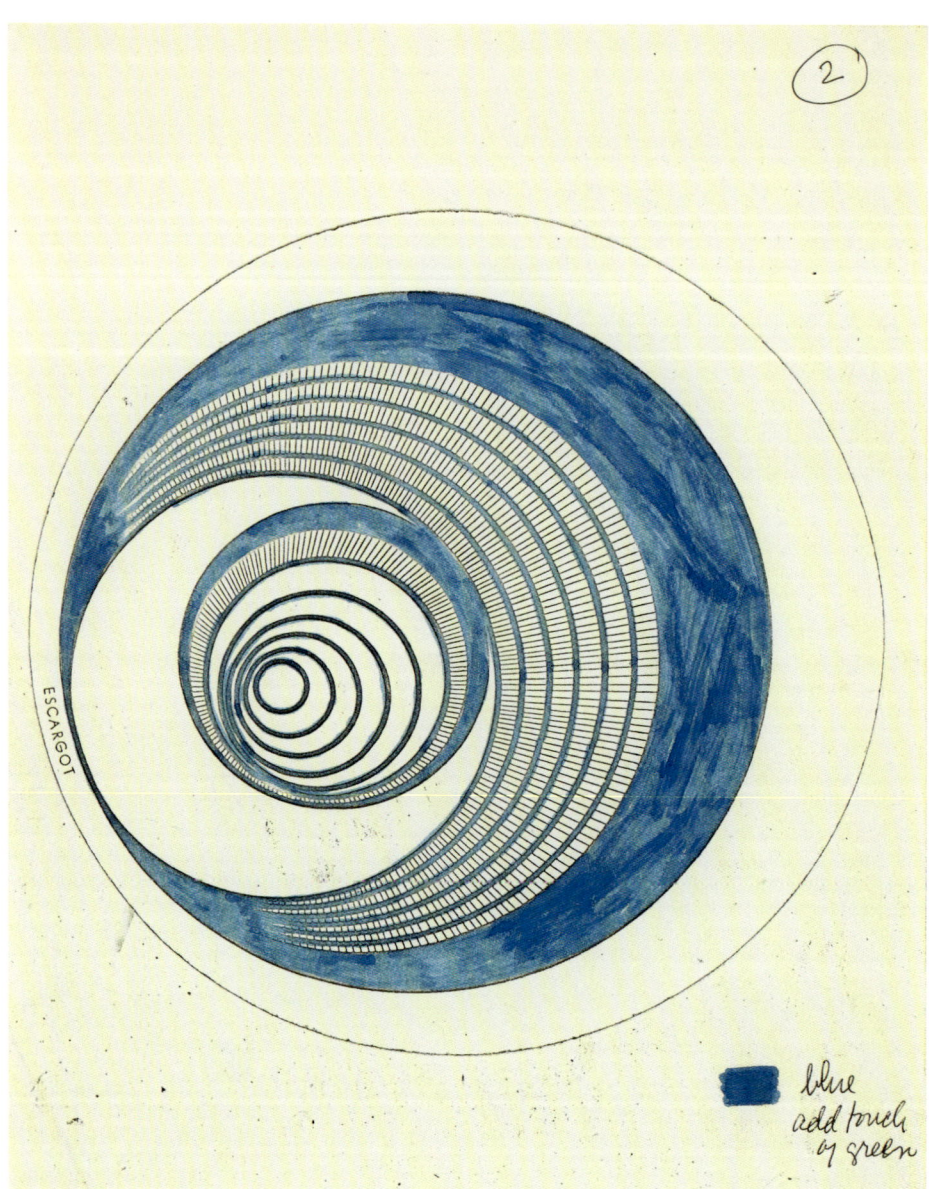

blue
add touch
of green

ESCARGOT

Duchamp Rotary Disc (ESCARGOT), 1969

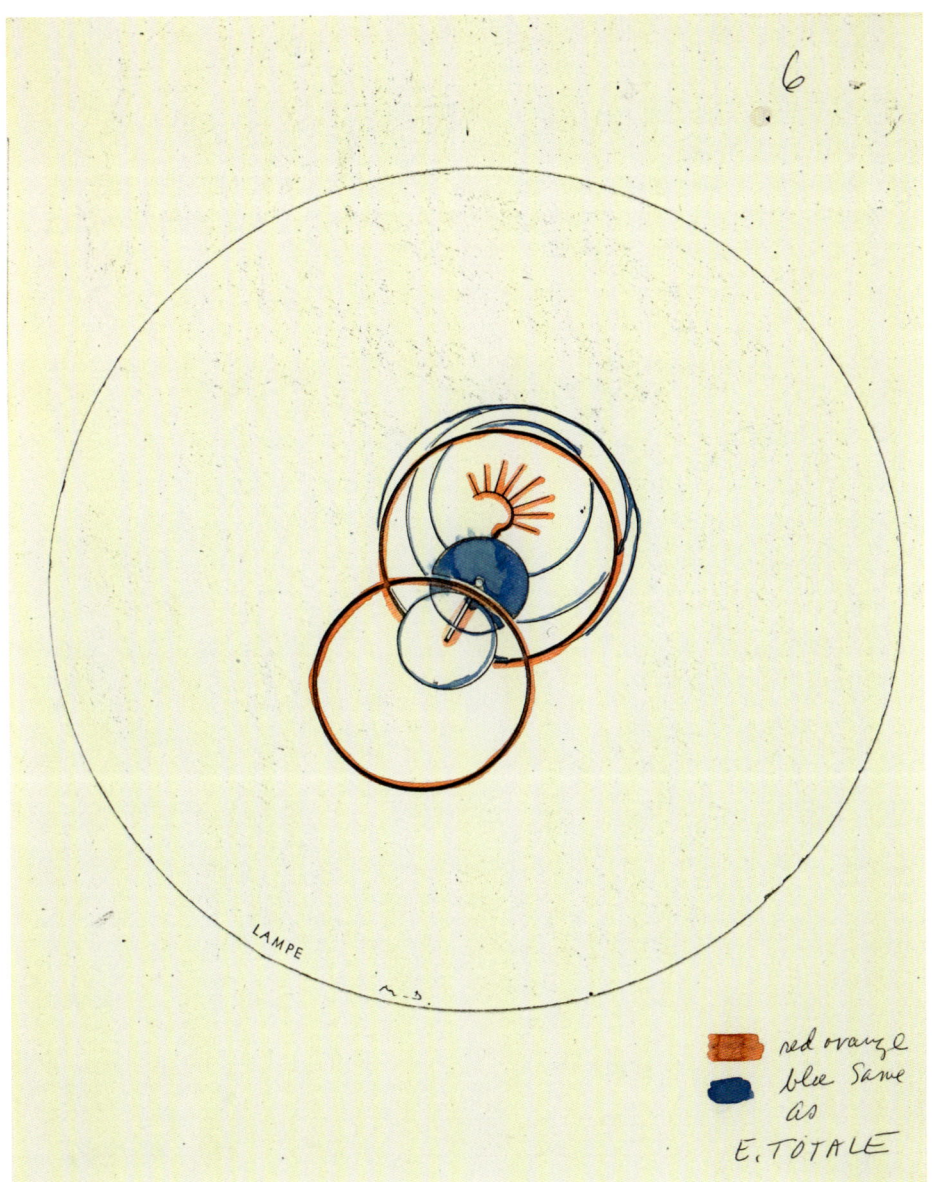

6

LAMPE

M.D.

red orange
blue same
as
E. TOTALE

Duchamp Rotary Disc (LAMPE), 1969   **85**

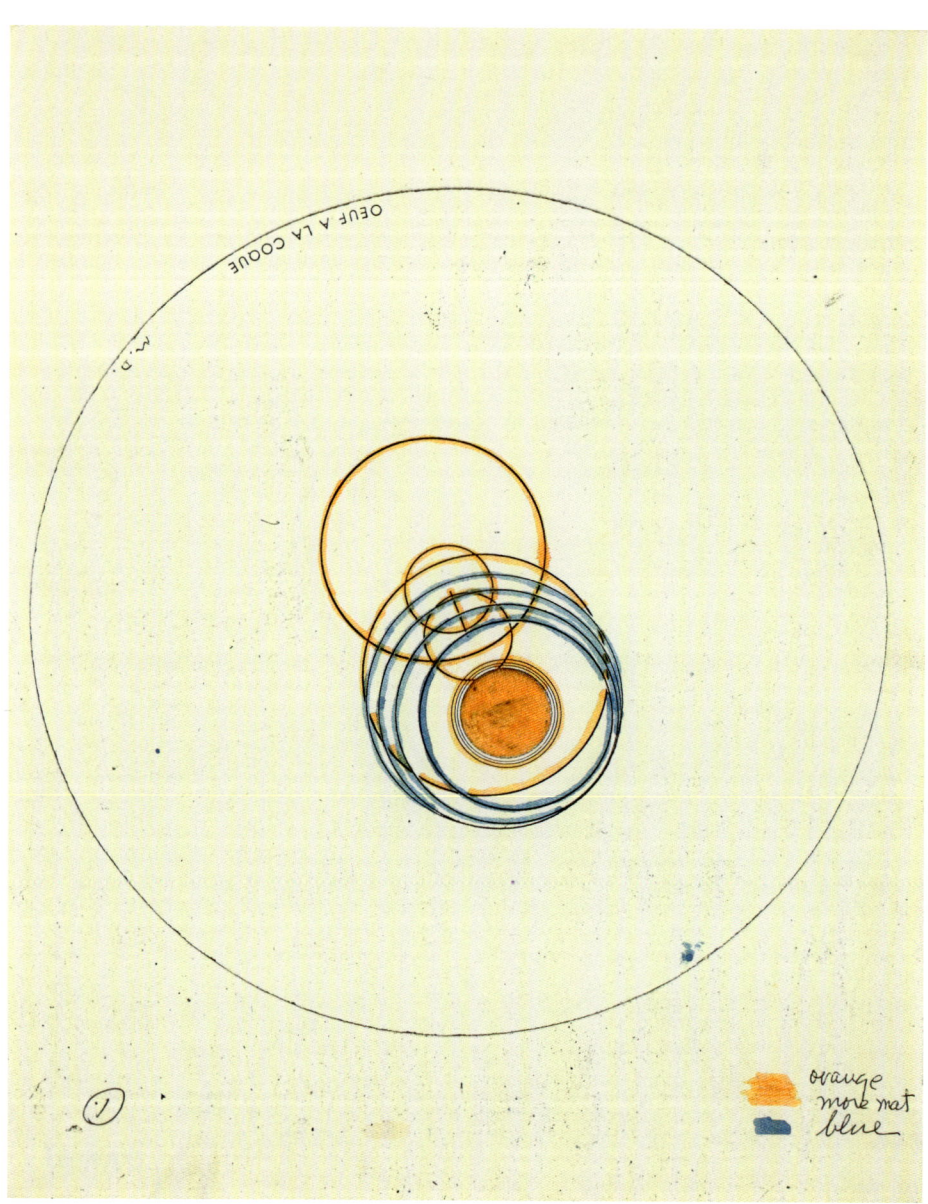

86 *Duchamp Rotary Disc* (OEUF A LA COQUE), 1969

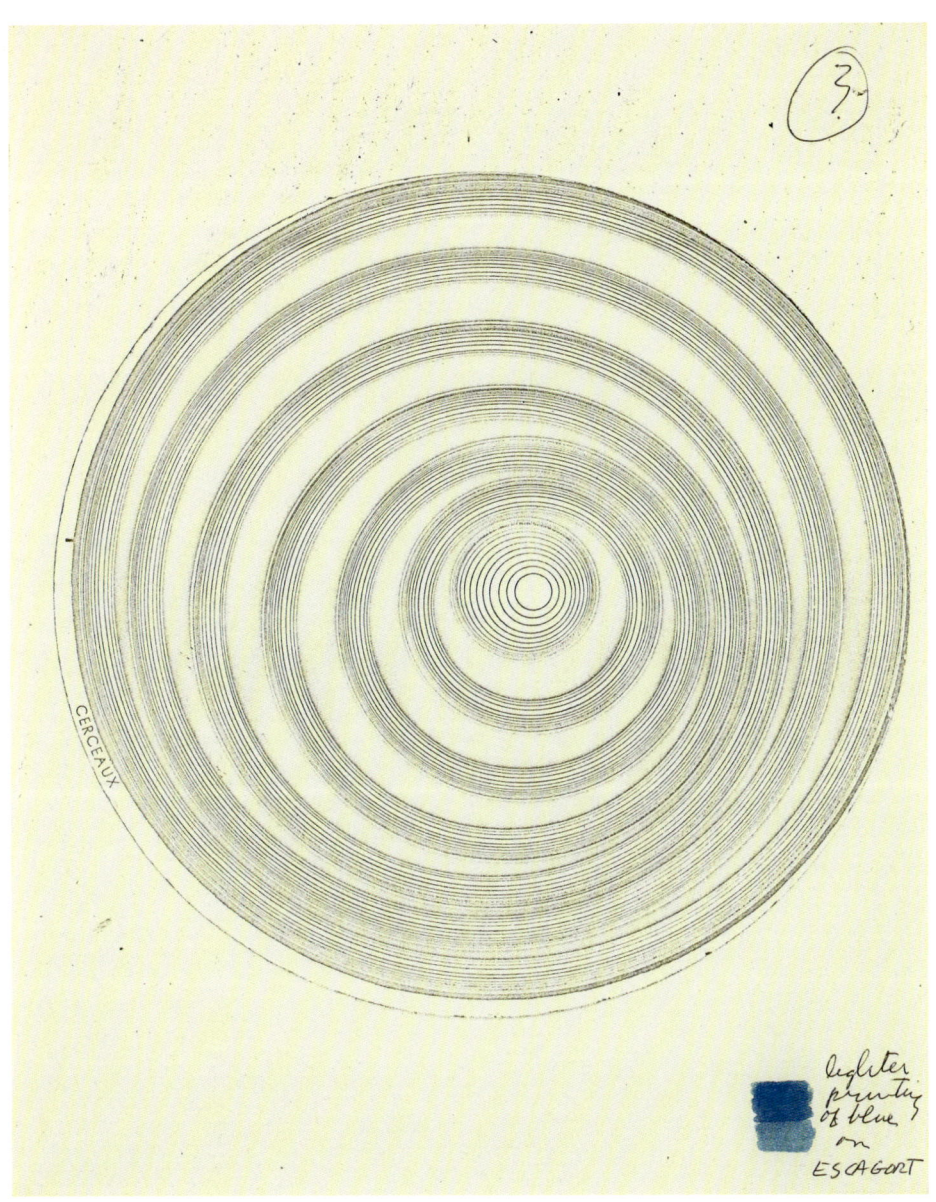

CERCEAUX

lighter
printing
of blue
on
ESCARGOT

Duchamp Rotary Disc (CERCEAUX), 1969   **87**

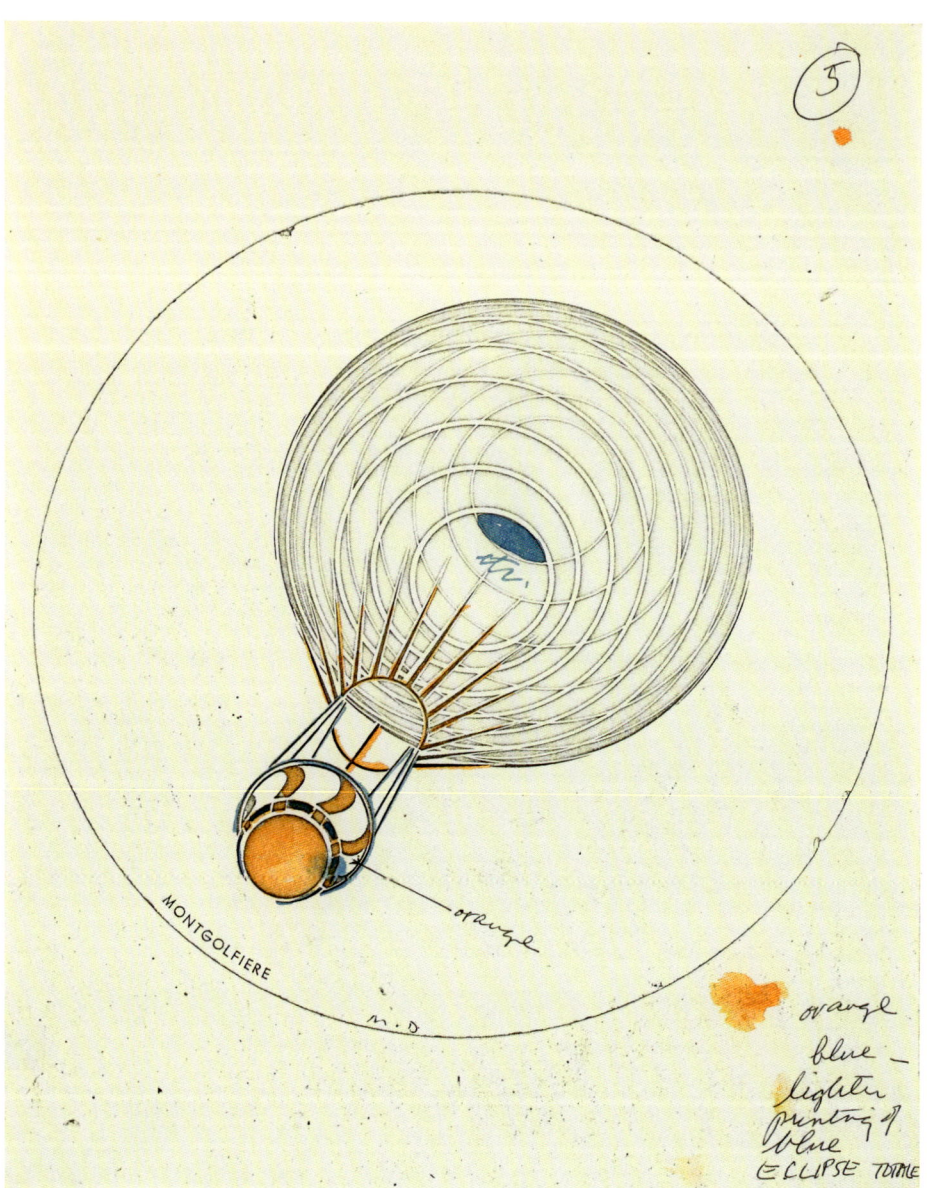

Duchamp Rotary Disc (MONTGOLFIERE), 1969

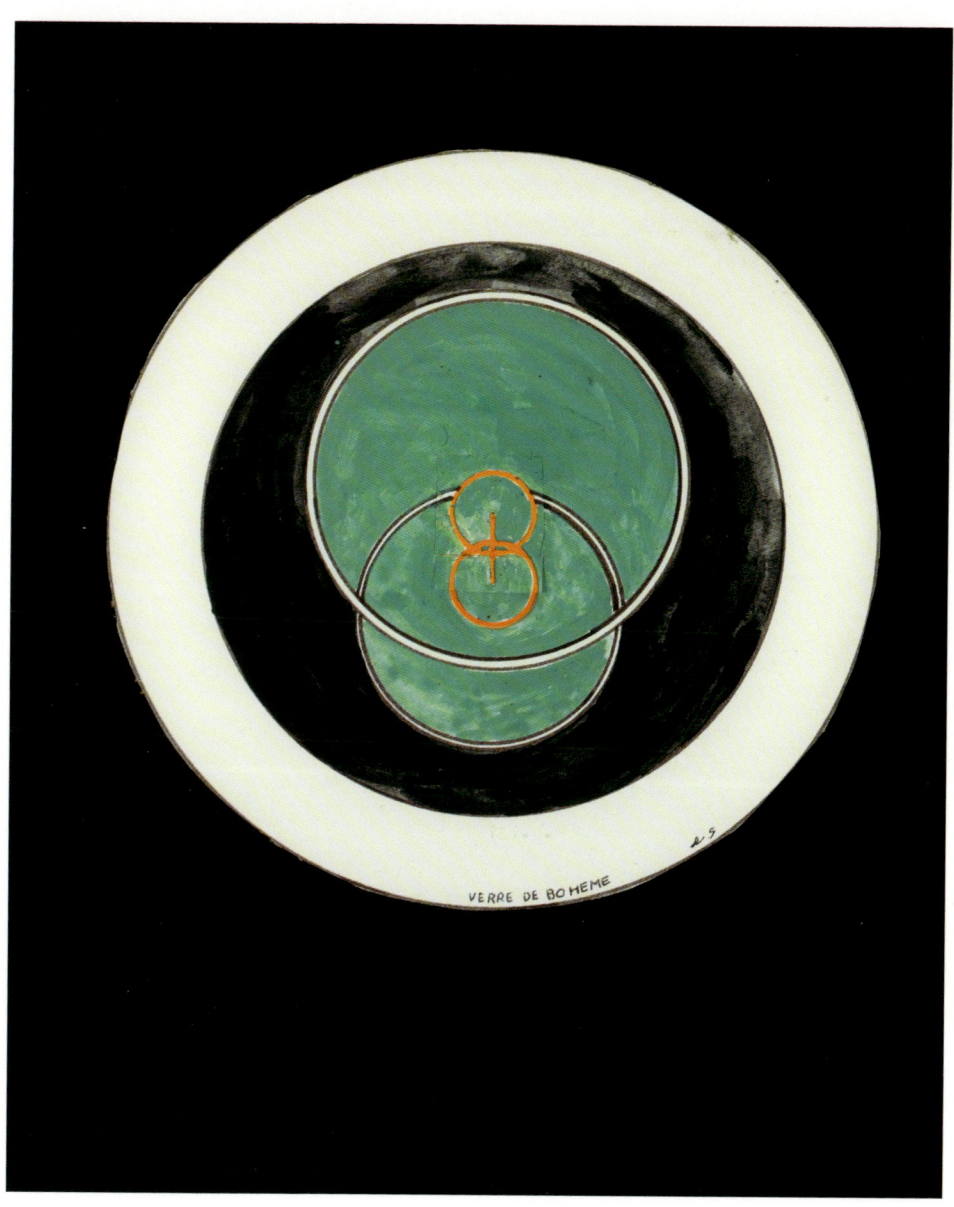

VERRE DE BOHEME

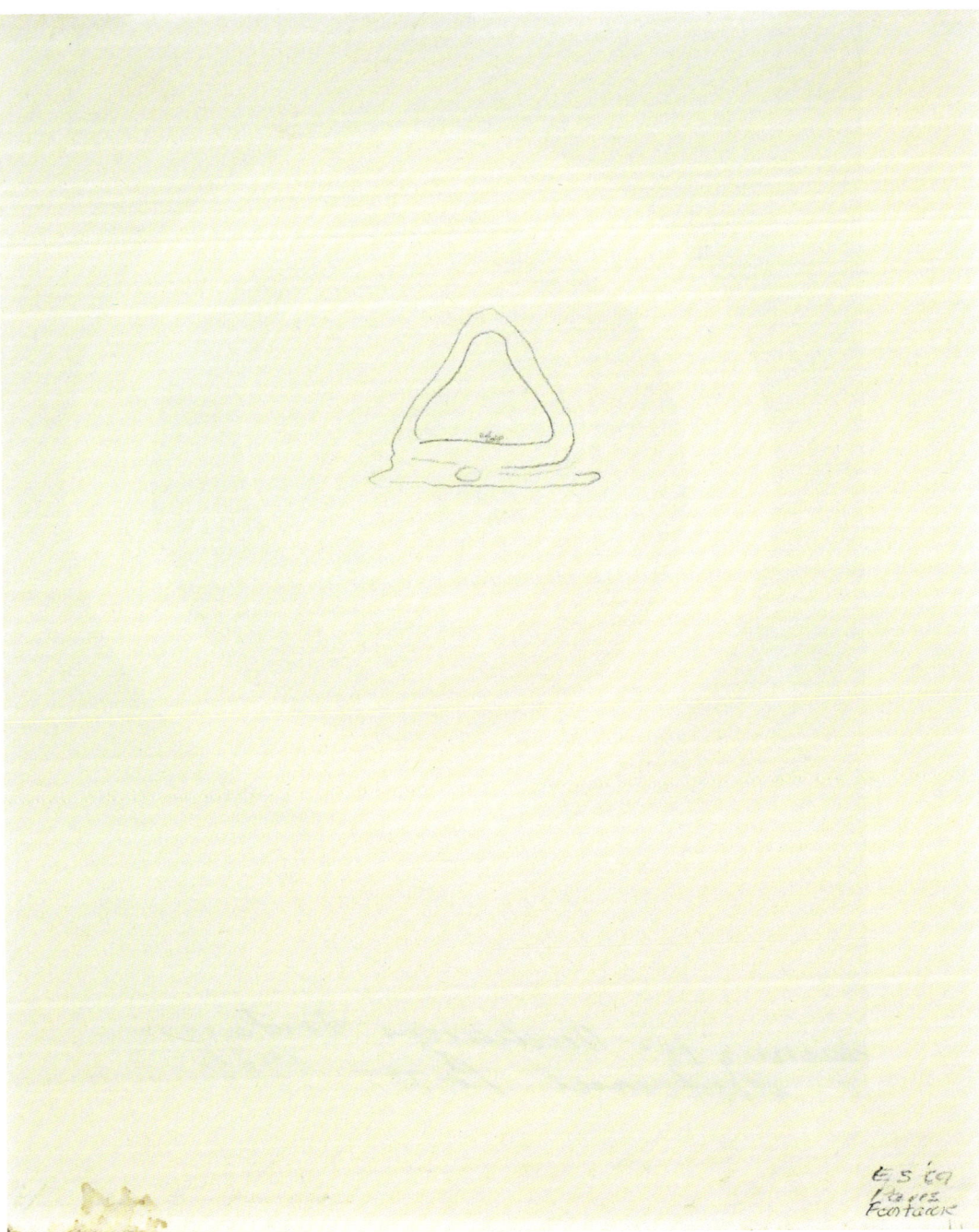

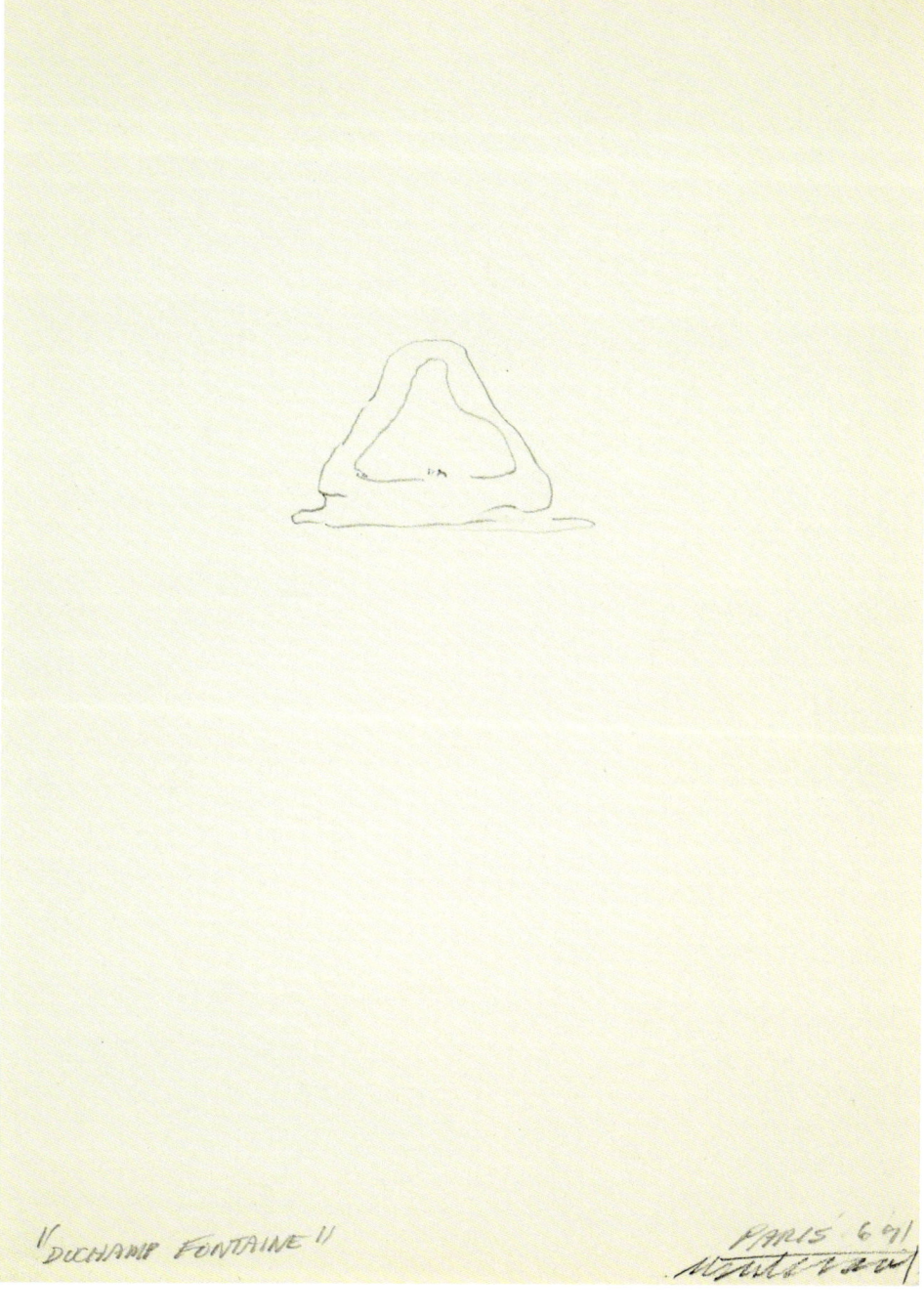

"DUCHAMP FONTAINE"

PARIS 6 91

SEVENTIES

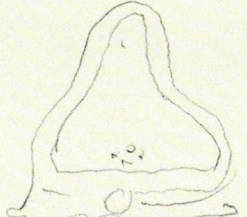

DUCHAMP FONTAINE

stutvart 70

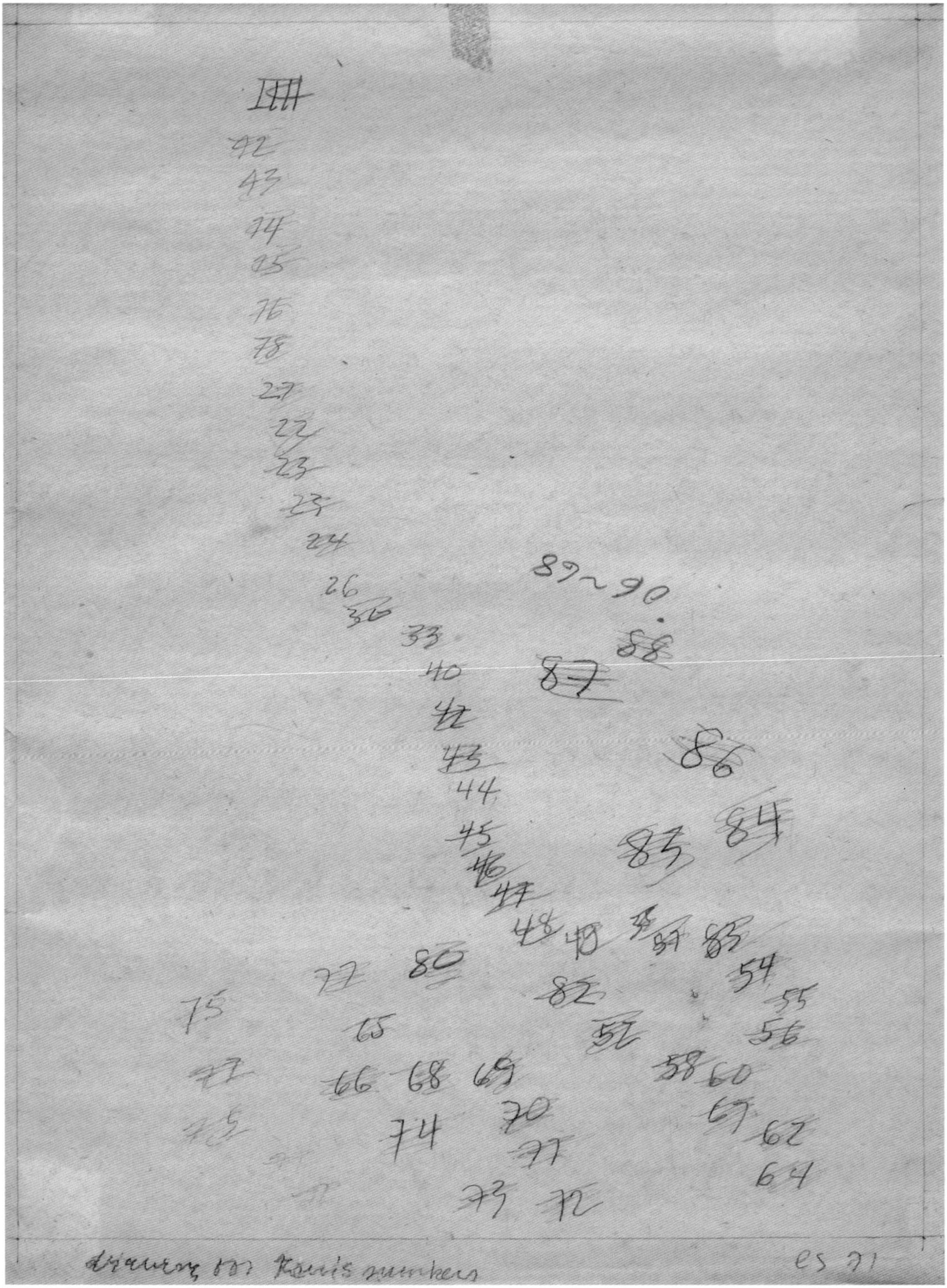

IIII

42
43
74
75
76
78
21
22
23
23
24
26
36 33
40
89~90
88
87
42
43
44
45
46 47
48 49
86
85 84
83 82
77 80
75
65
47
66 68 69
74
70
77
73 72
82
52
58 60
63
29
62
64
54
55
56

drawing for Beuys numbers

es 71

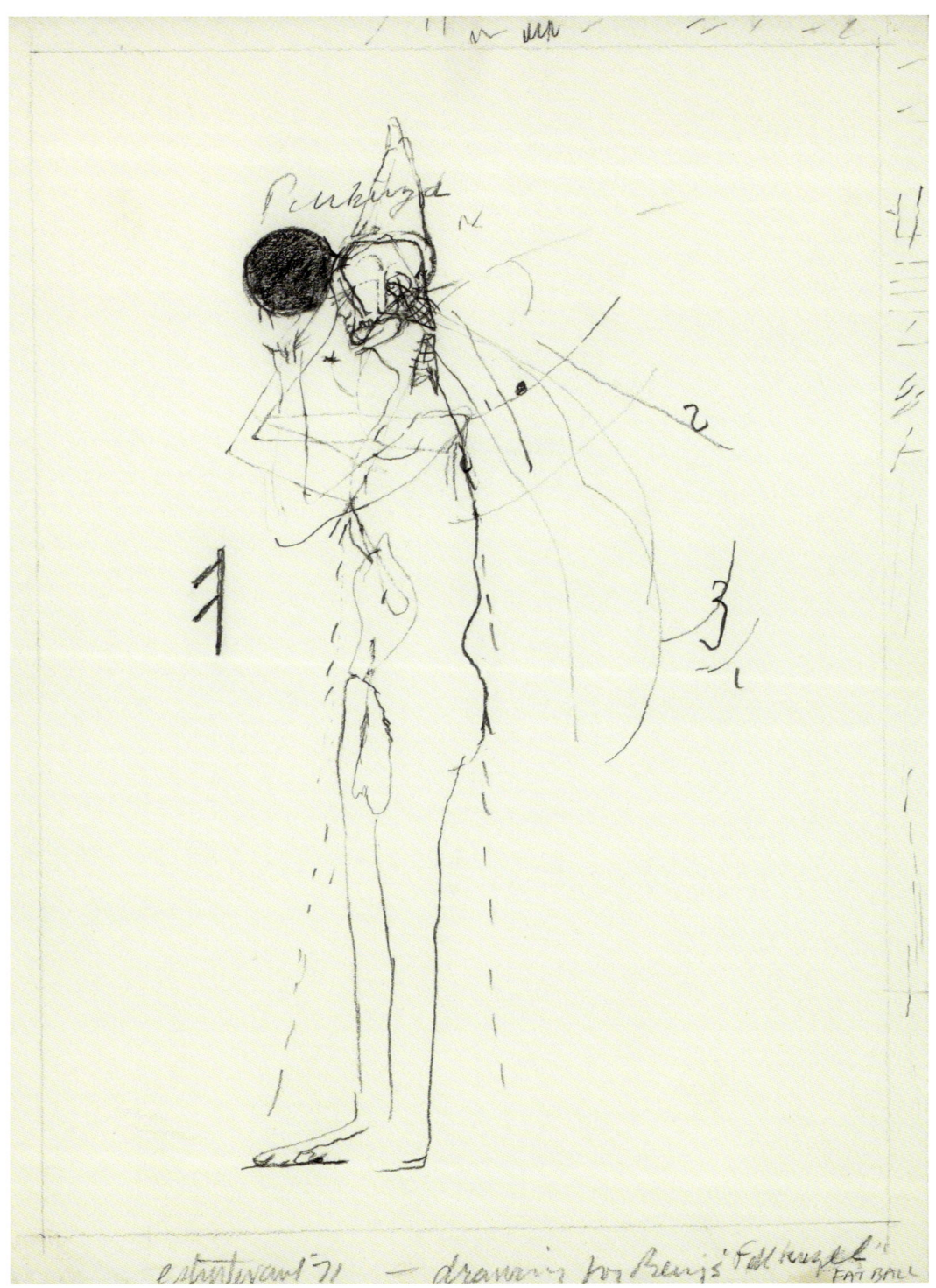

Drawing for Beuys Fettkugel, 1971 **97**

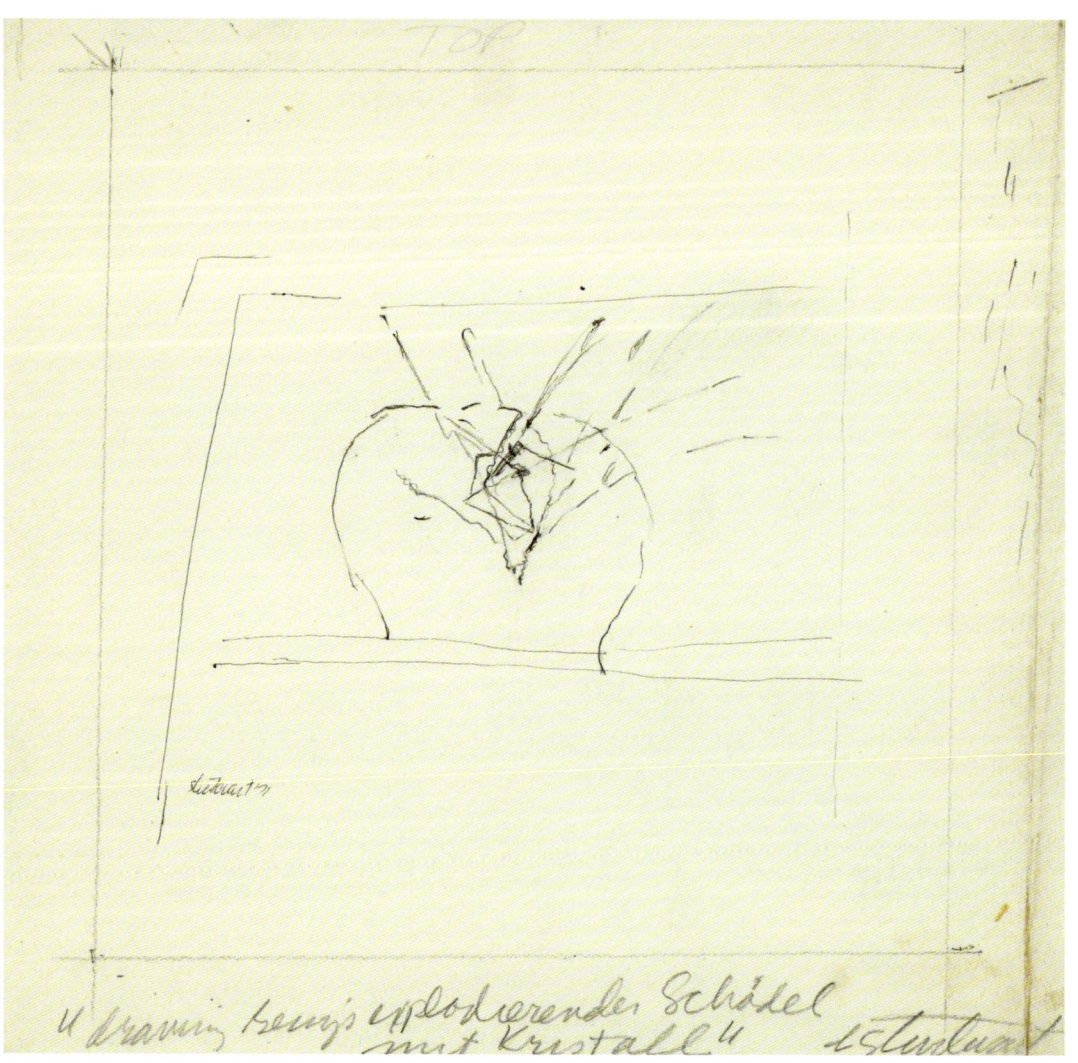

Drawing Beuys explodierender Schädel mit Kristall, 1971

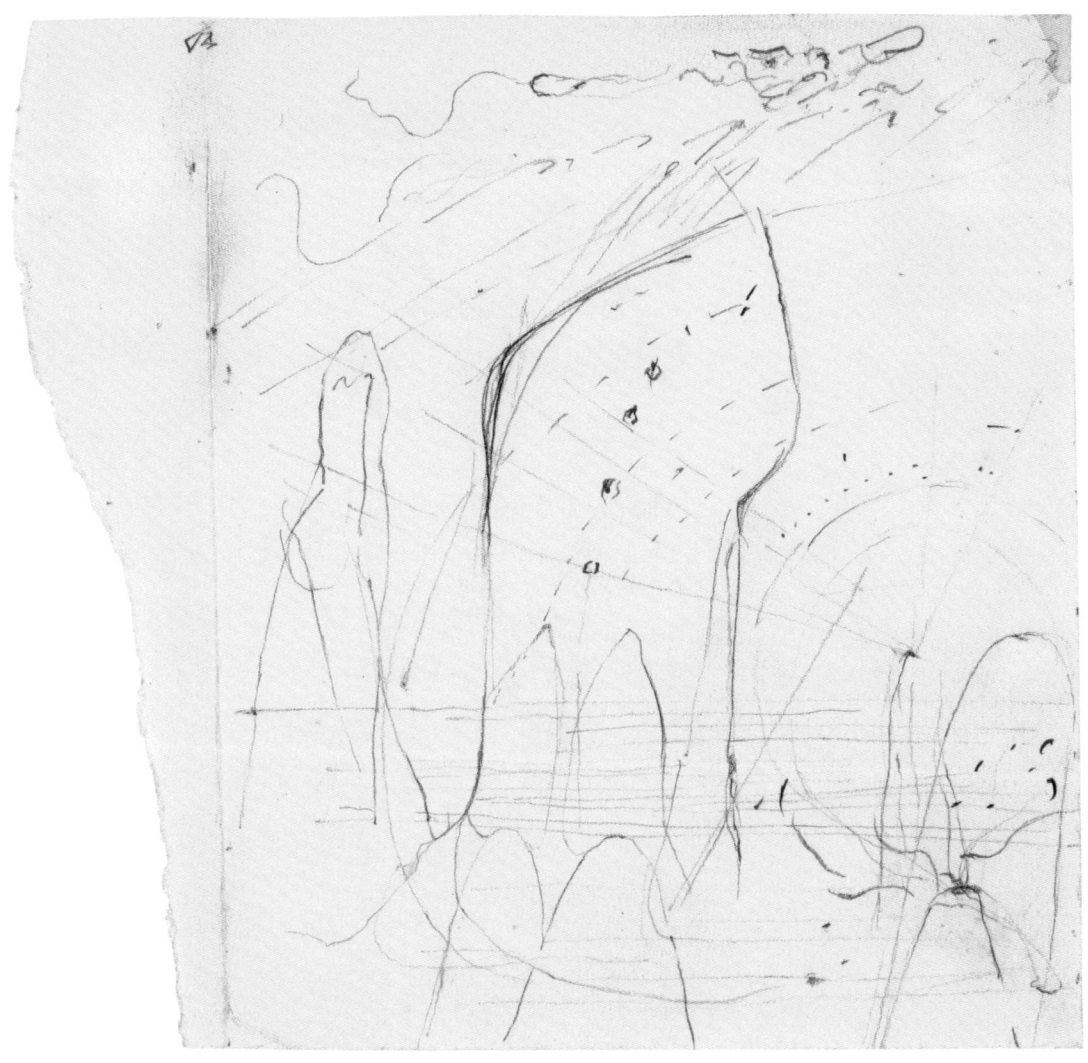

Drawing for Beuys Sonne Meer Steine Himmel, 1971 **99**

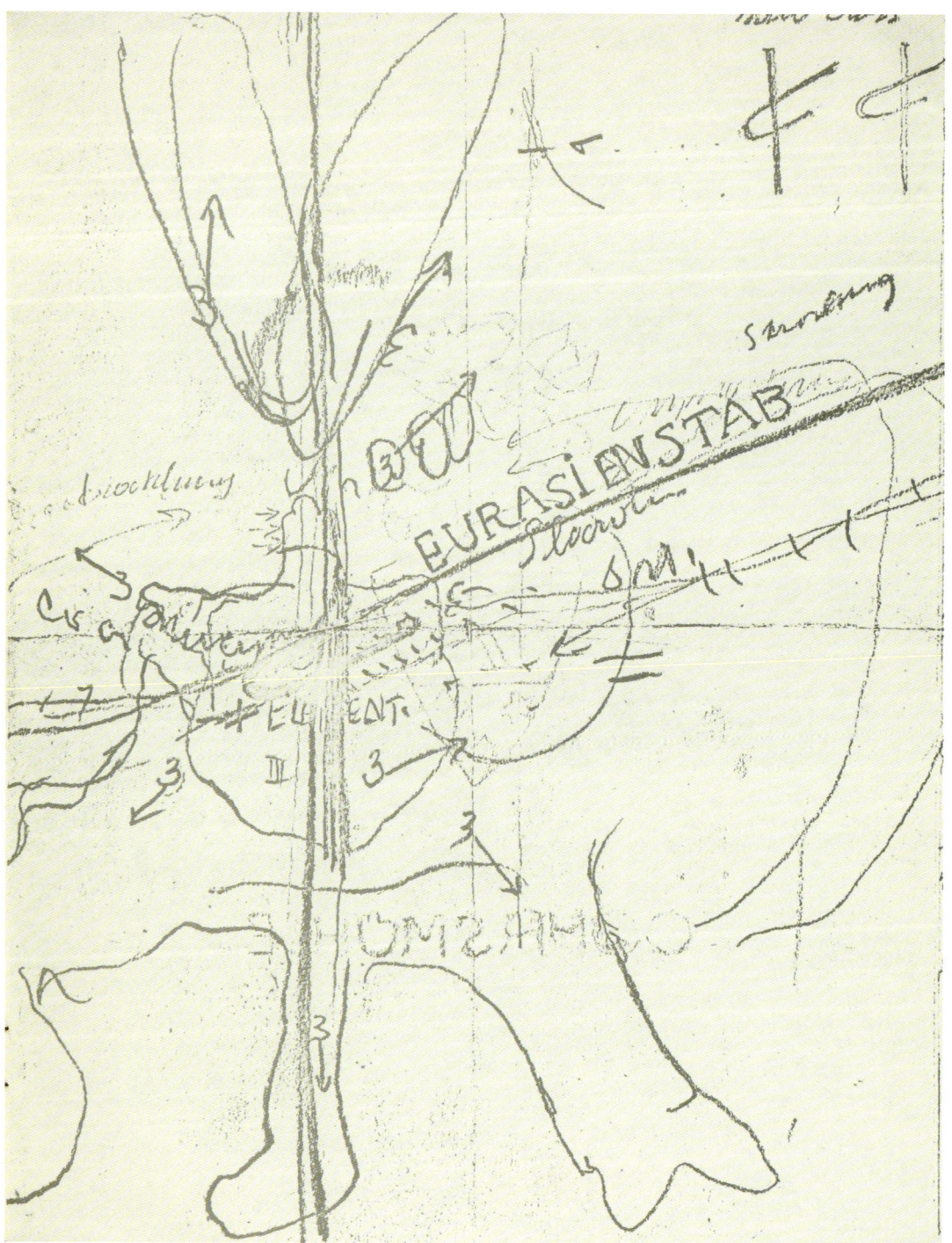

100 *Drawing for Beuys Aktion Eurasienstab*, 1971

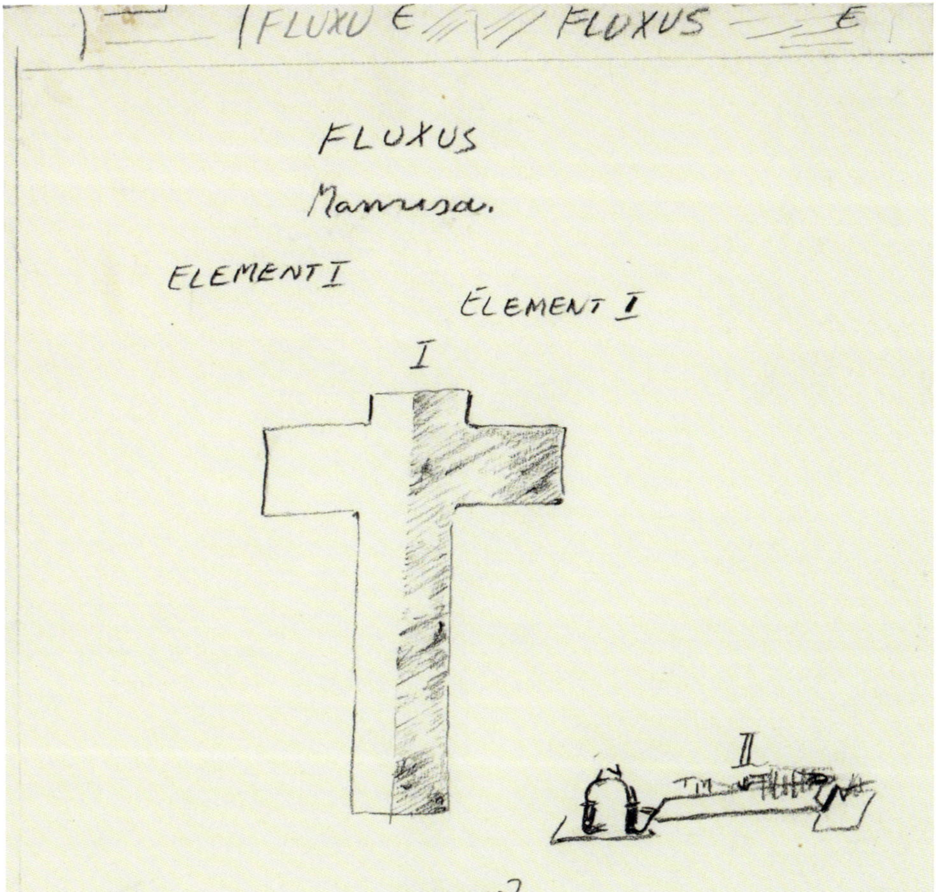

FLUXUS

Manresa.

ELEMENT I

ELEMENT I

I

NUN?

N + Element II Ju Element I urseifgenbrgen?

NUN? Ns? Element I Ju Element II nunnervorgerlagen?

Bjon Neugold . ral Tontrontanufnedand.
Tontana geralen suging

Bjönro N zradim nunagebrgu.

Drawing for Beuys Aktion Manresa
171

EIGHTIES

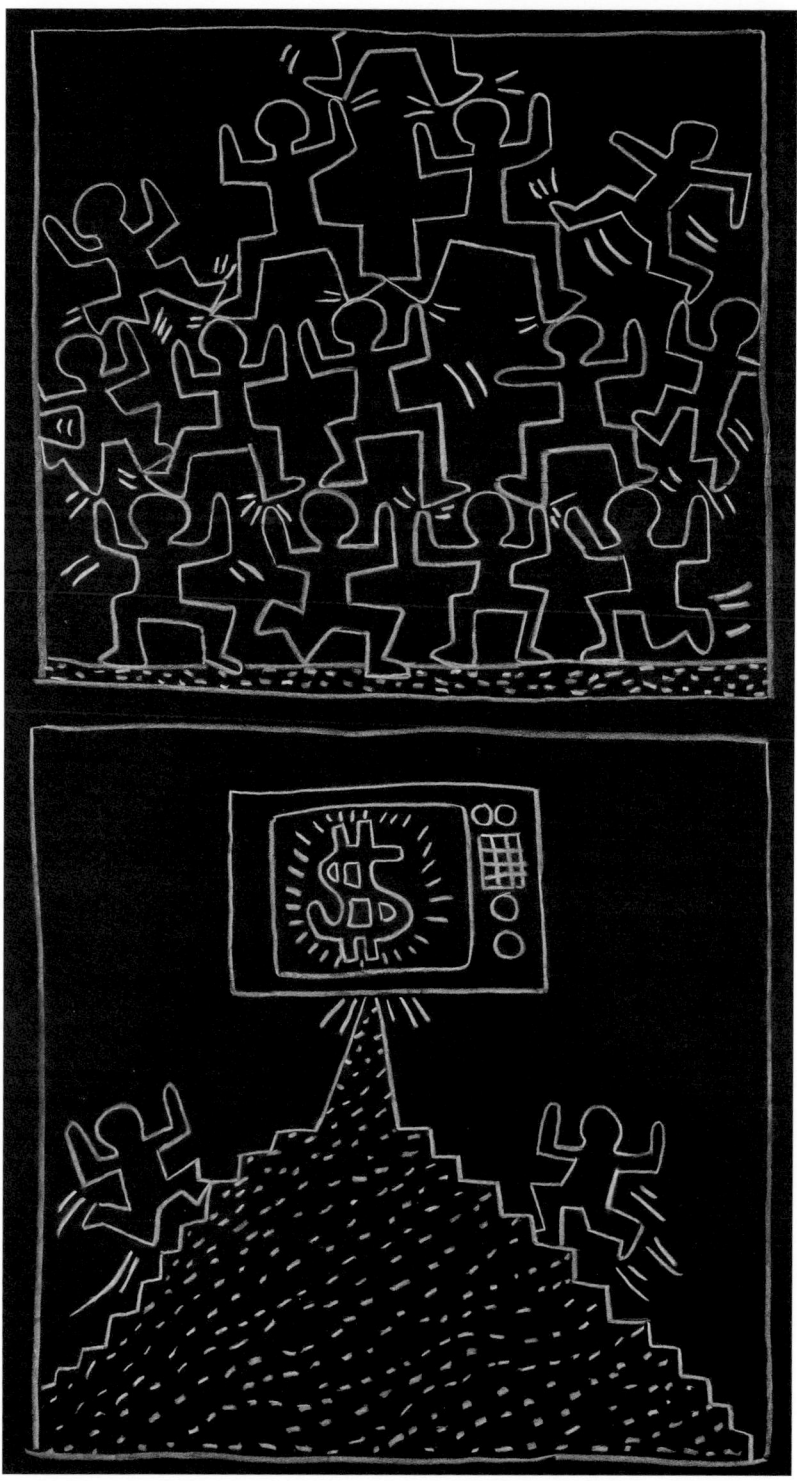

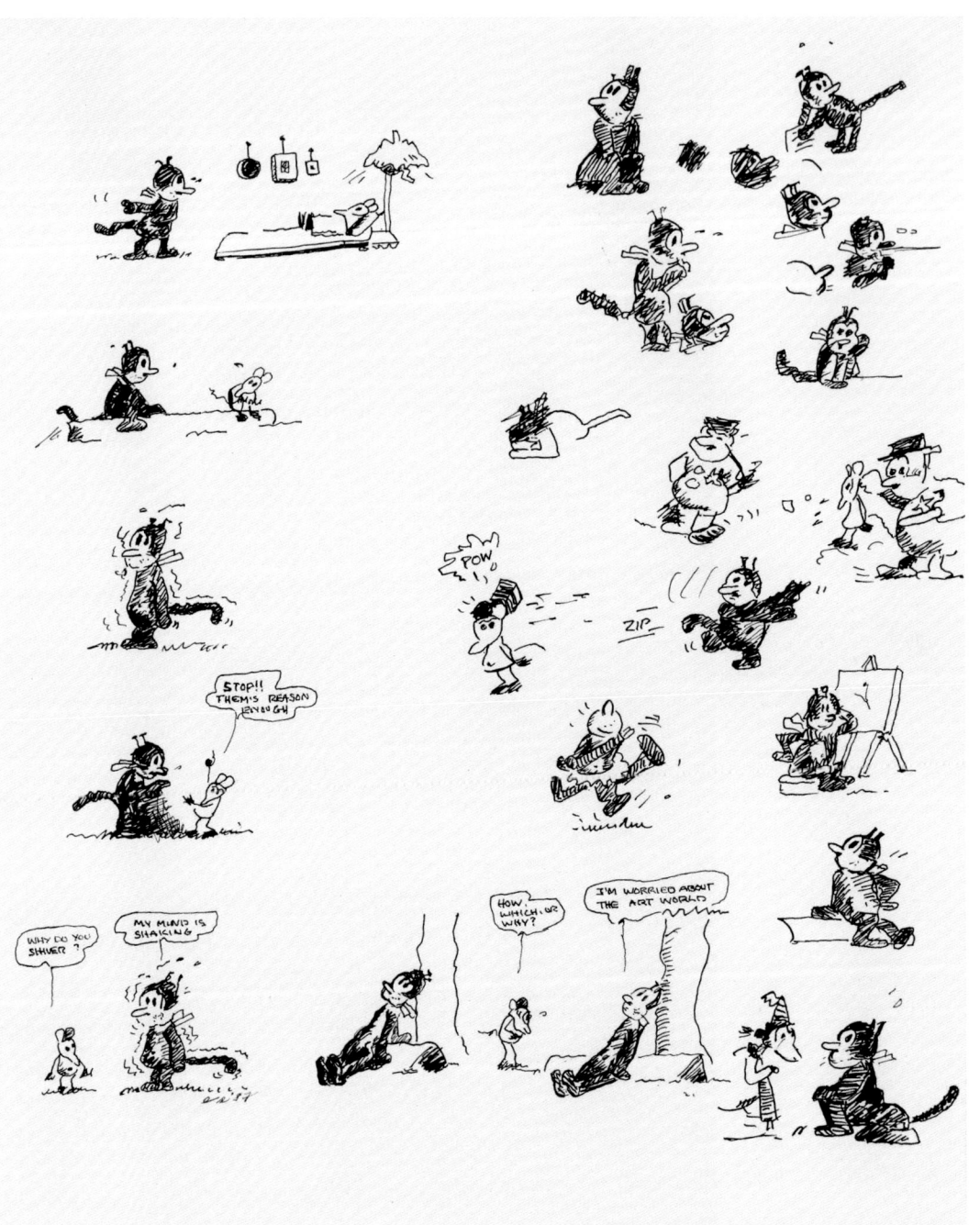

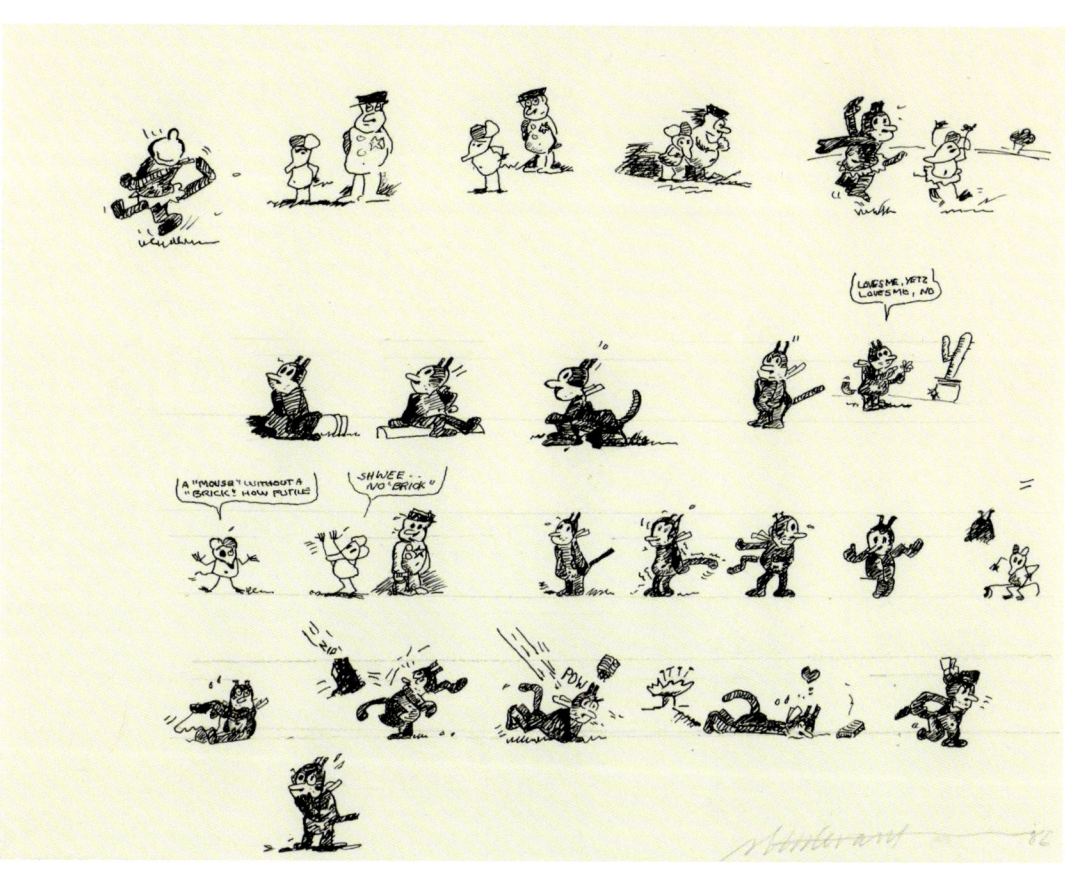

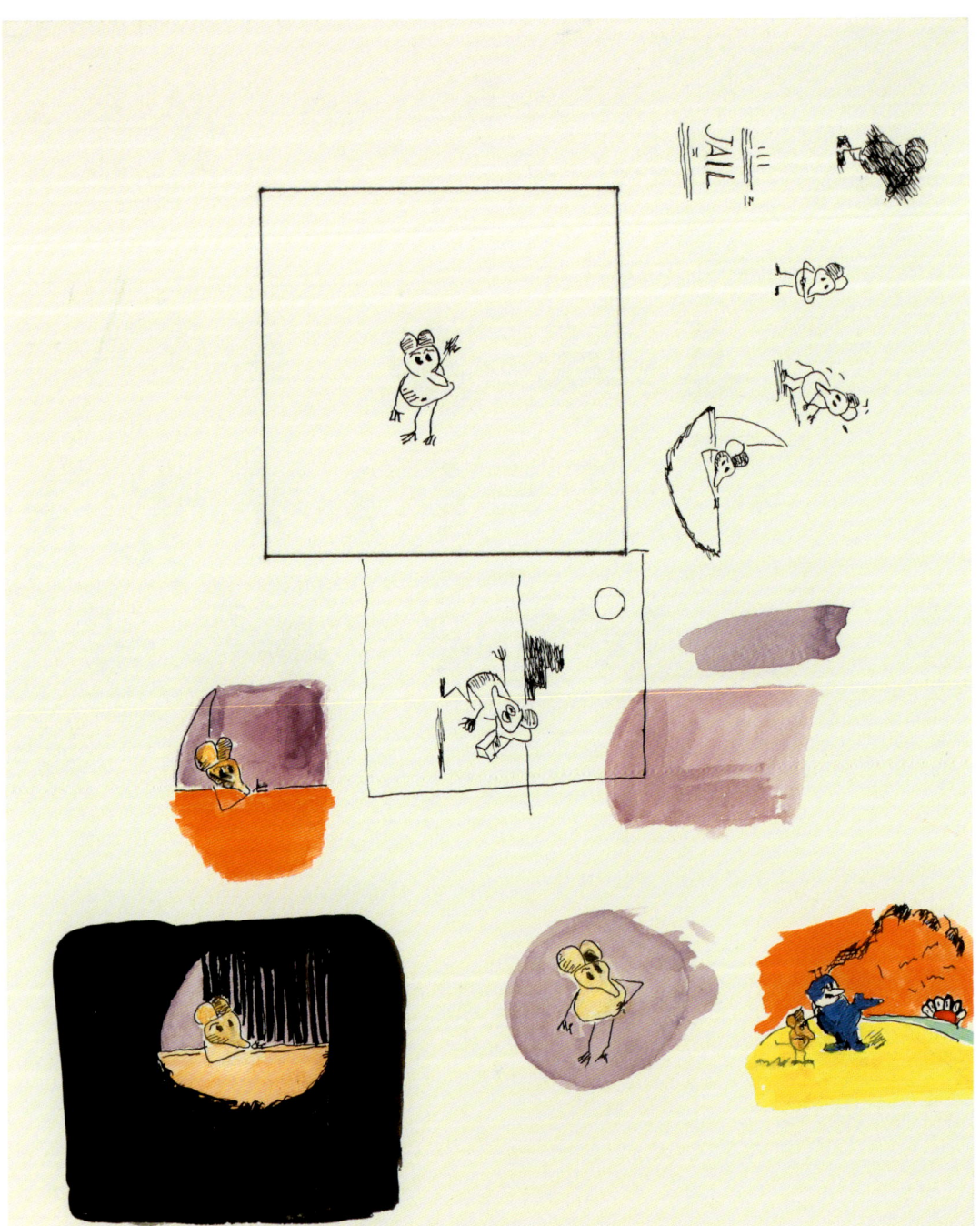

108 *Study for Krazy Kat*, 1986

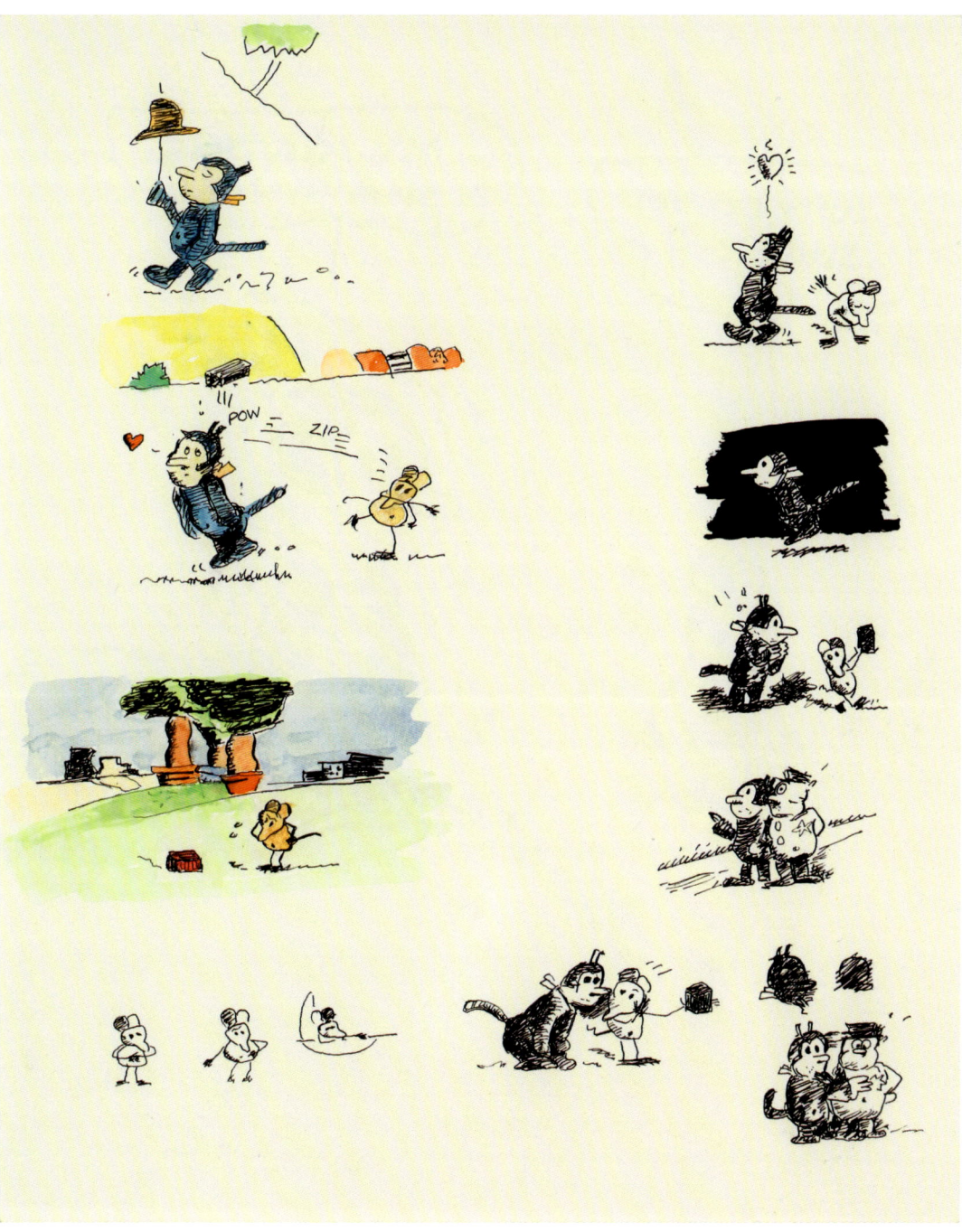

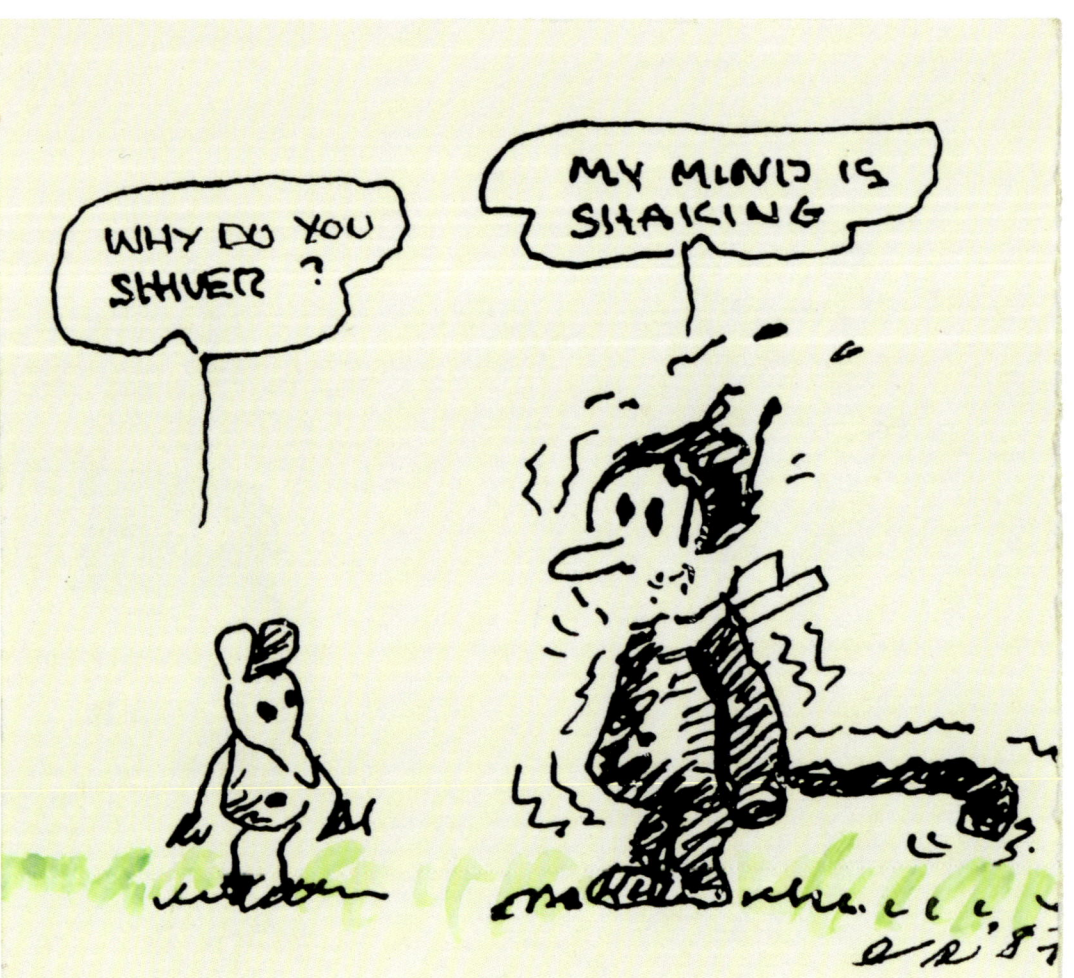

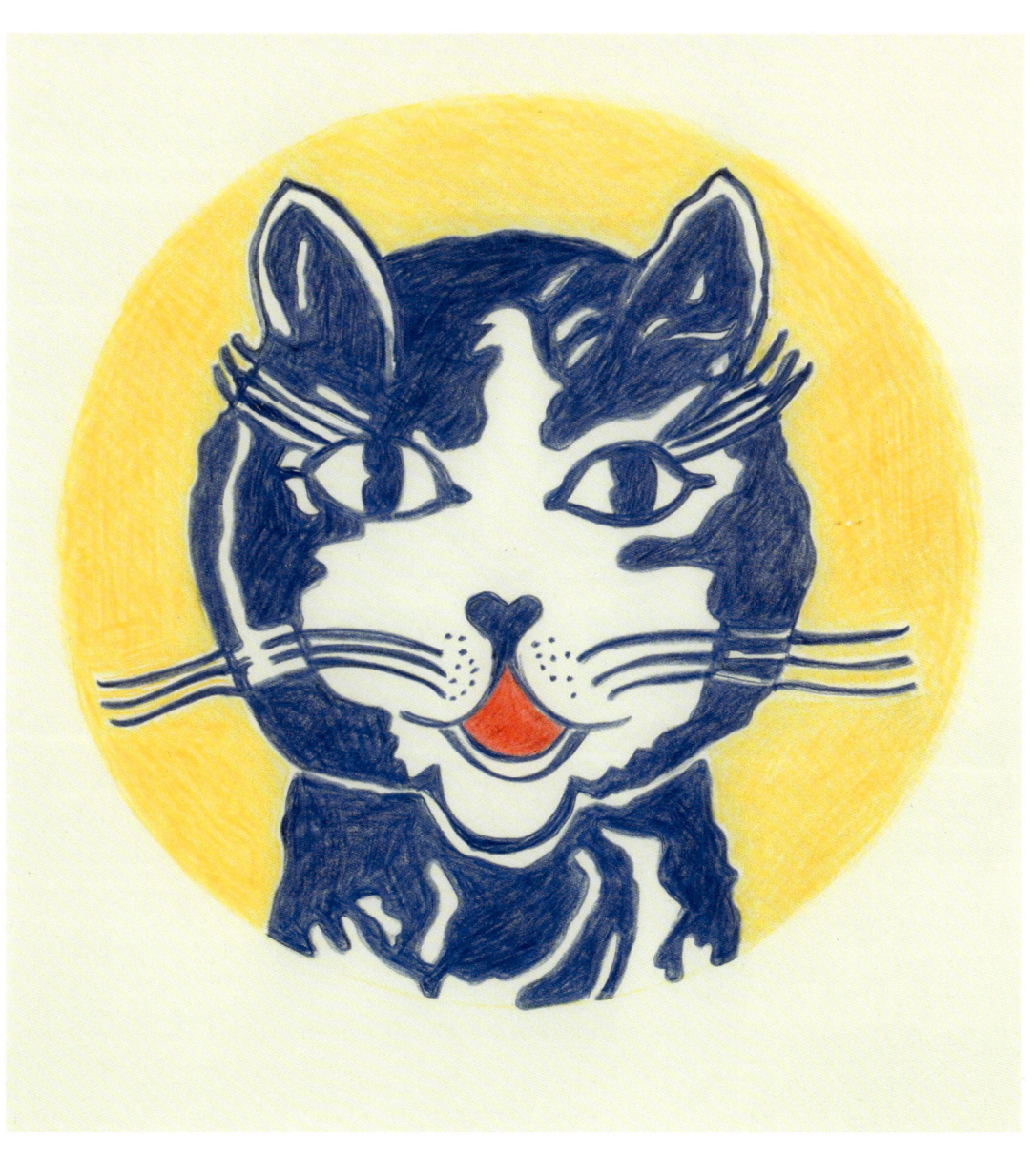

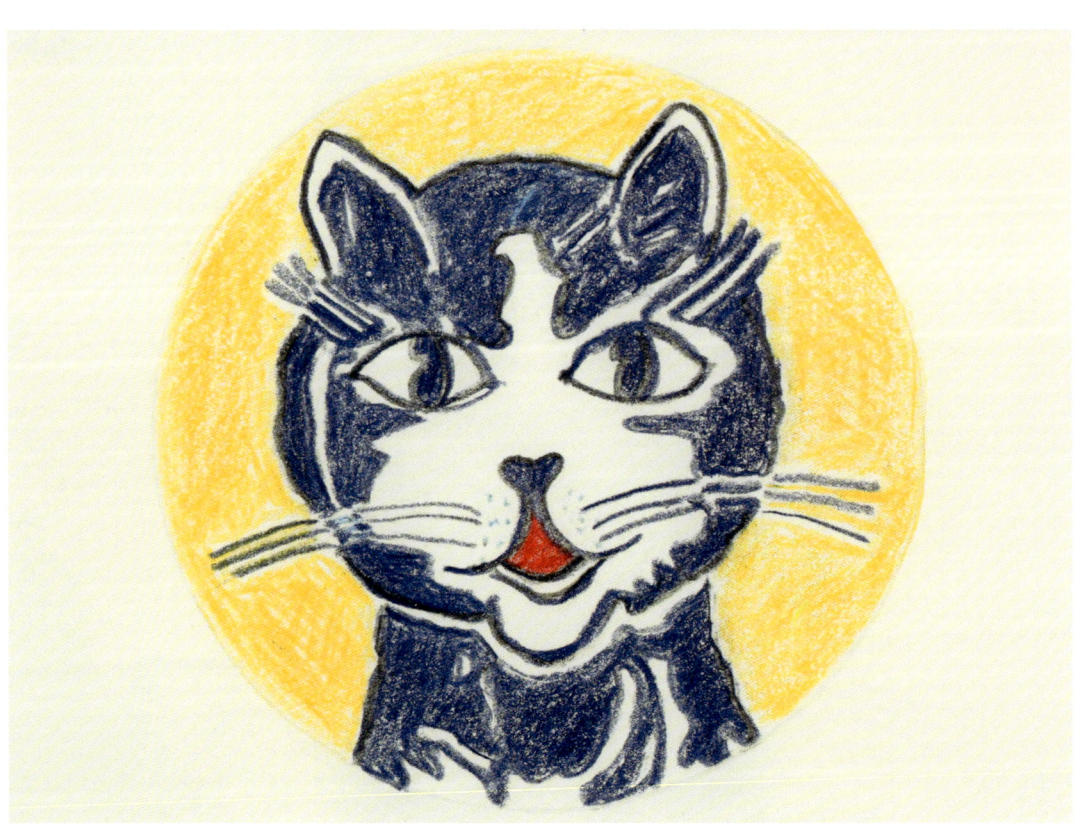

Lichtenstein Laughing Cat, 1988

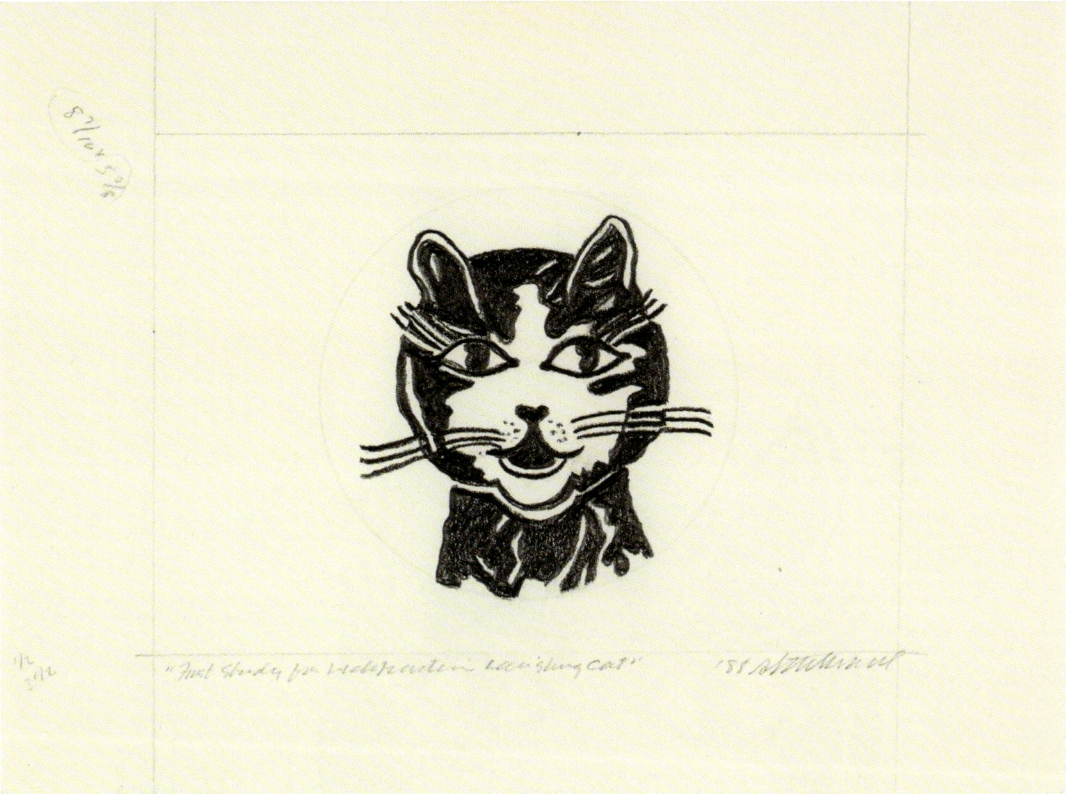

First Study for Lichtenstein Laughing Cat, 1988

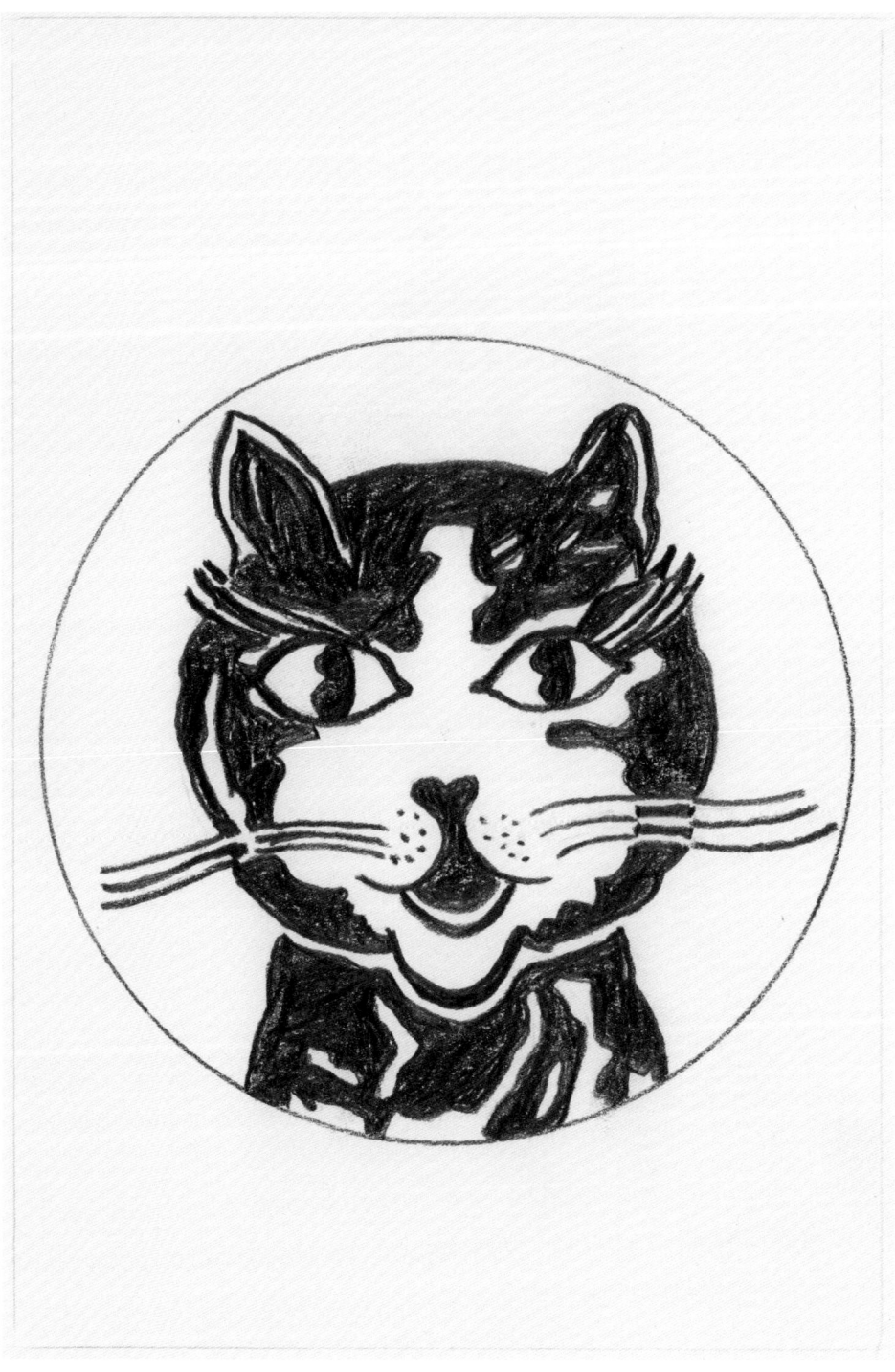

114   *Study for Lichtenstein Laughing Cat, 1988*

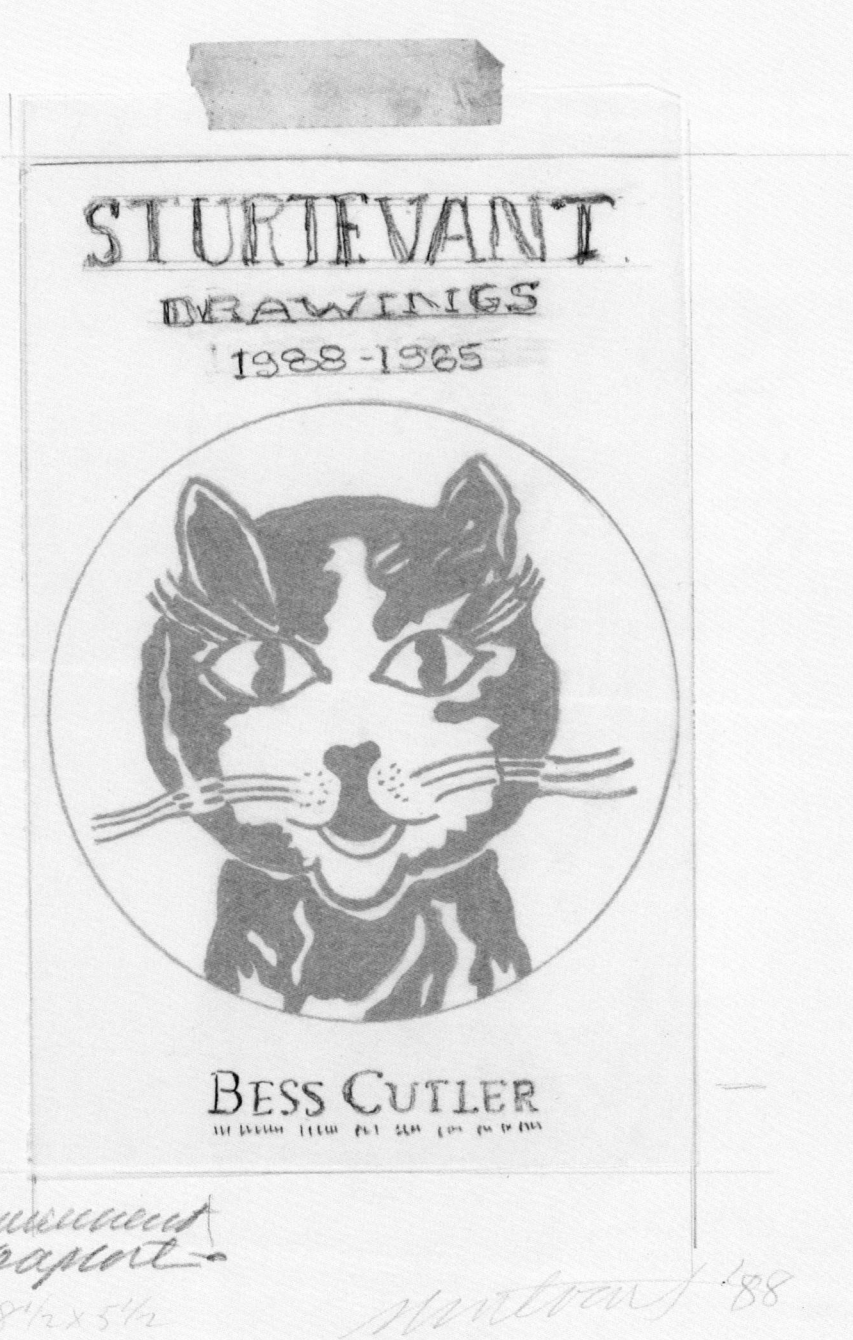

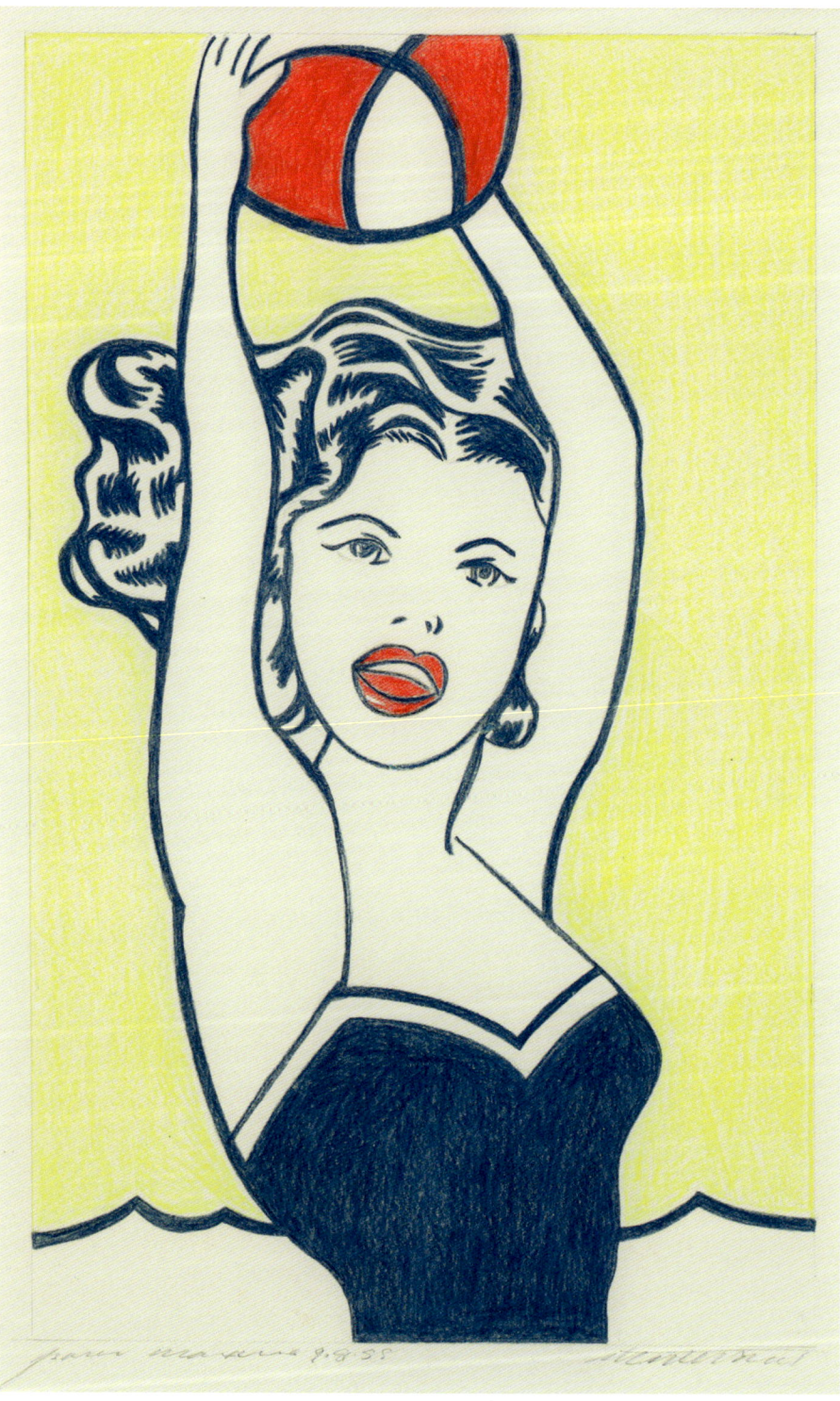

116 *Study for Lichtenstein Girl with Ball,* 1988

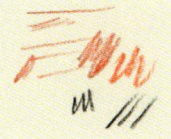

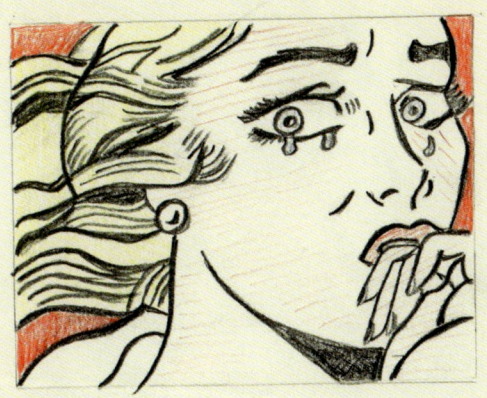

sternbant lichstein study '88

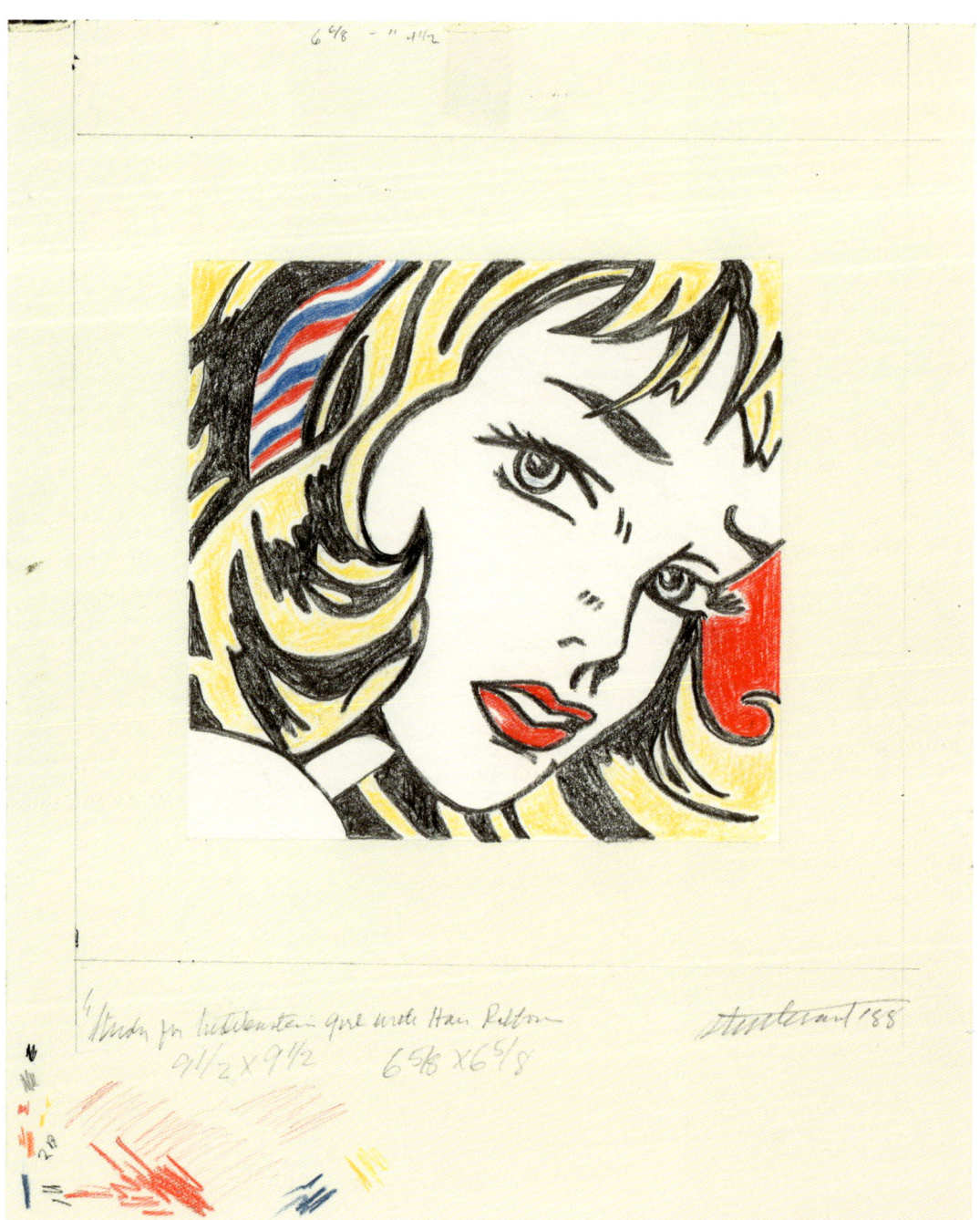

Study for Lichtenstein Girl with Hair Ribbon, 1988

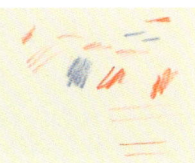

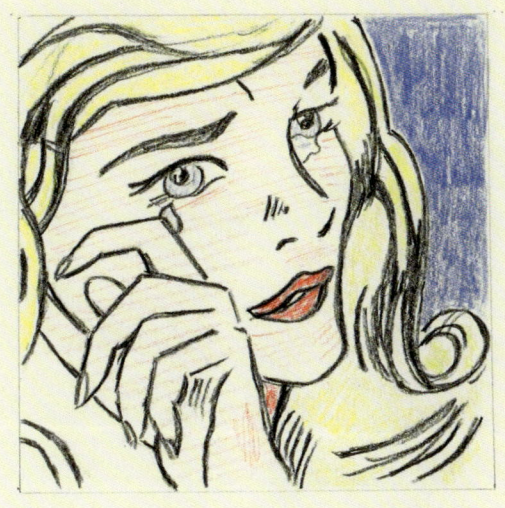

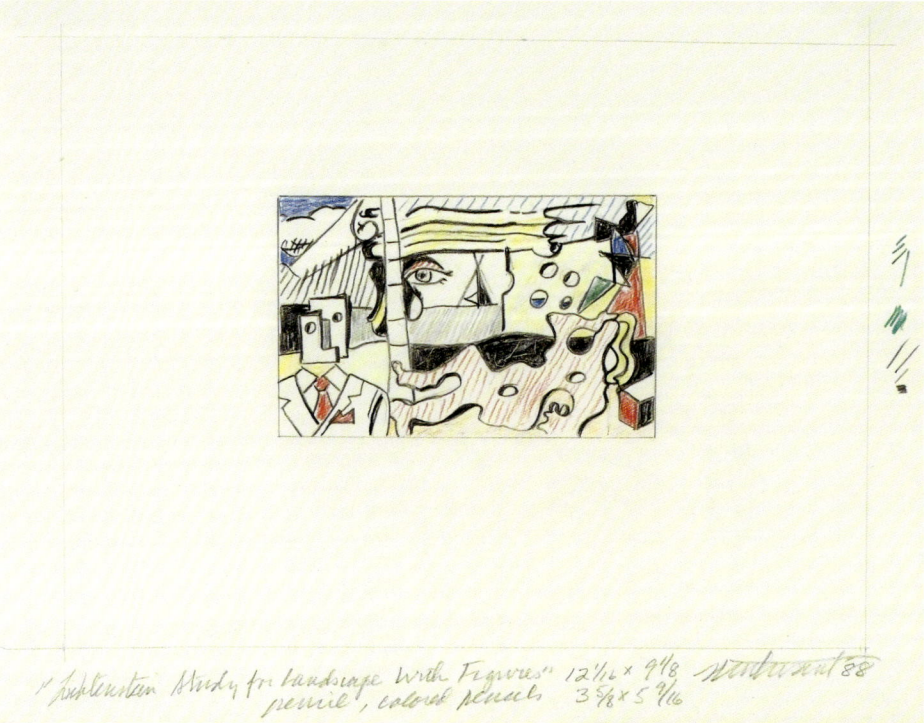

"Lichtenstein Study for Landscape With Figures" 12¹¹/₁₆ × 9⅛   *Rosenthal* 88
pencil, colored pencils   3⅝ × 5 ⁹/₁₆

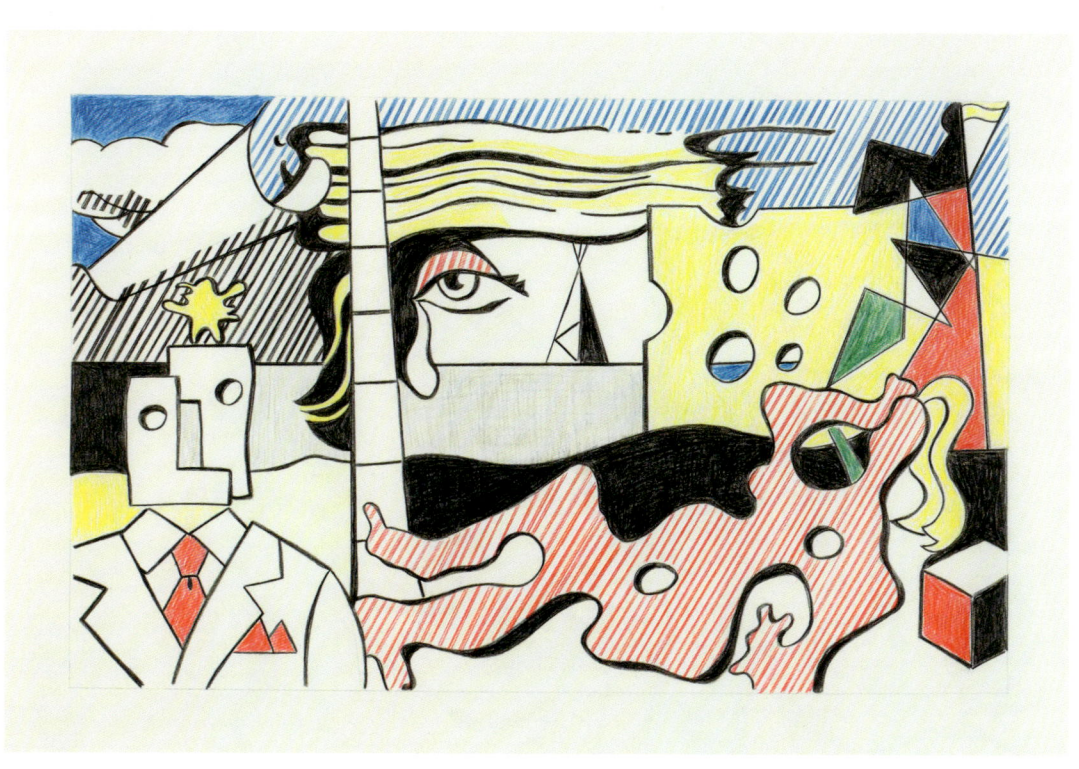

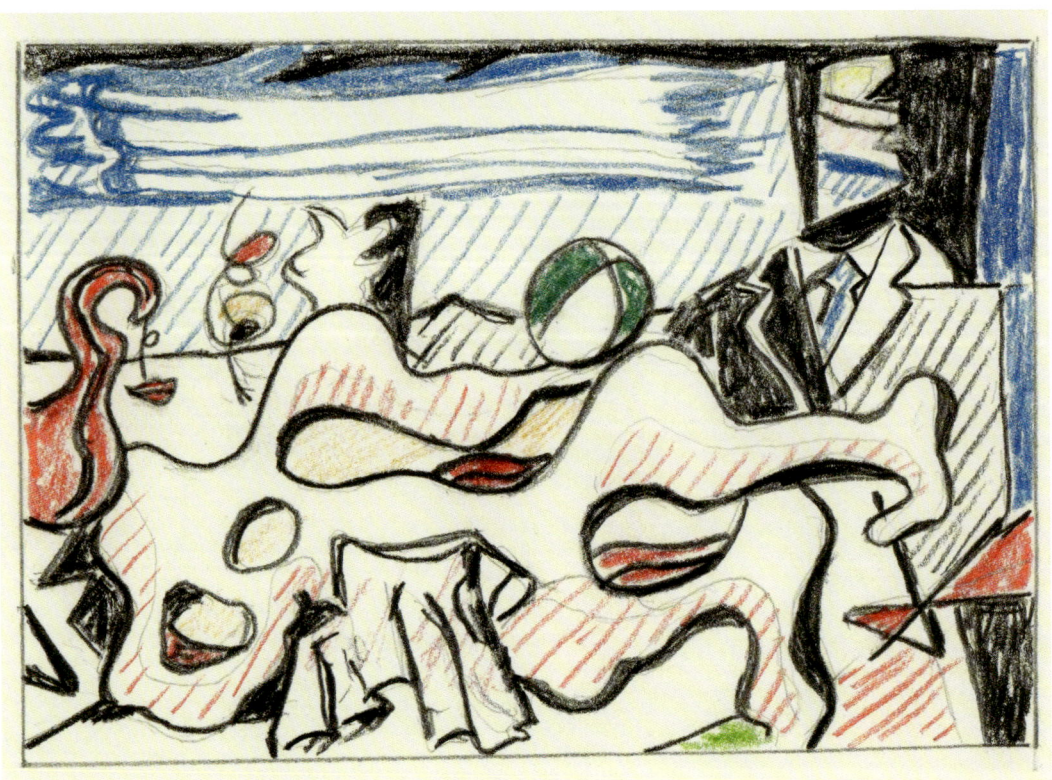

Lichtenstein Study for Reclining Nude, 1988

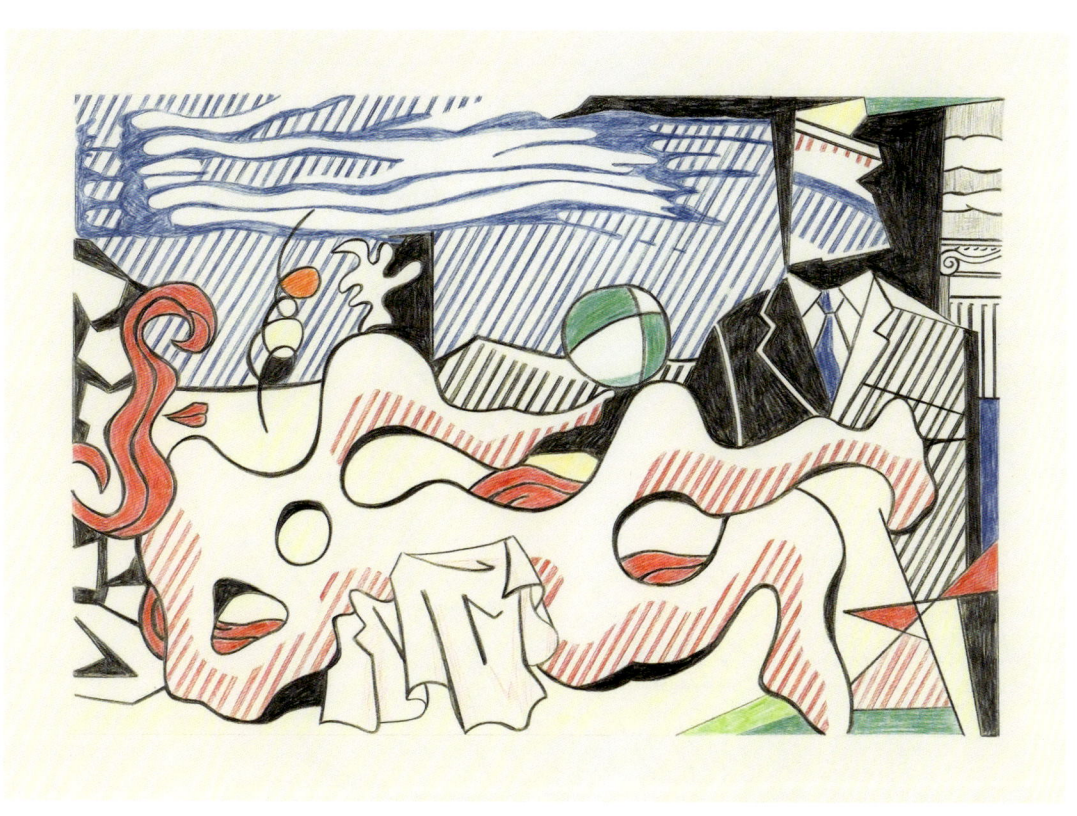

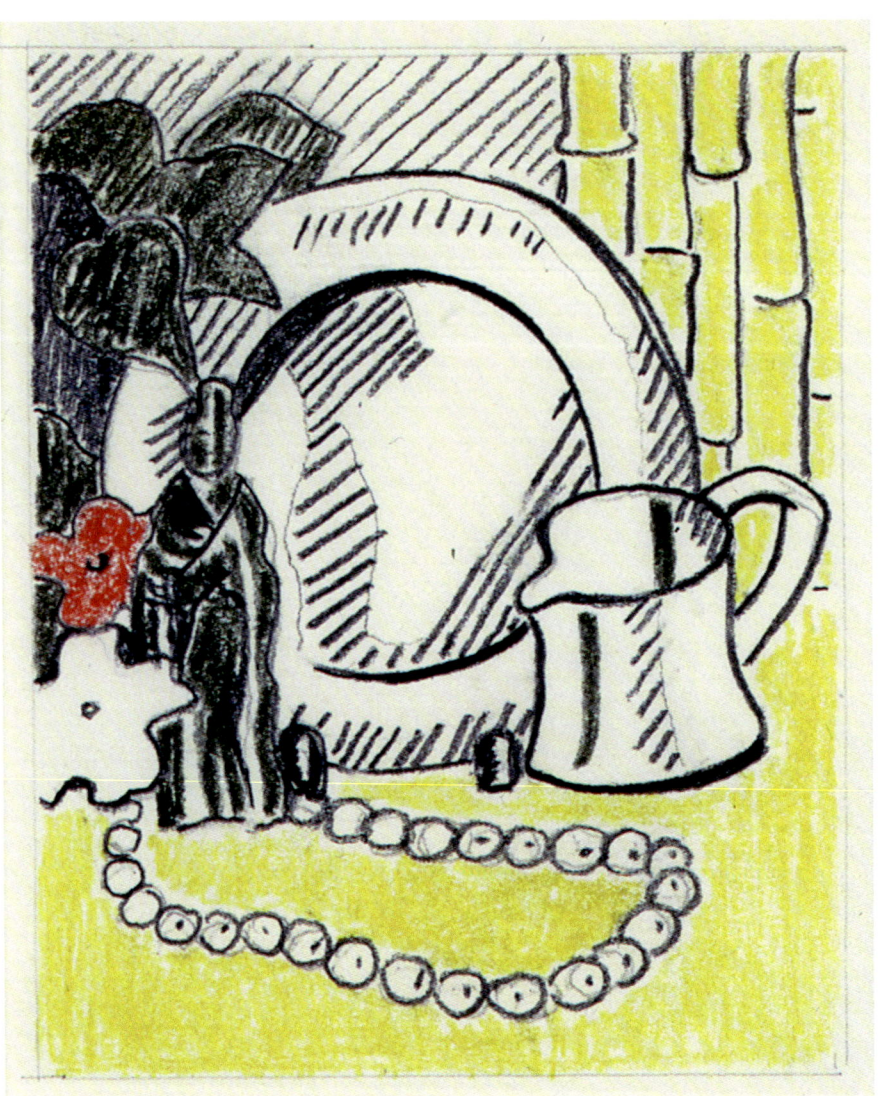

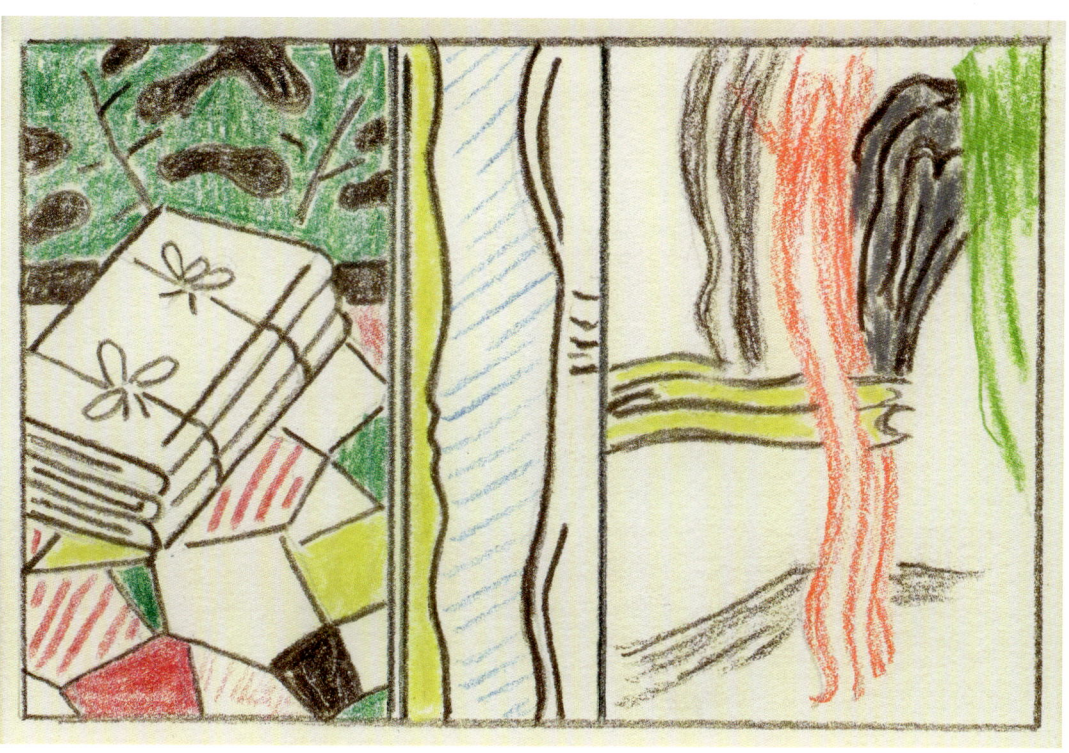

"Lichtenstein Study for Female Head"
10 5/8 X 8 1/2   3 7/16 X 3 3/16   Roÿ Lichtenstein 88
pencil, colored pencils

for Madame R. Nerta
Affection   Marie

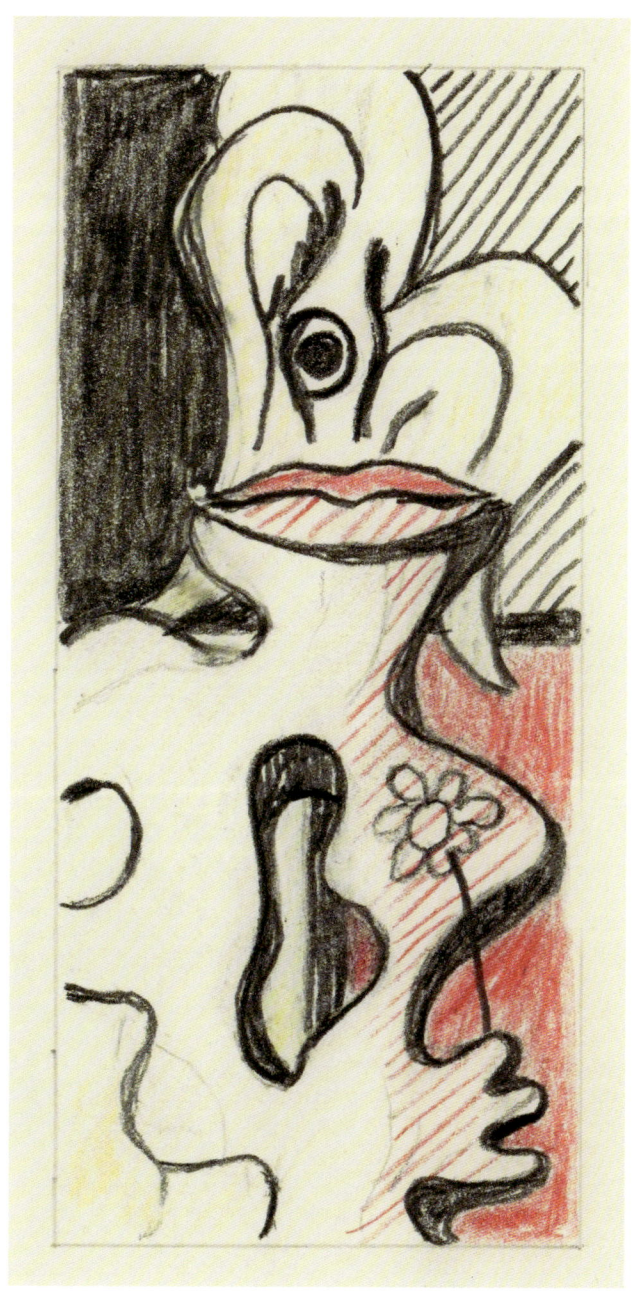

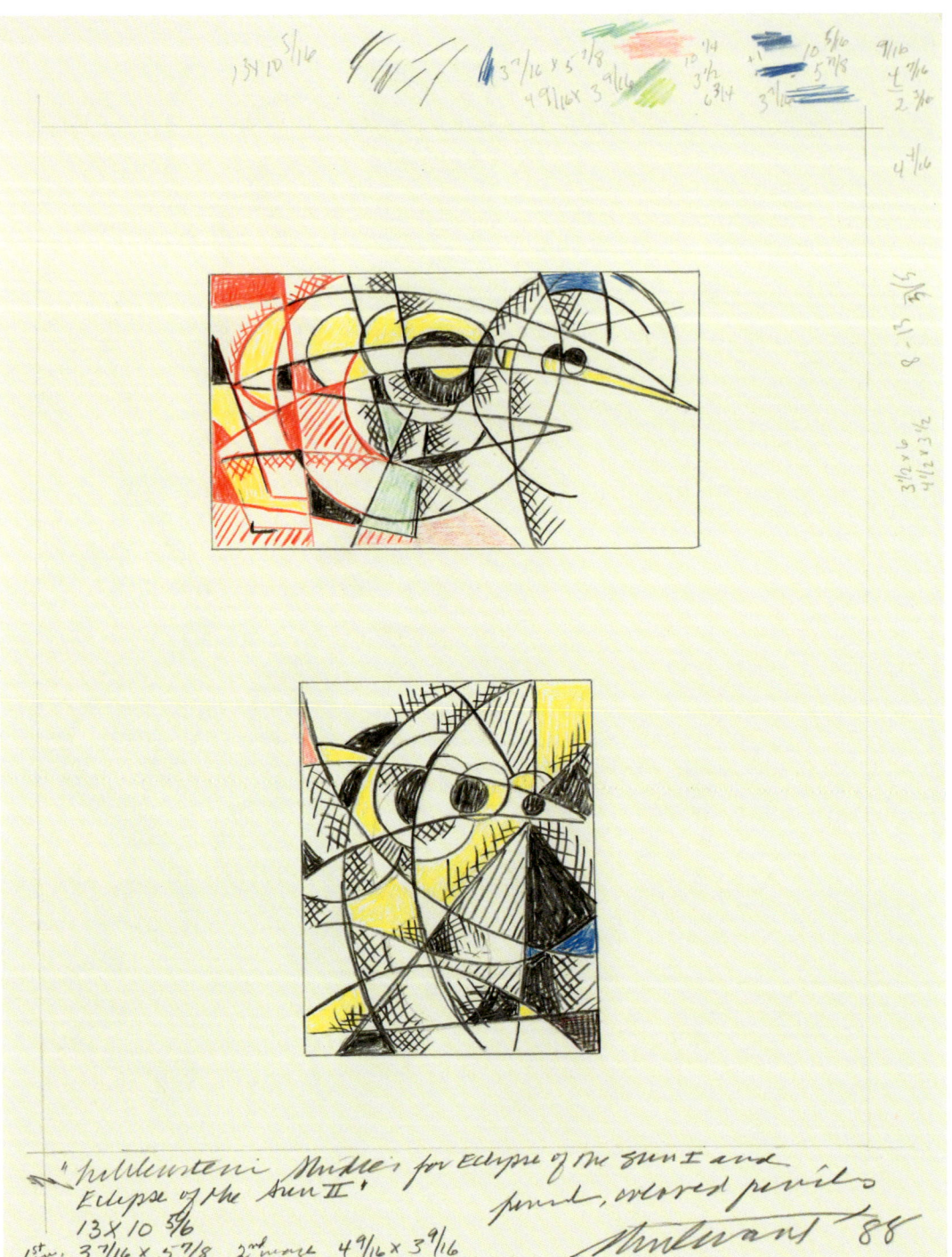

Lichtenstein Studies for Eclipse of the Sun I and Eclipse of the Sun II, 1988

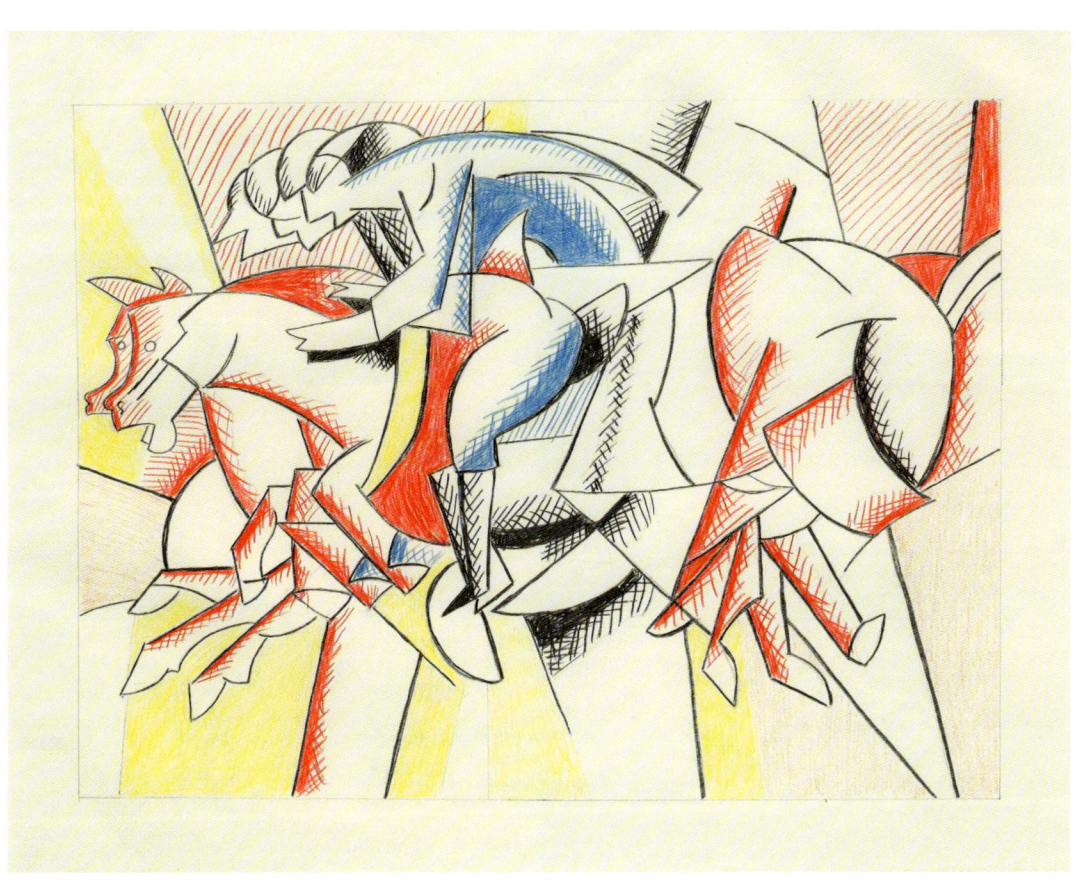

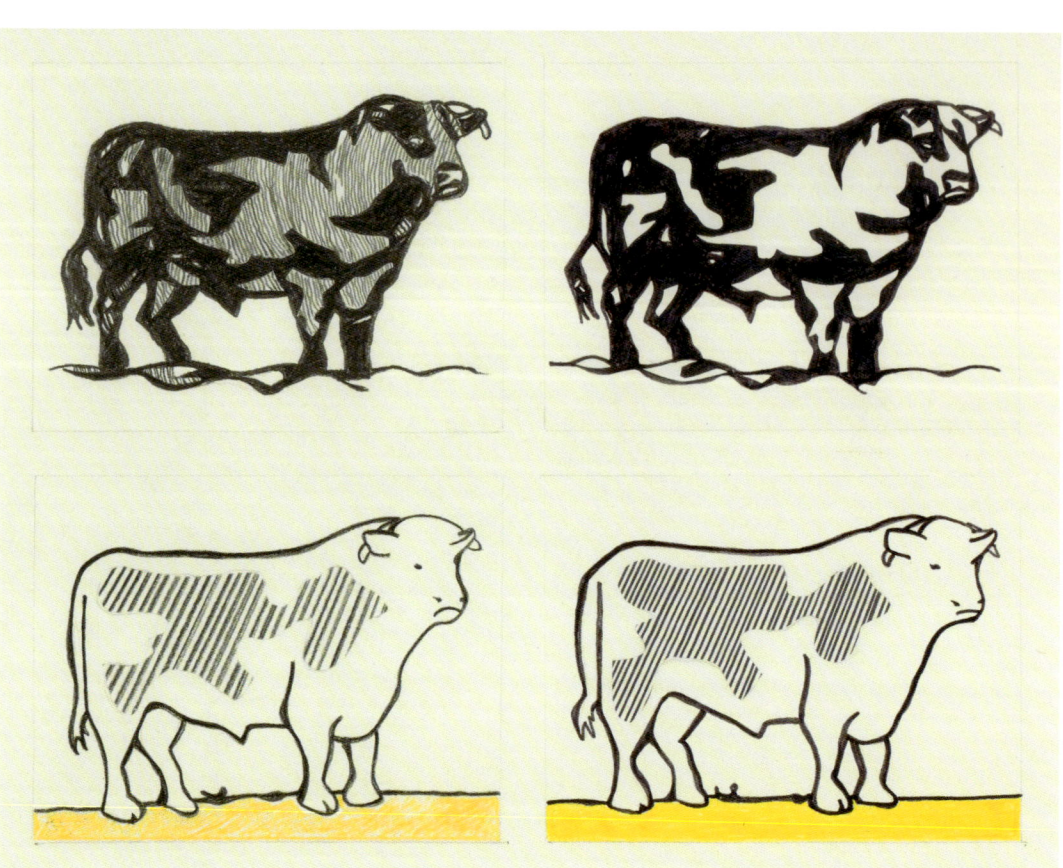

Study for Lichtenstein Bull I and II, 1988

NINETIES

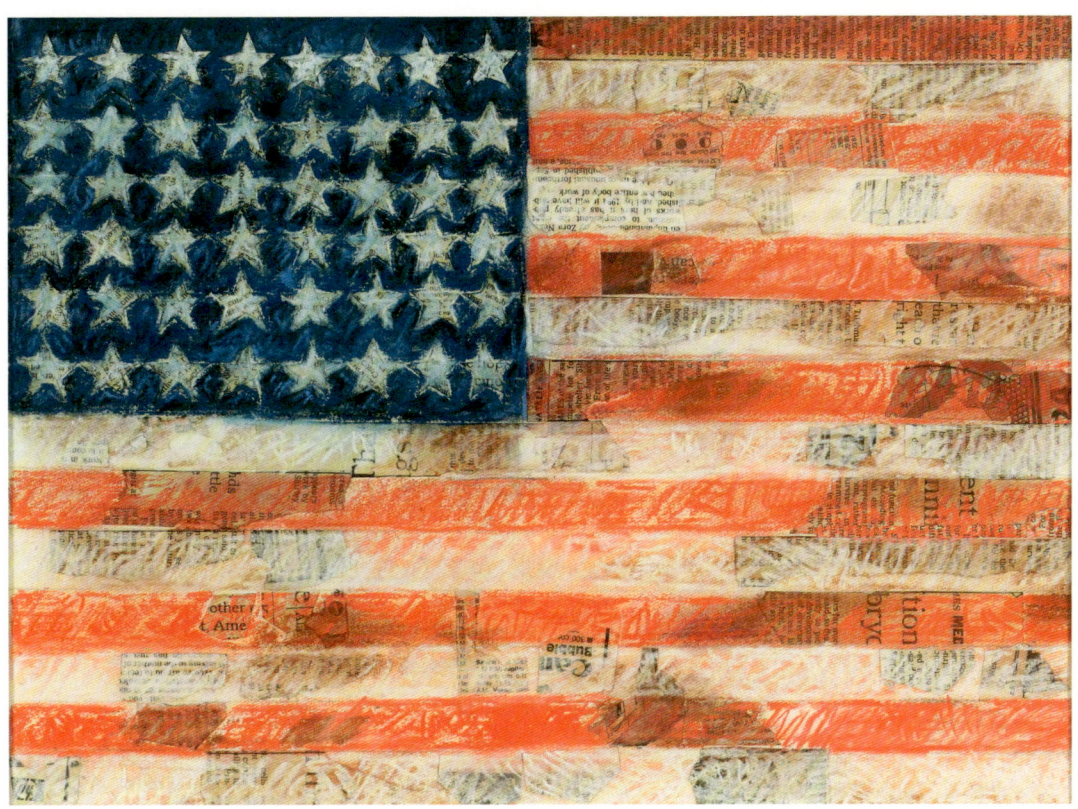

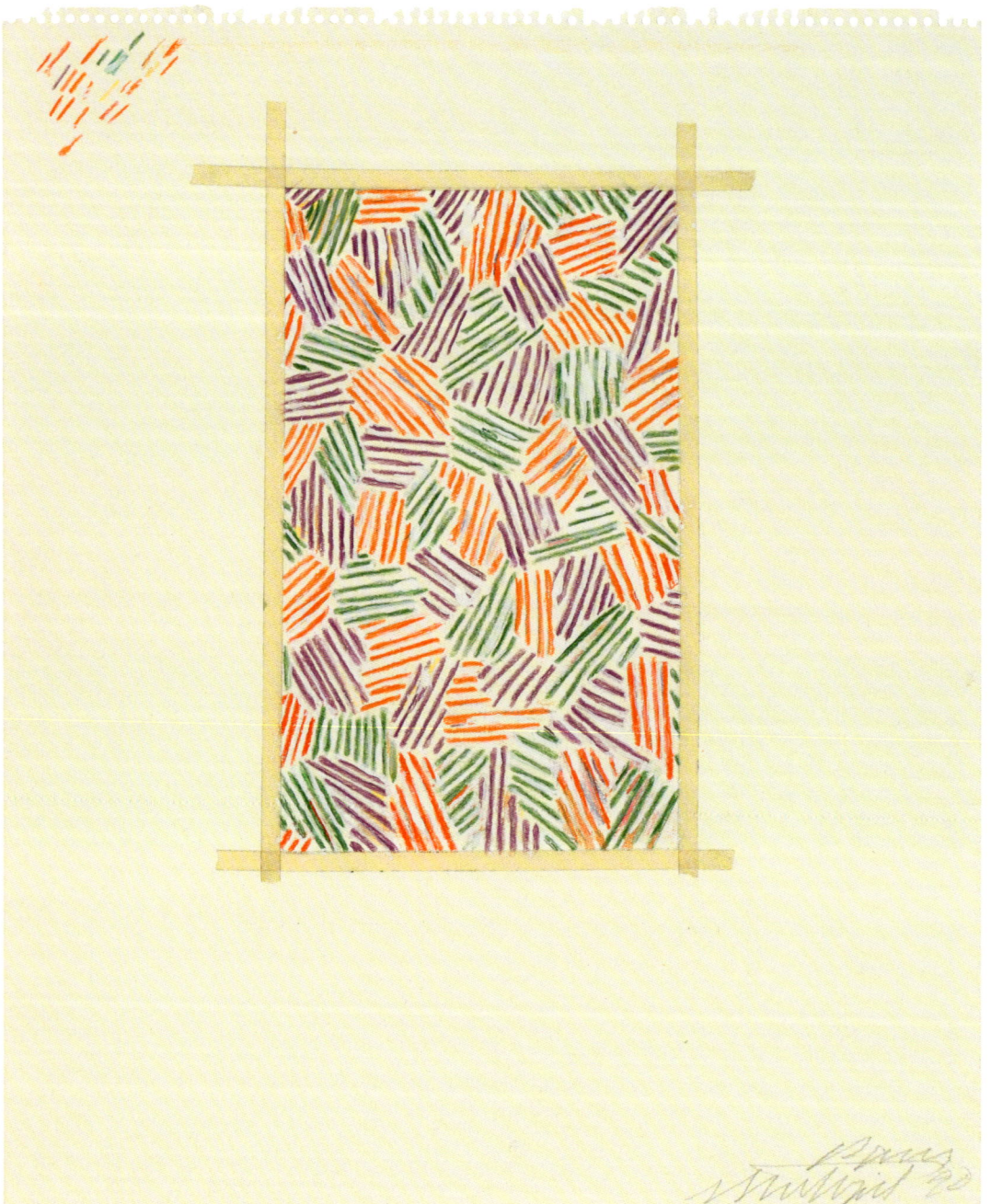

134   Untitled (Johns), 1990

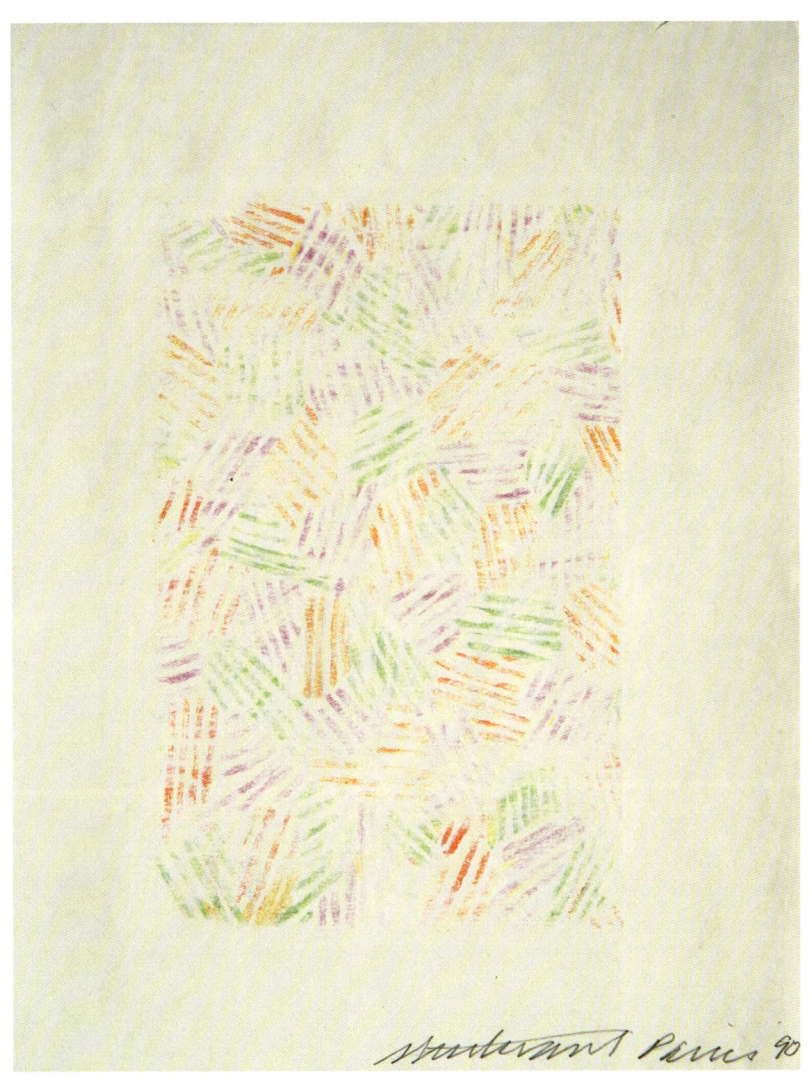

Untitled (Johns), 1990   **135**

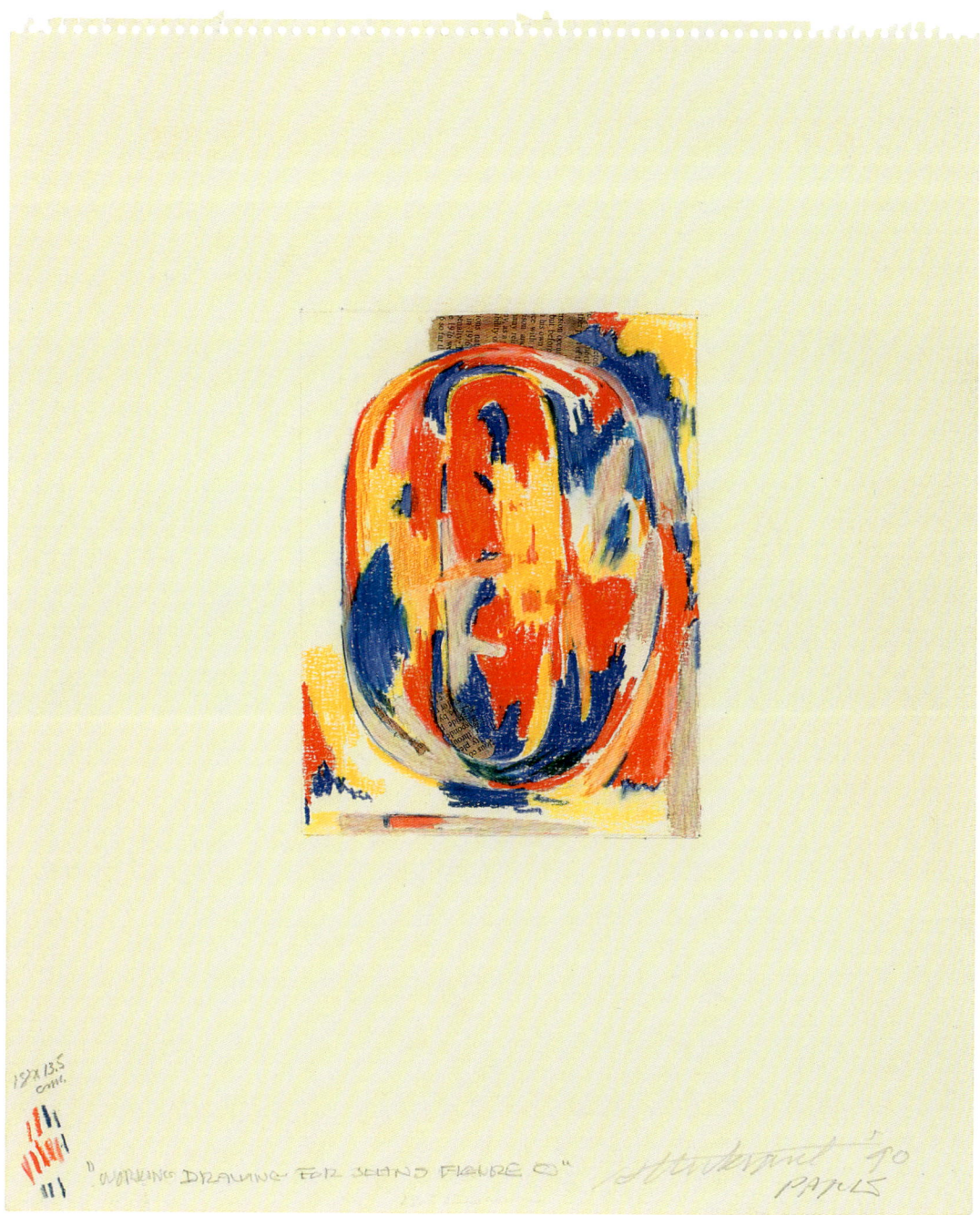

19 X 13.5
cm.

"WORKING DRAWING FOR JOHNS FIGURE 0"   90
PAULS

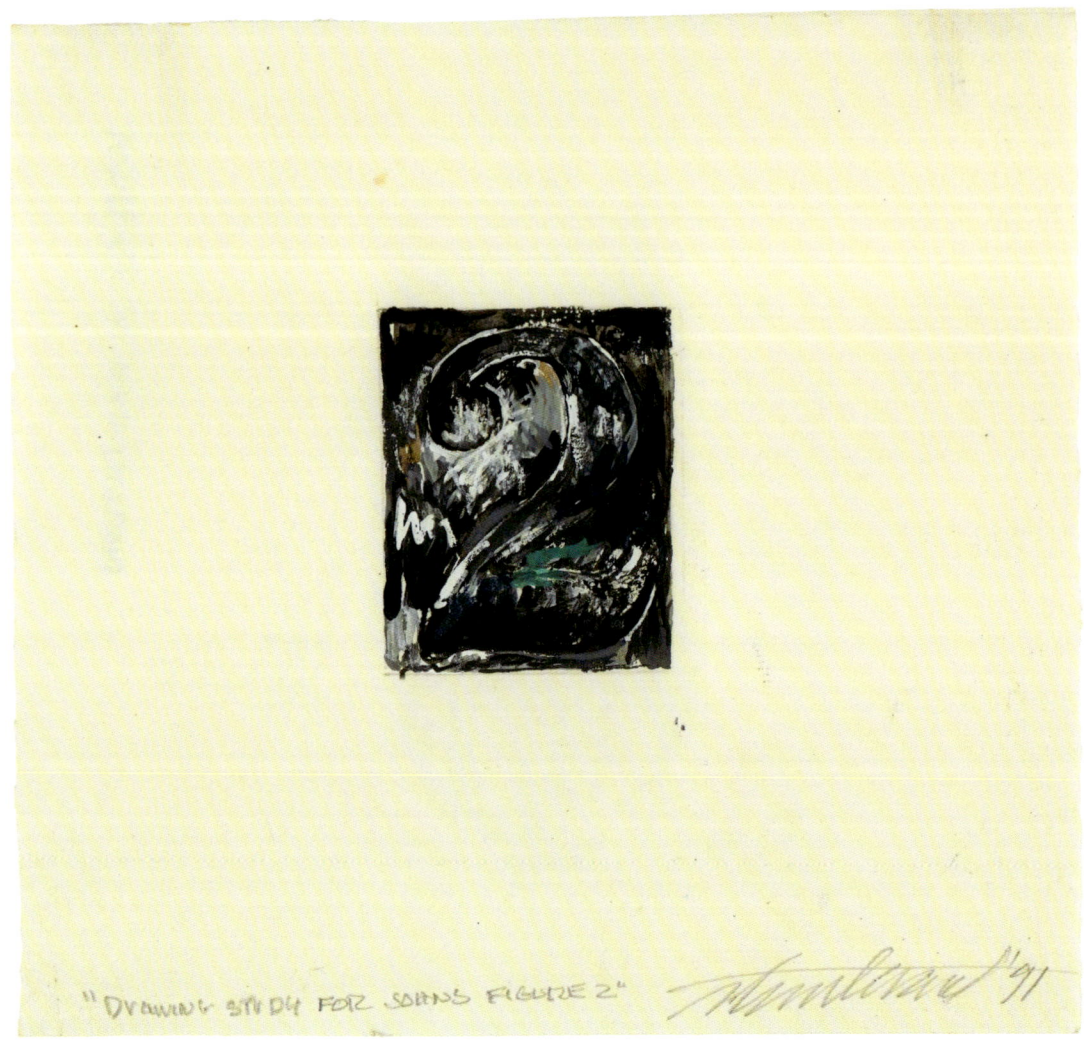

" DRAWING STUDY FOR JOHNS FIGURE 2"

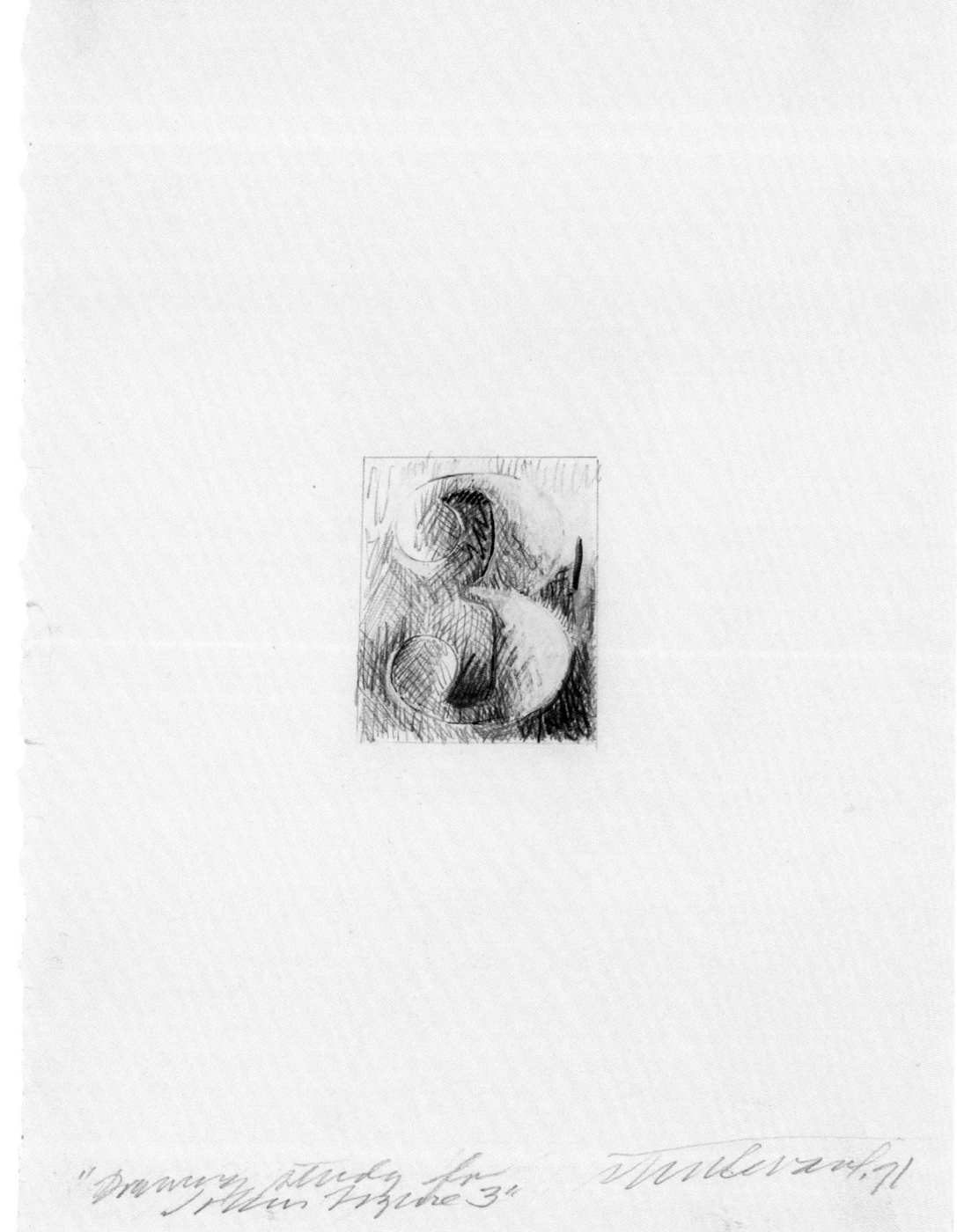

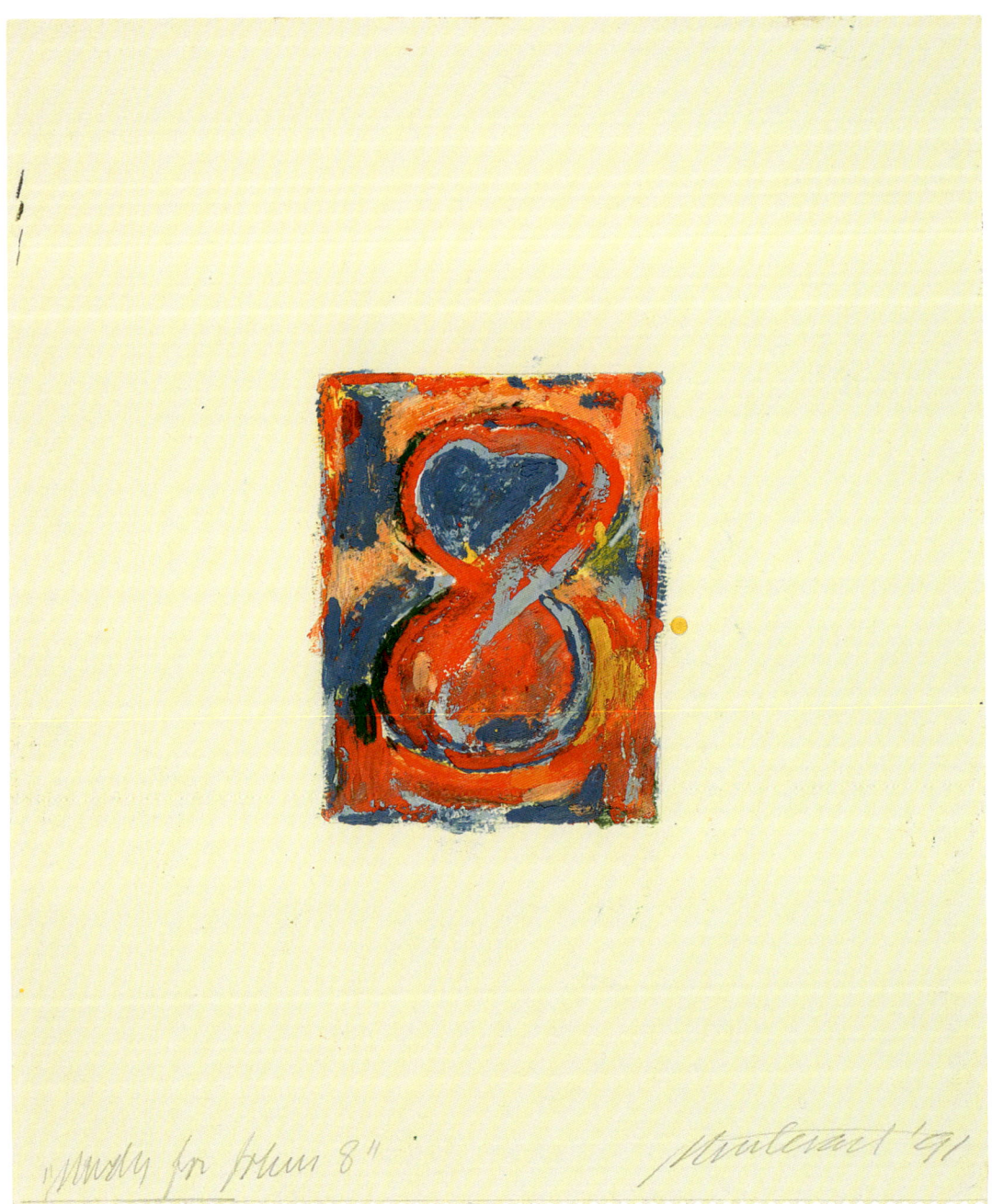

„Study for Johns 8"   Winterart '91

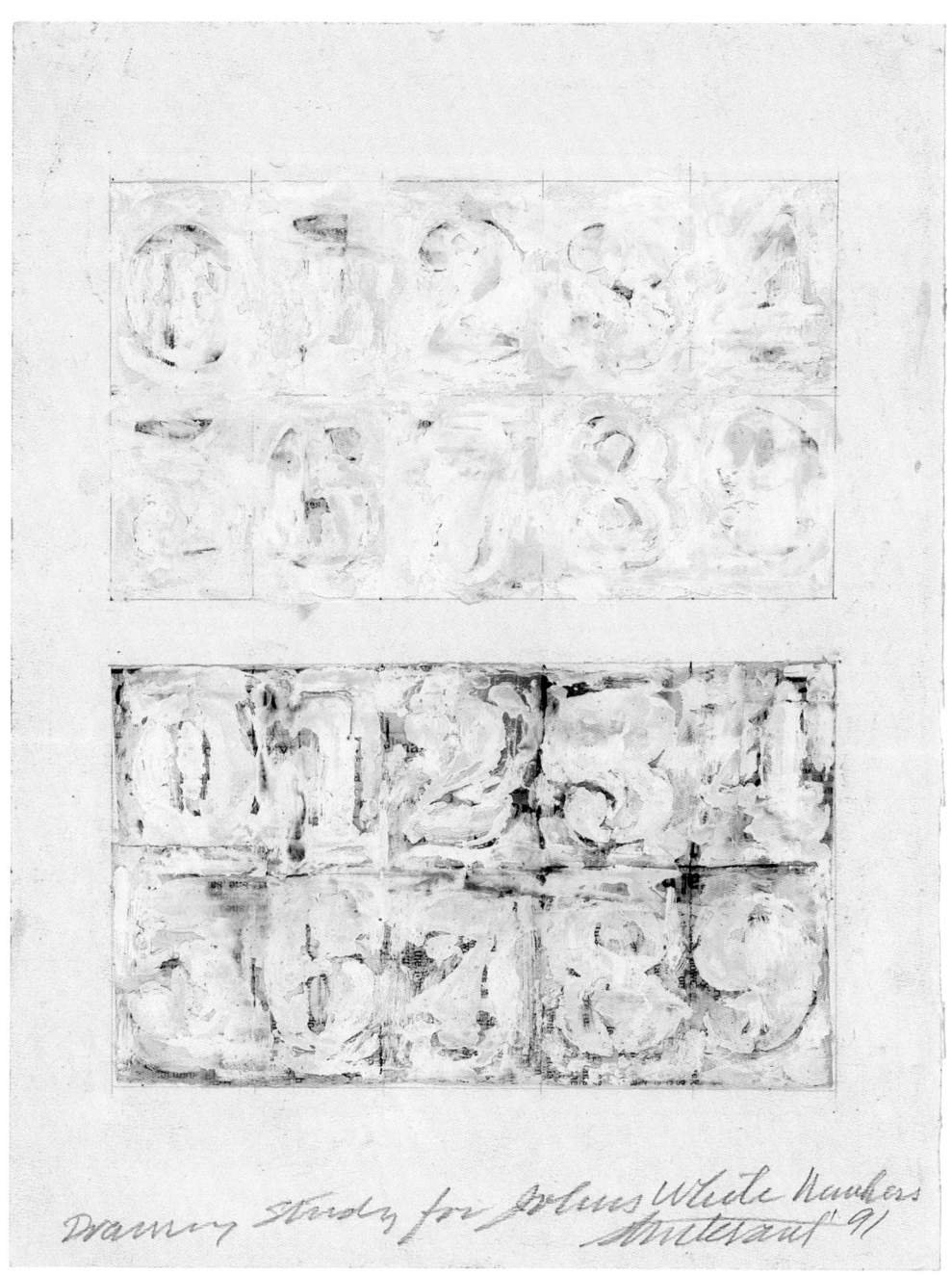

Drawing Study for Johns White Numbers, 1991

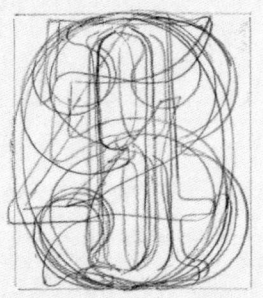

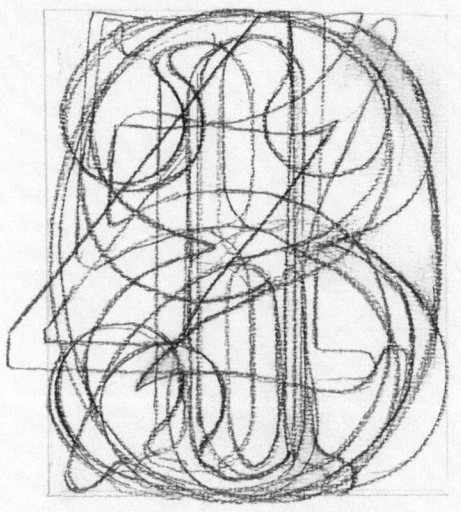

"JOHNS NUMBERS"   Sturtevant 91

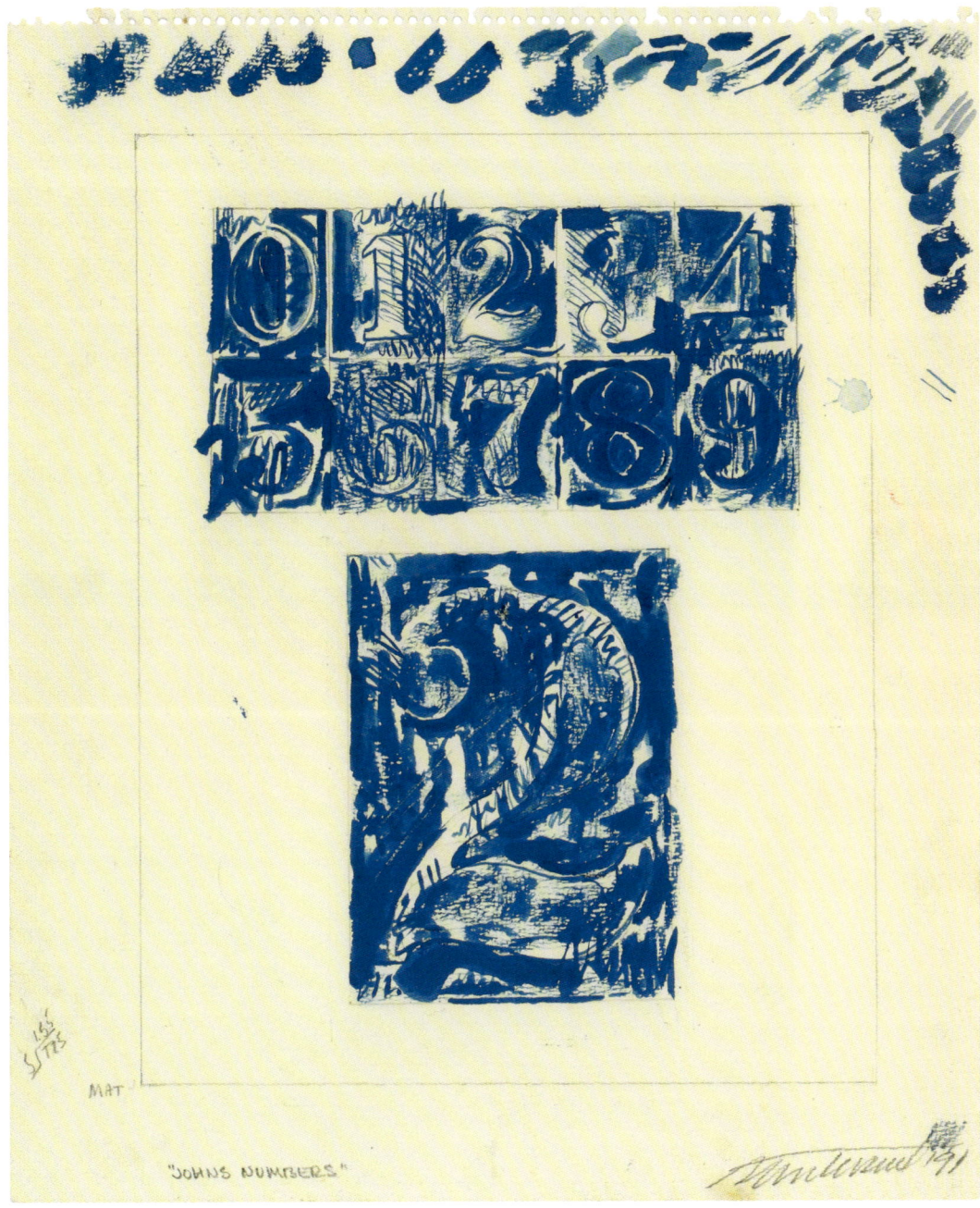

"JOHNS NUMBERS"

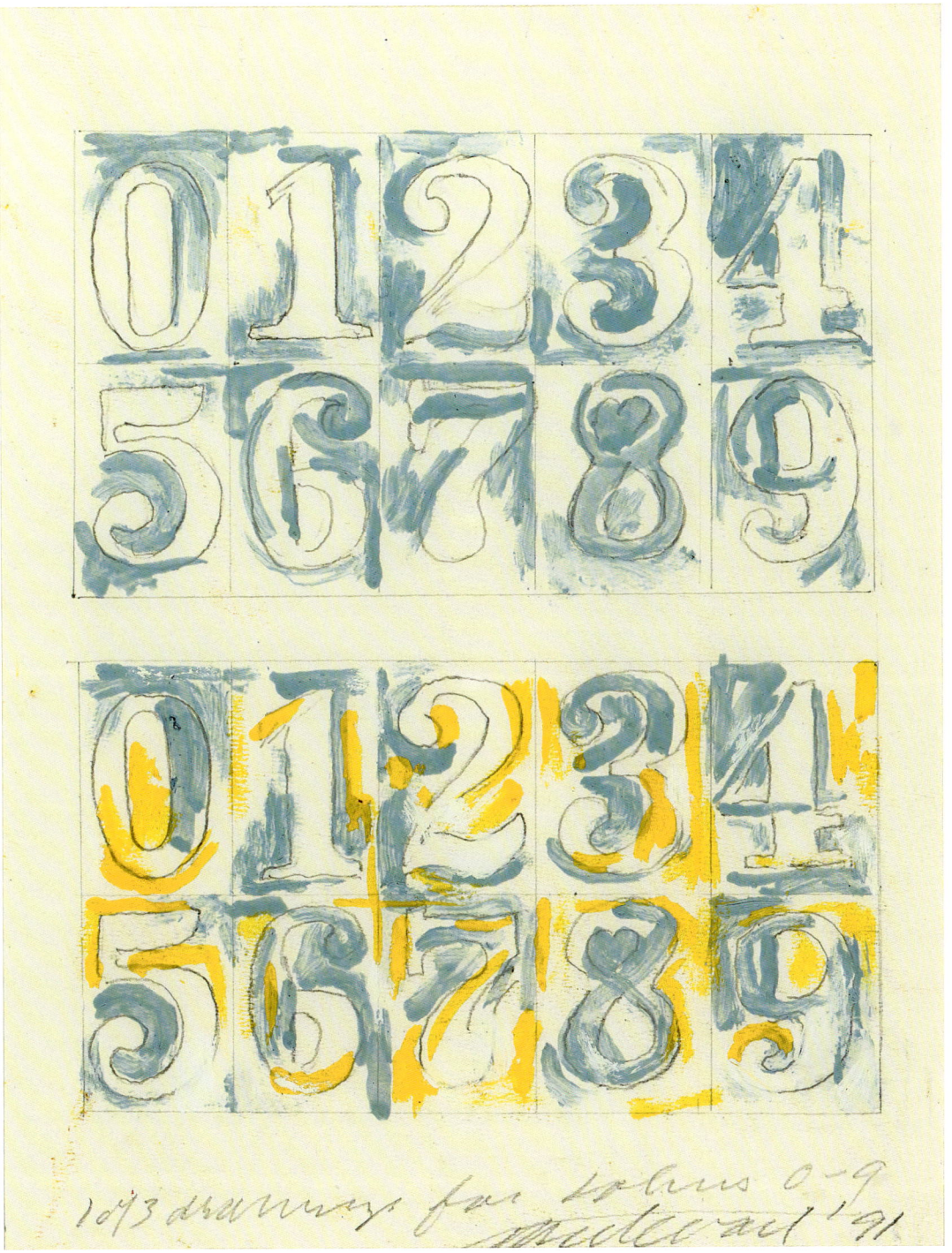

1 of 3 Drawings for Johns 0–9, 1991   **147**

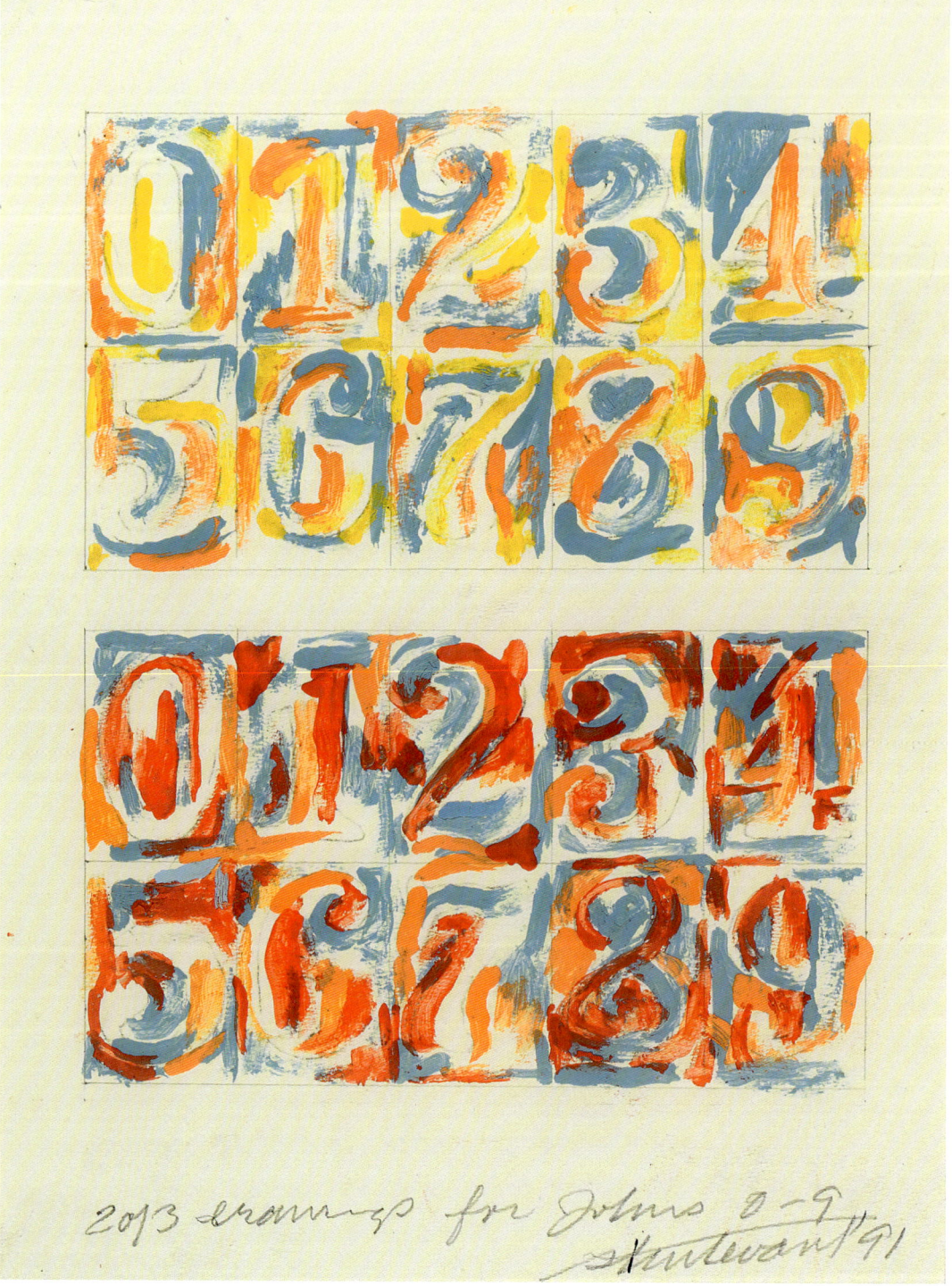

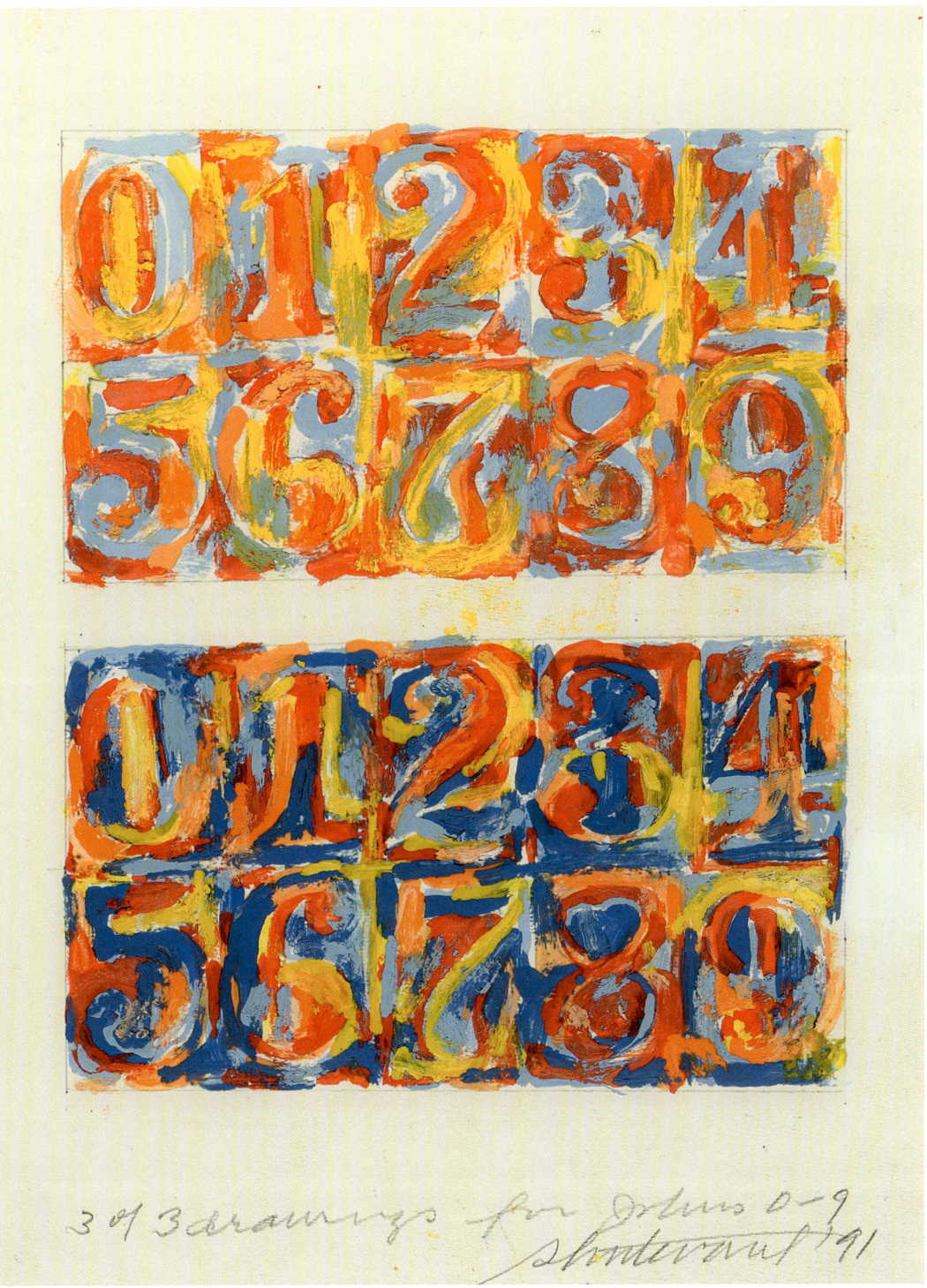

3 of 3 drawings for Johns 0–9
shintermut '91

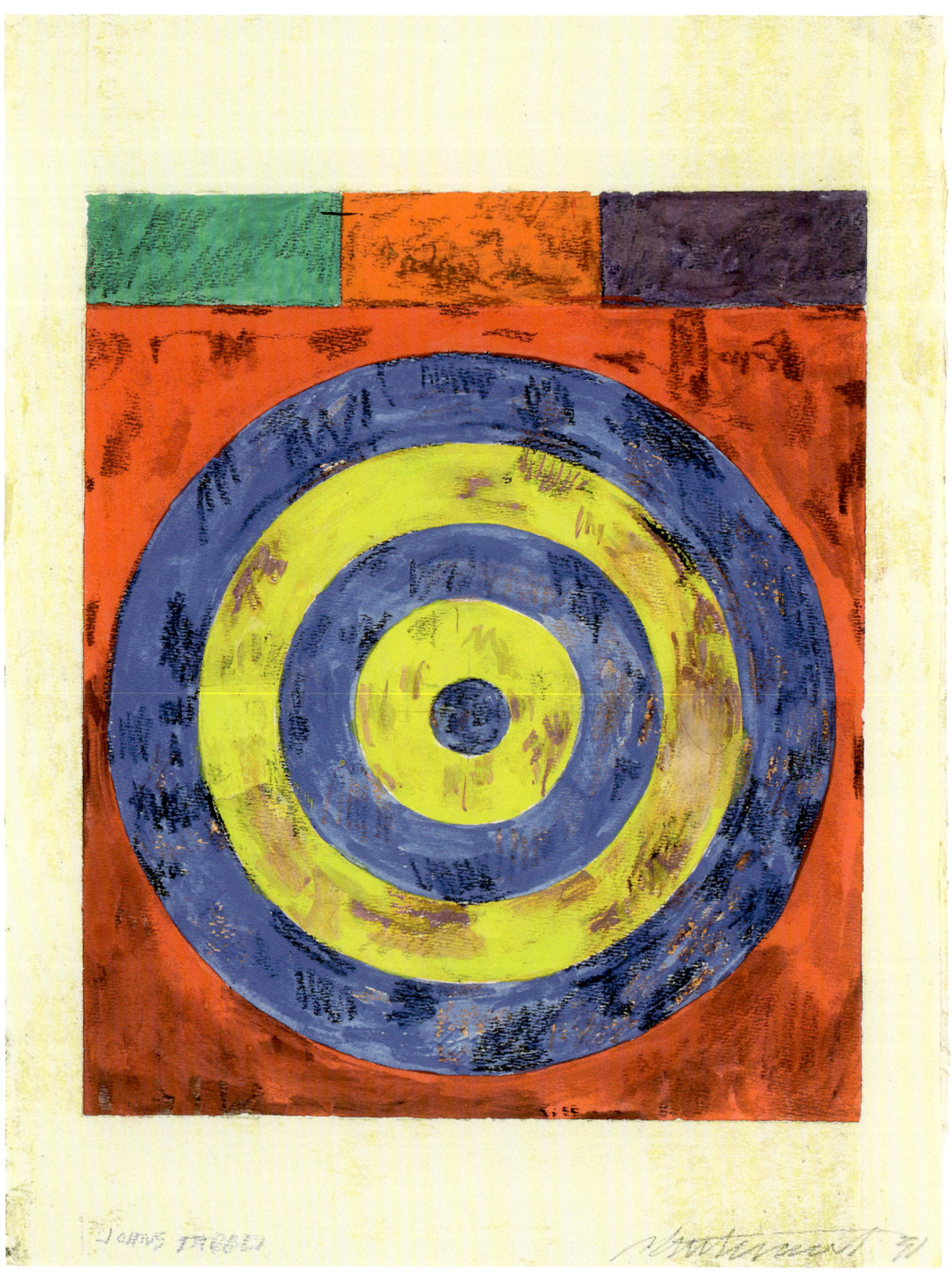

150 *Johns Target*, 1991

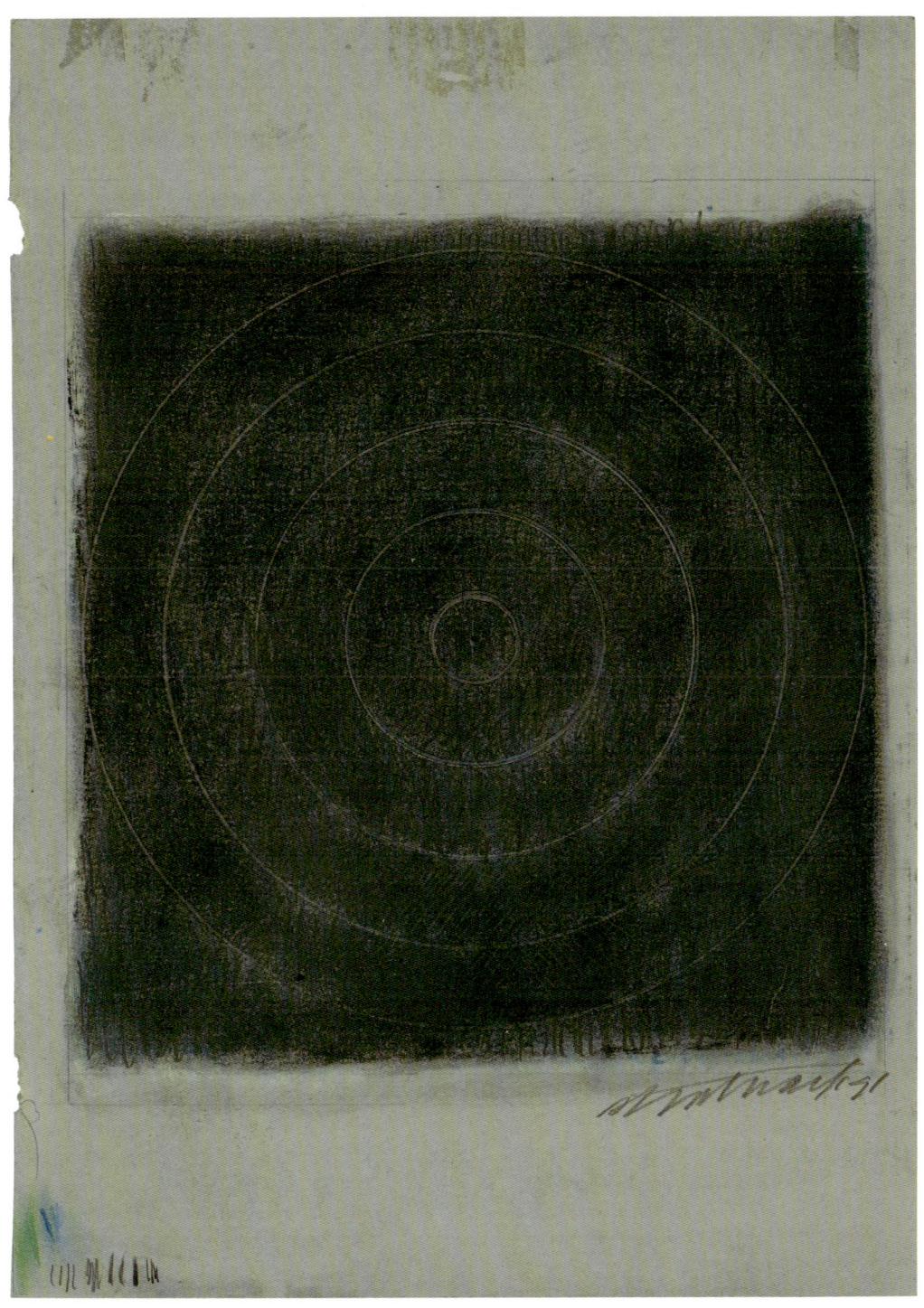

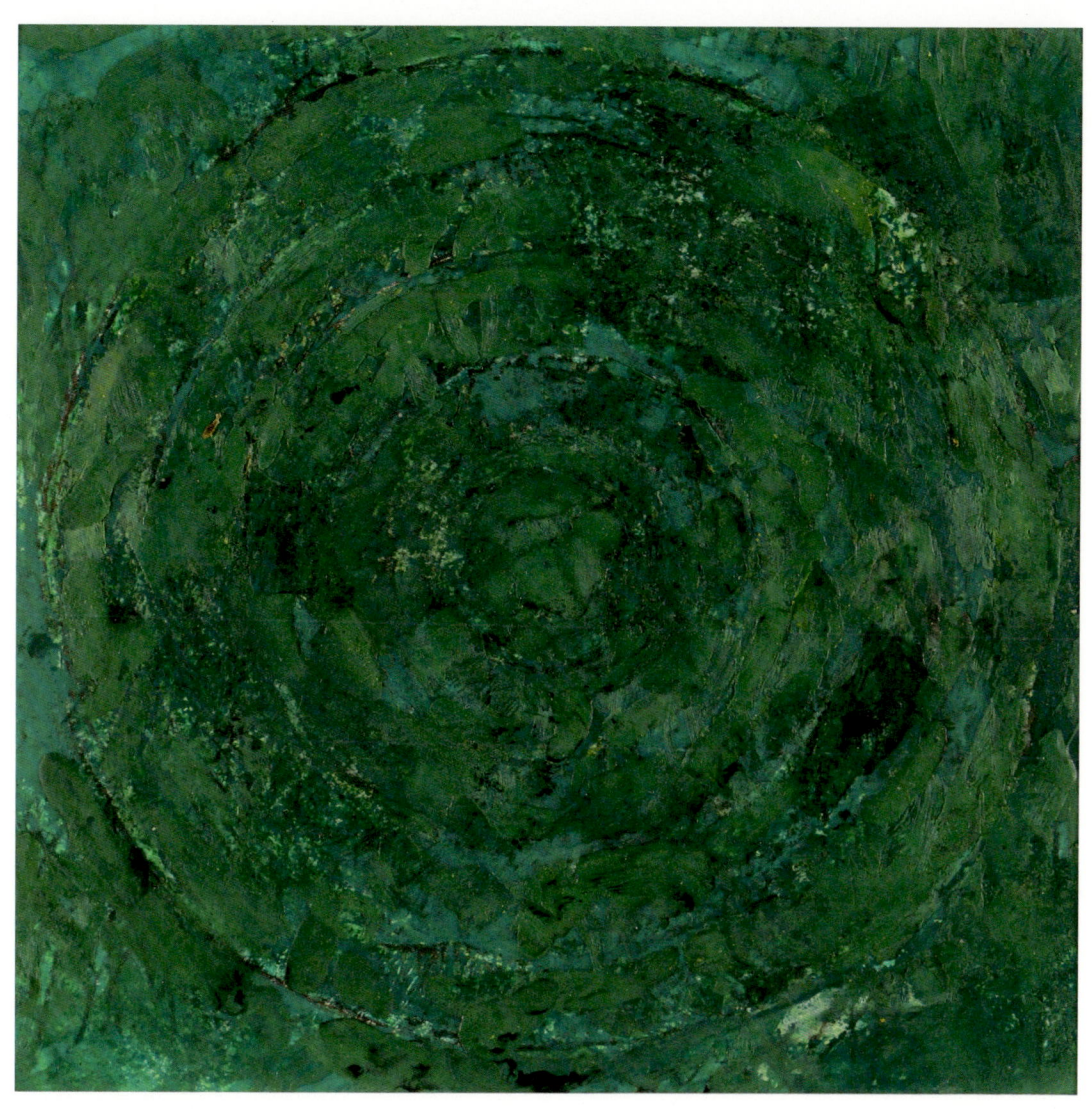

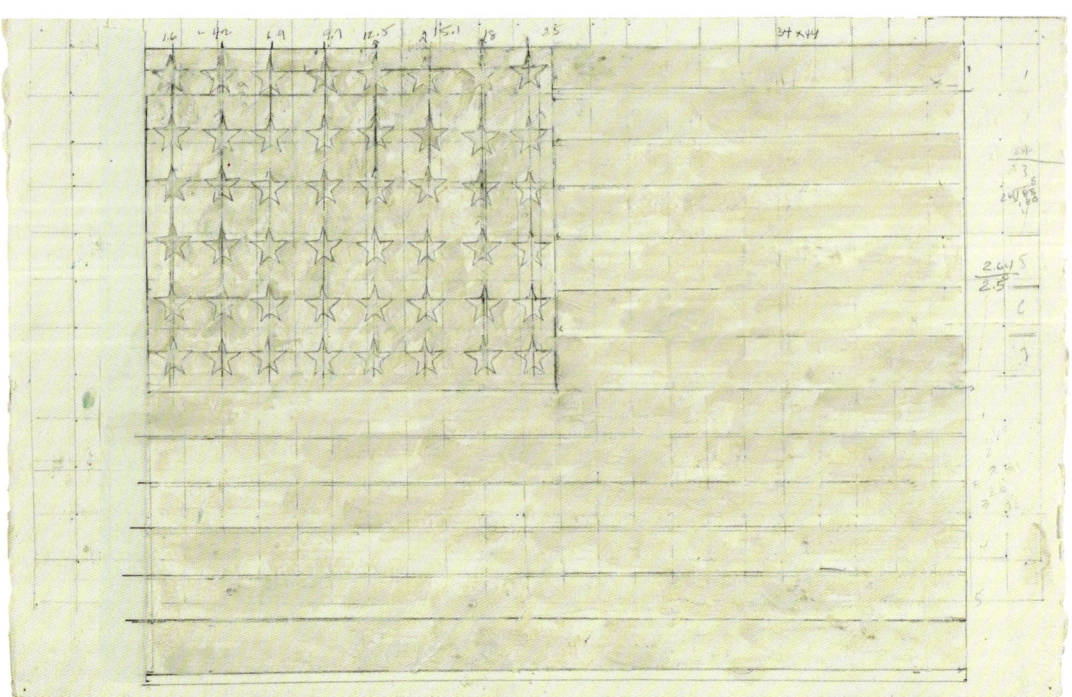

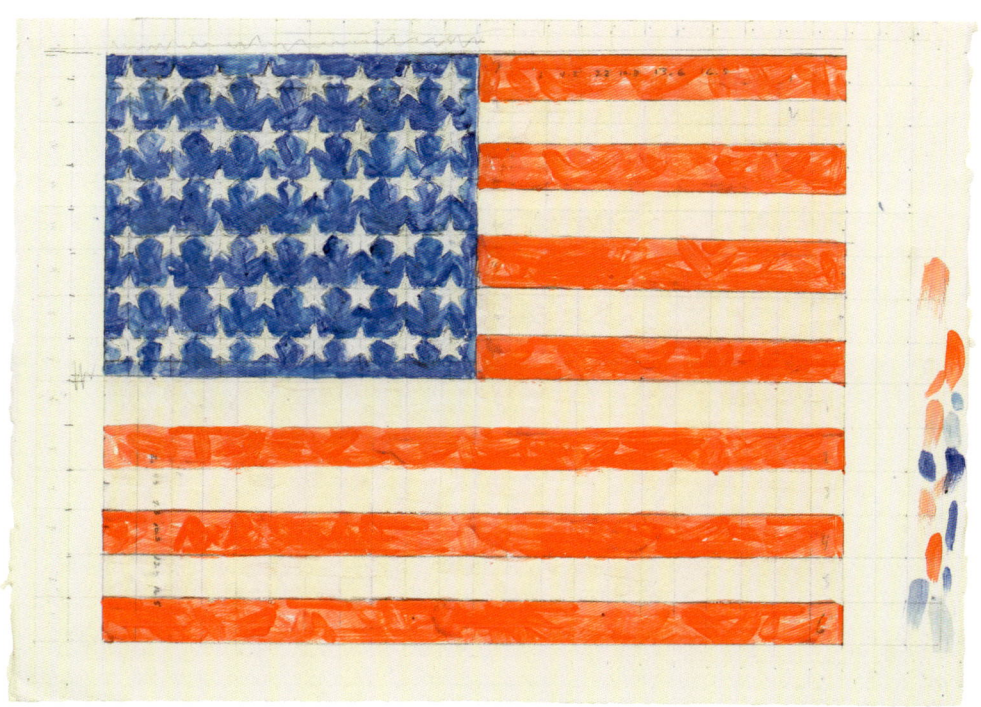

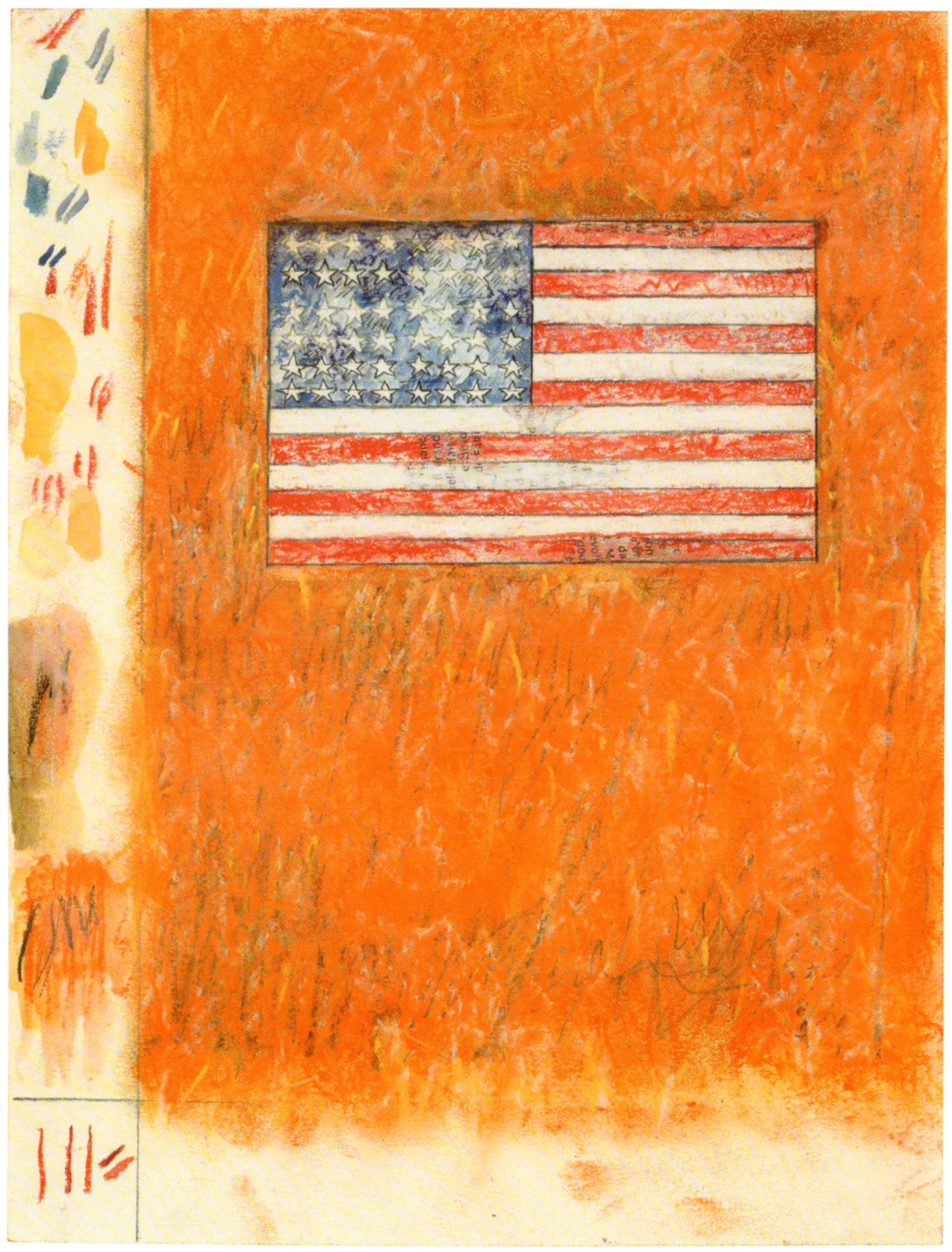

Study for Johns Flag on Orange Ground, 1991   **157**

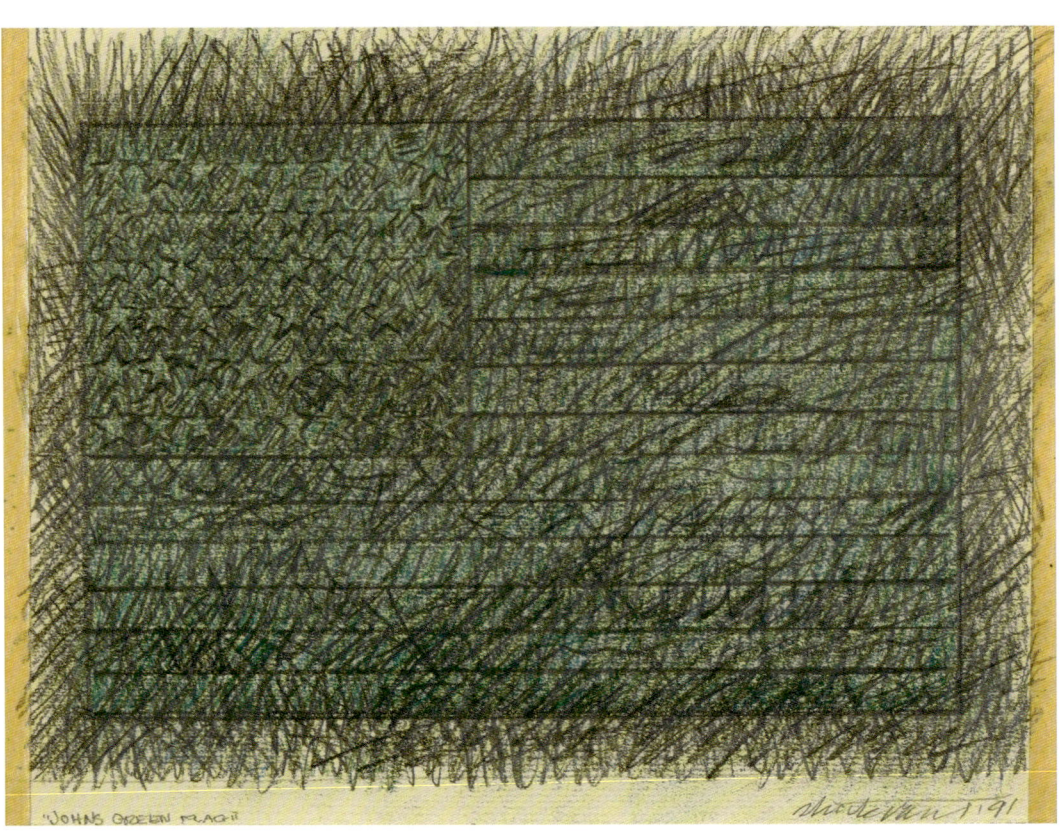

"JOHNS GREEN FLAG"

158   *Johns Green Flag*, 1991

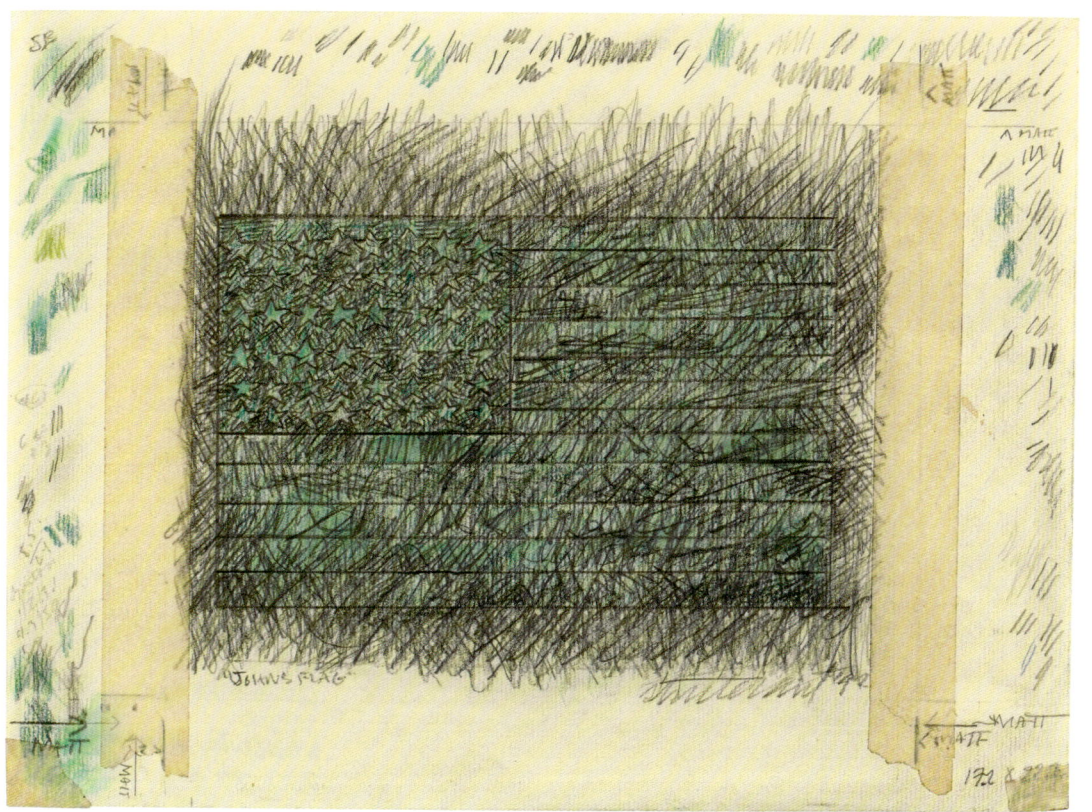

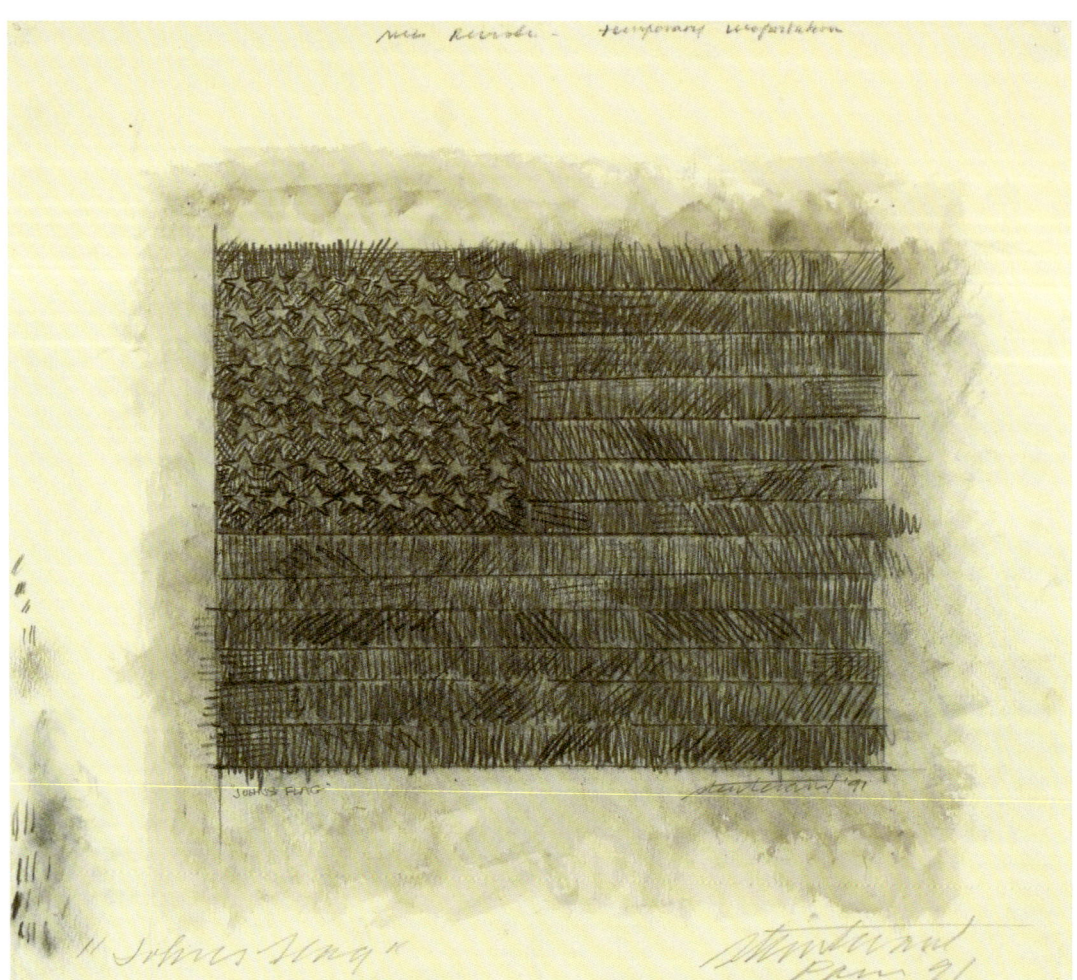

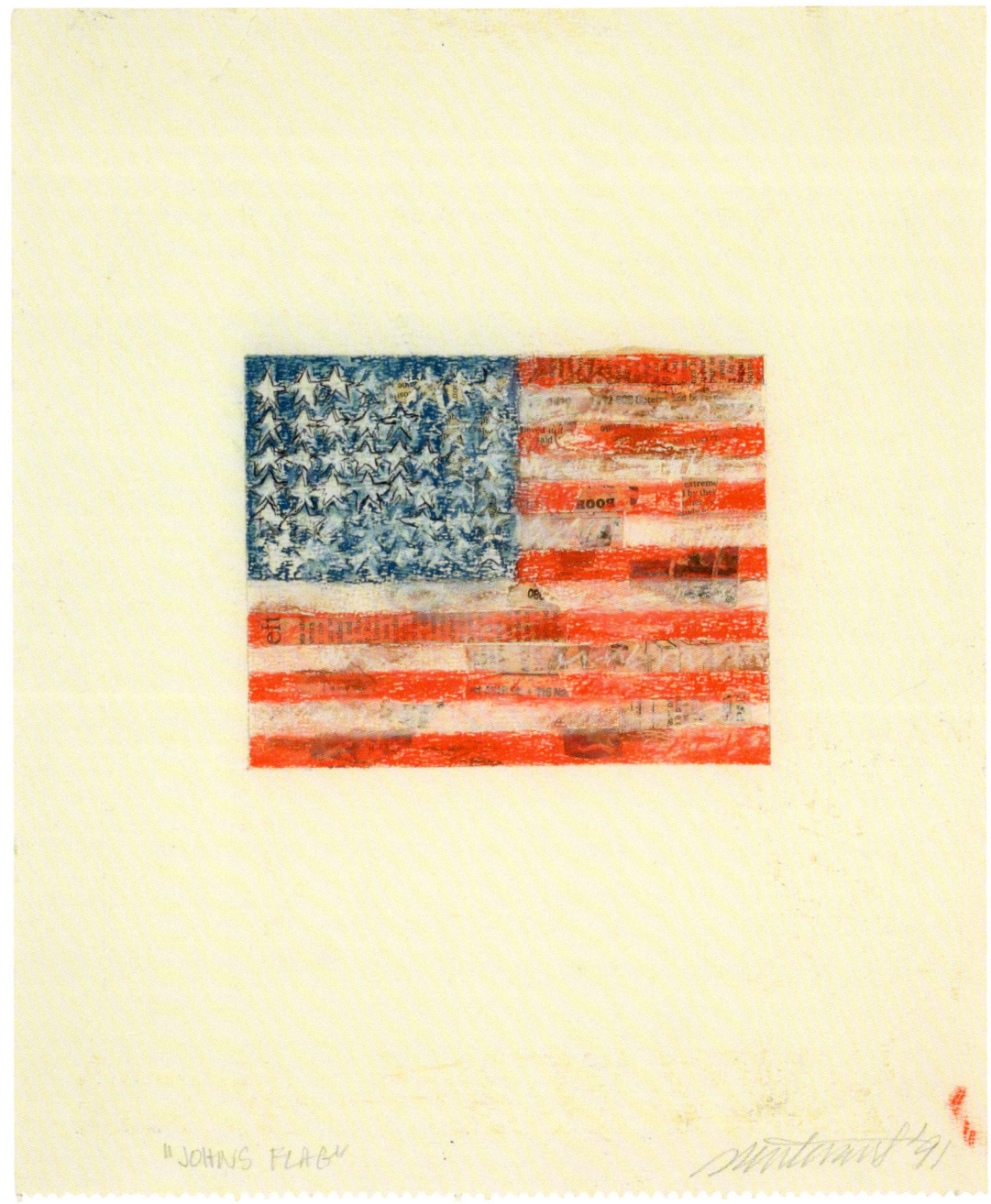

"JOHNS FLAG"

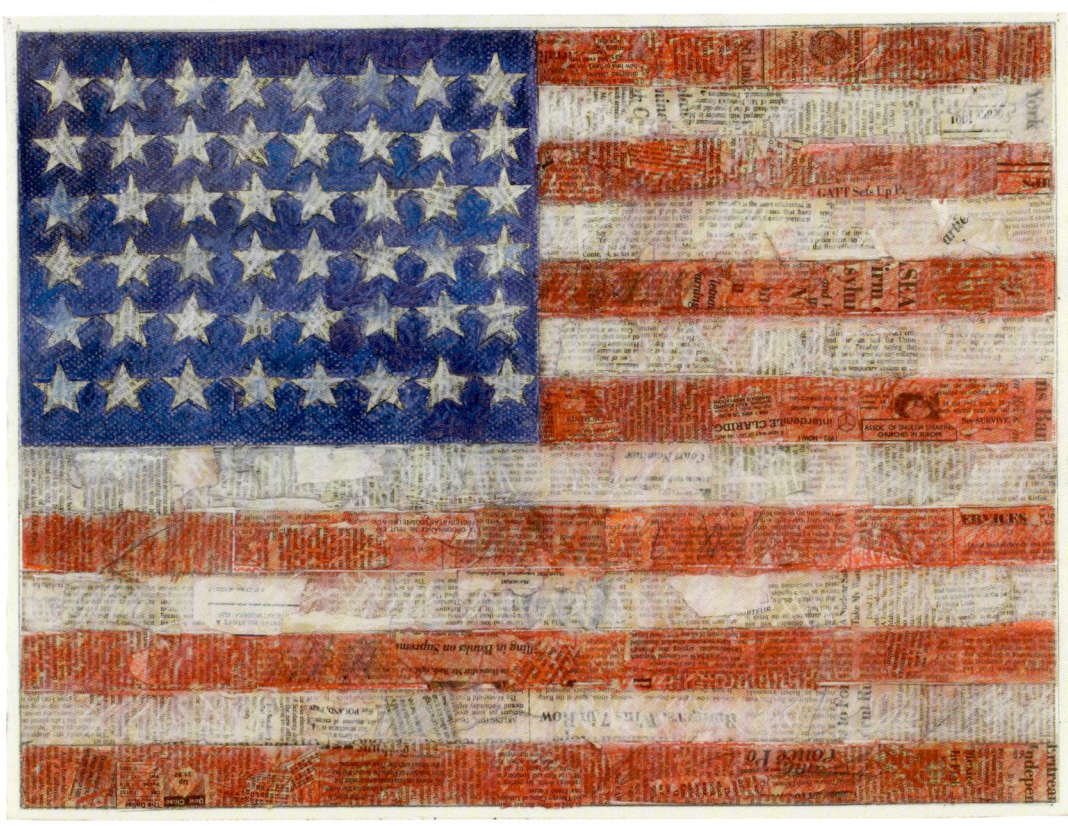

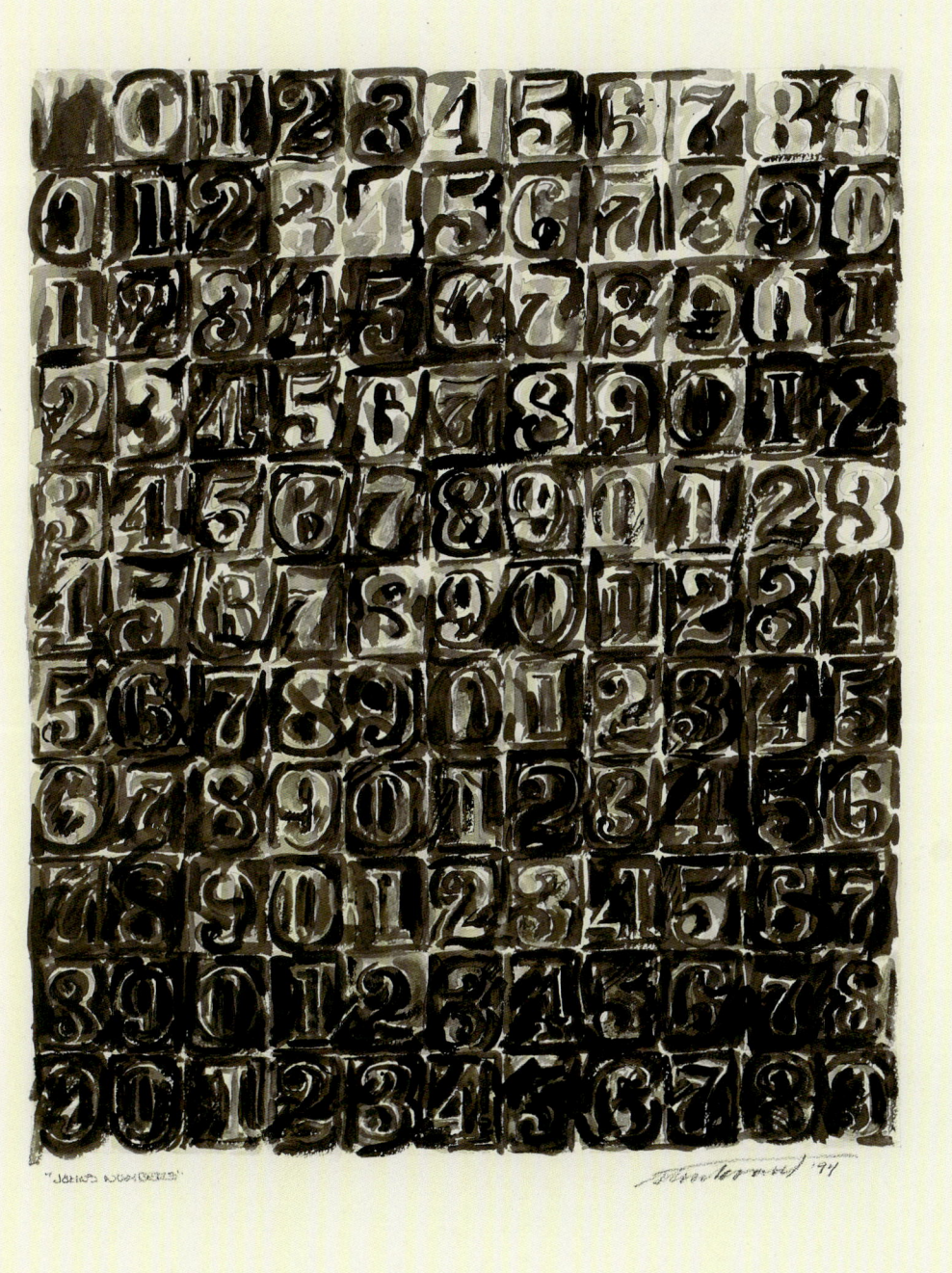

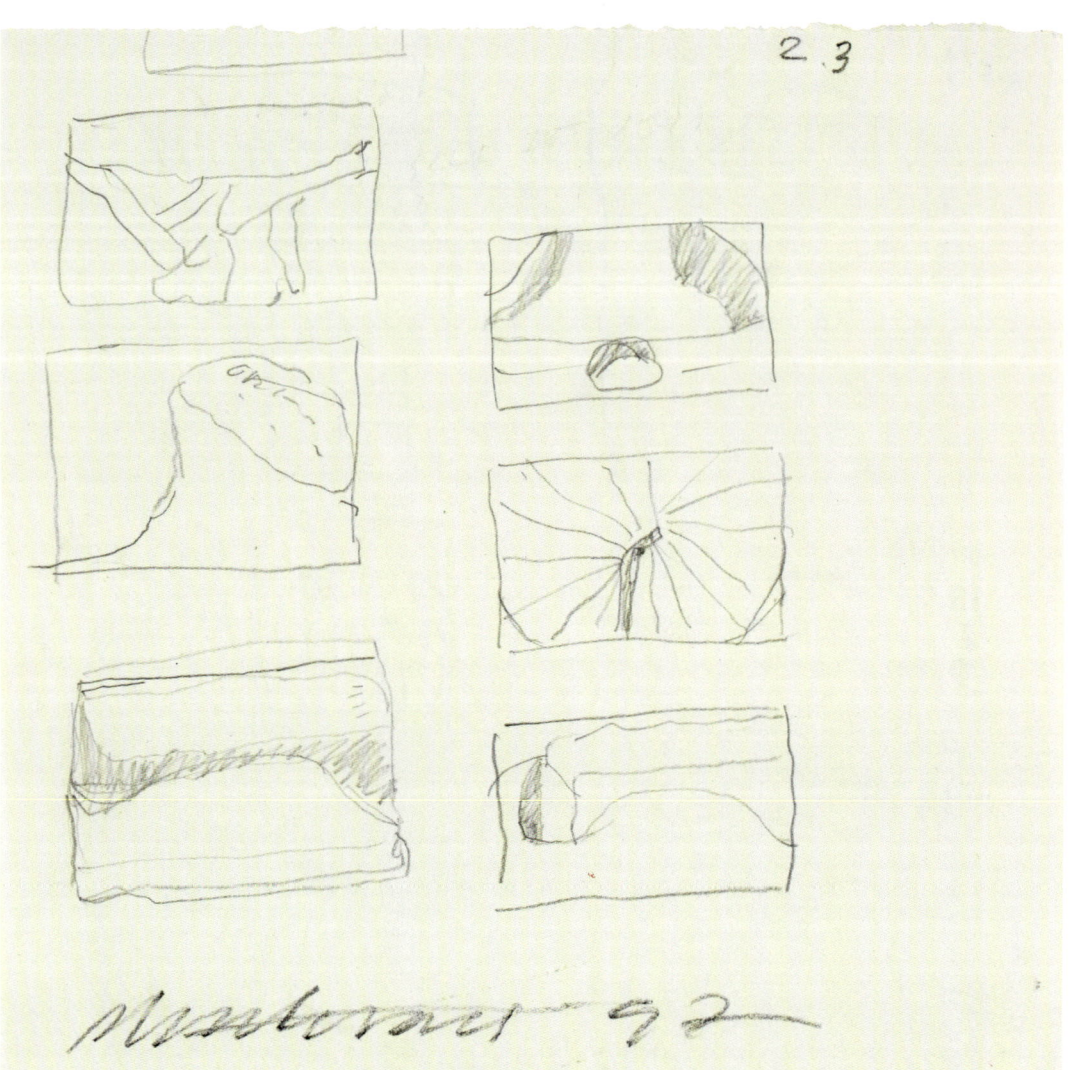

NOUGHTIES

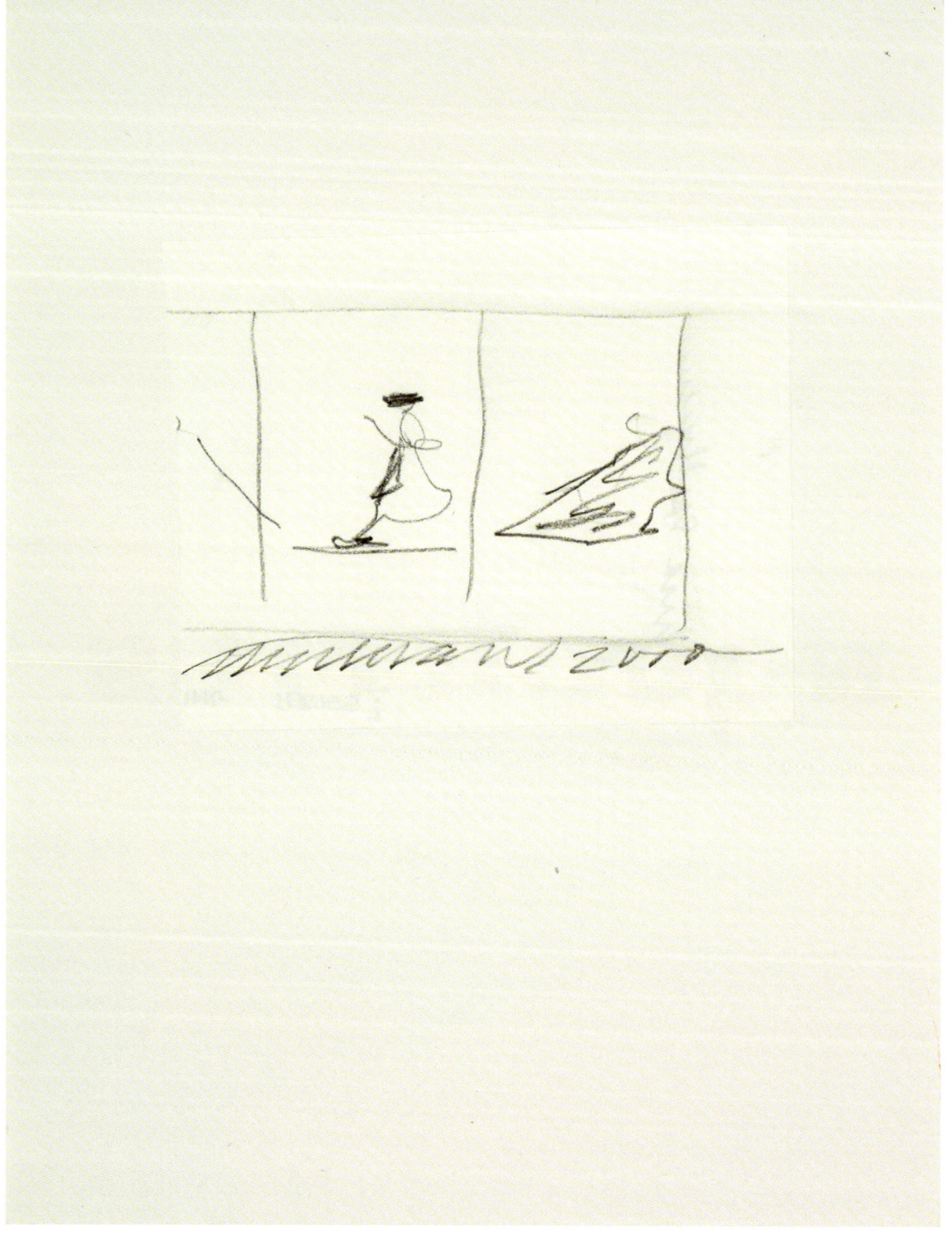

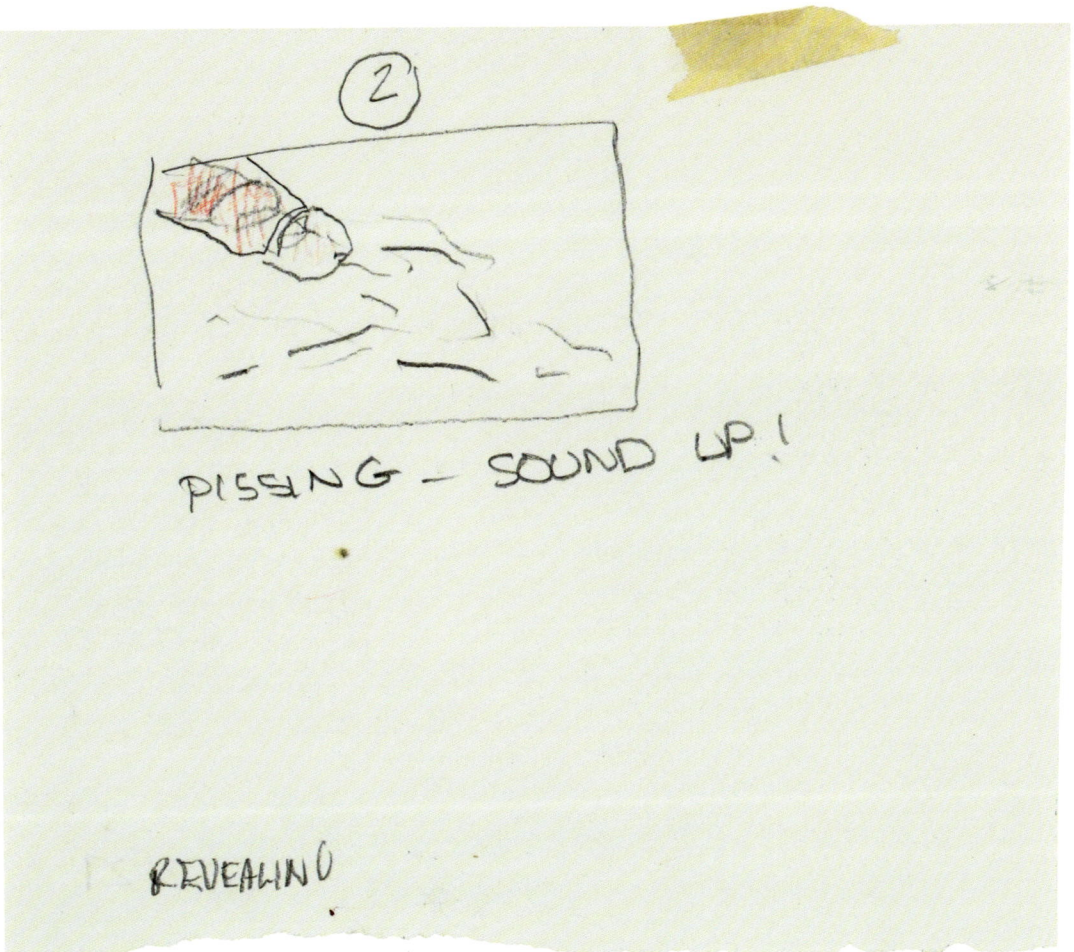

PISSING — SOUND UP!

R.EVEALING

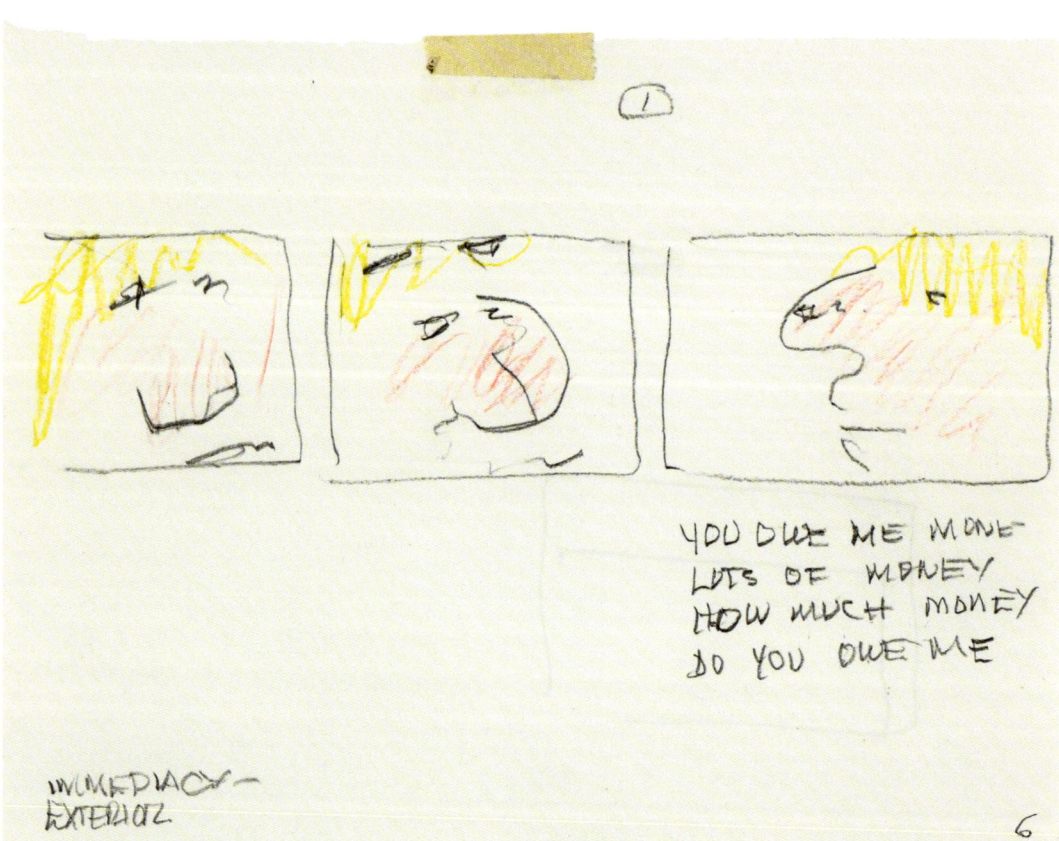

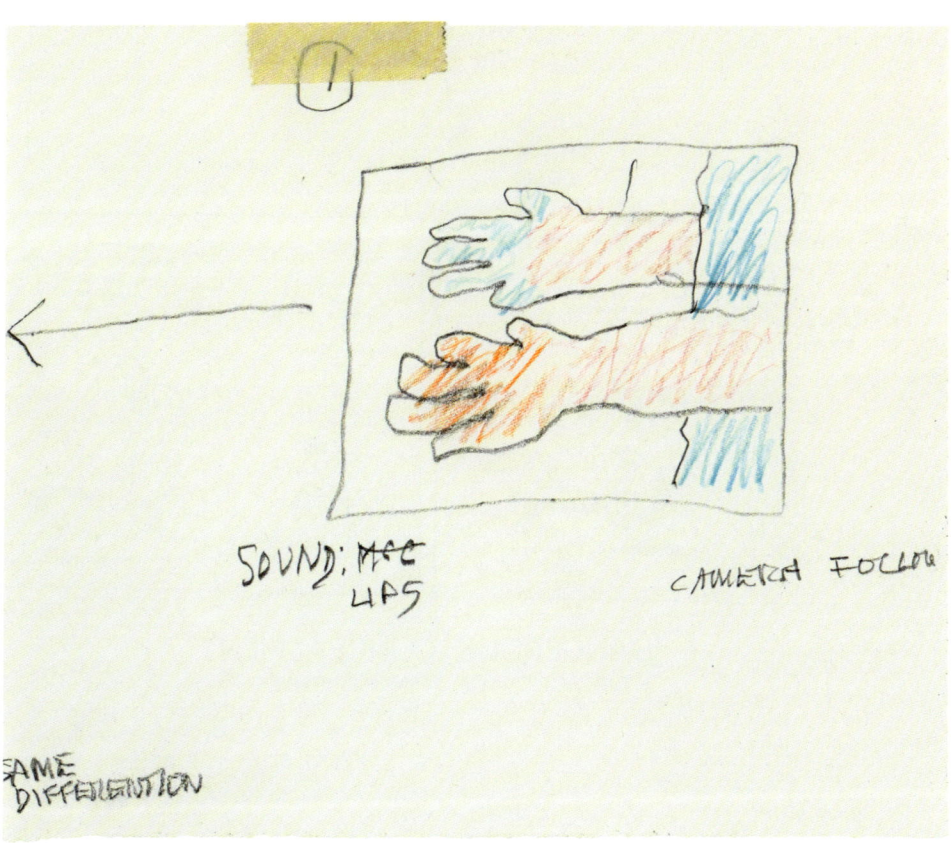

SOUND: MFC
LAS

CAMERA FOLLOW

SAME
DIFFERENTION

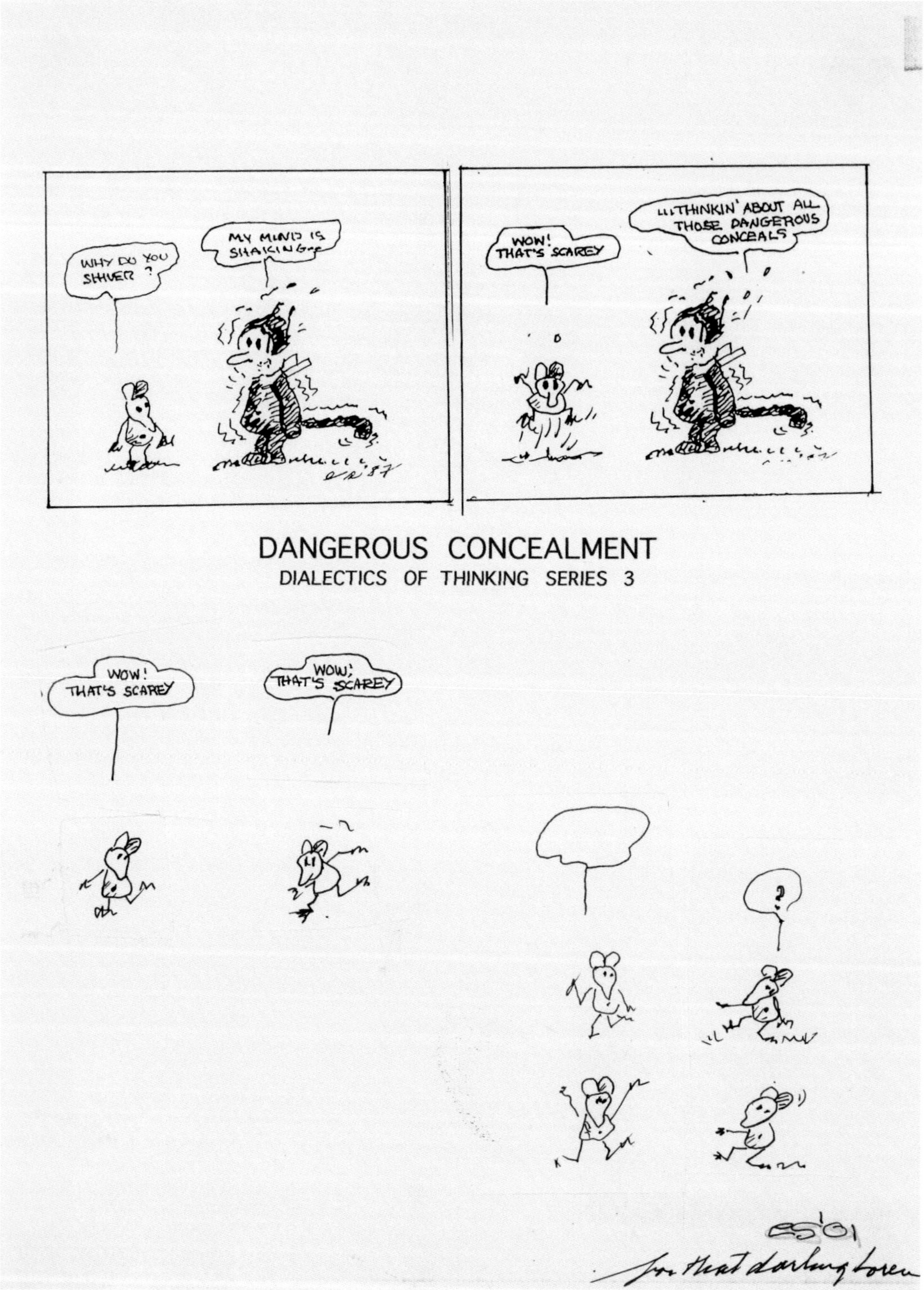

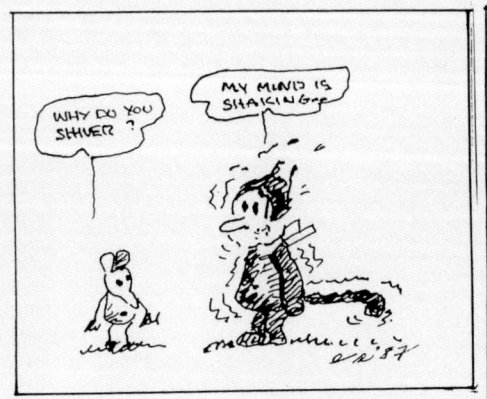
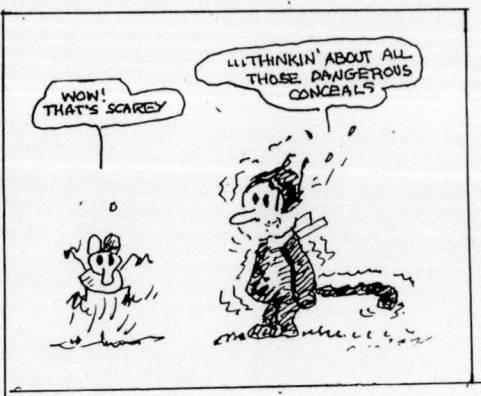

DANGEROUS CONCEALMENT
DIALECTICS OF THINKING SERIES 3

ARTIST'S BOOKS

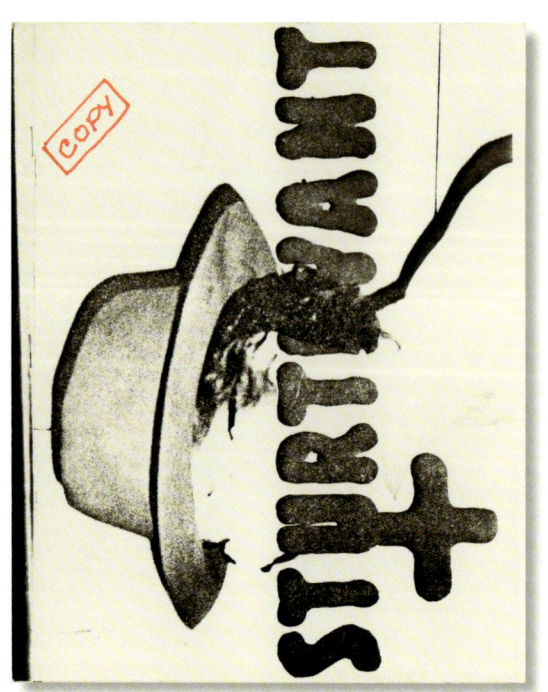

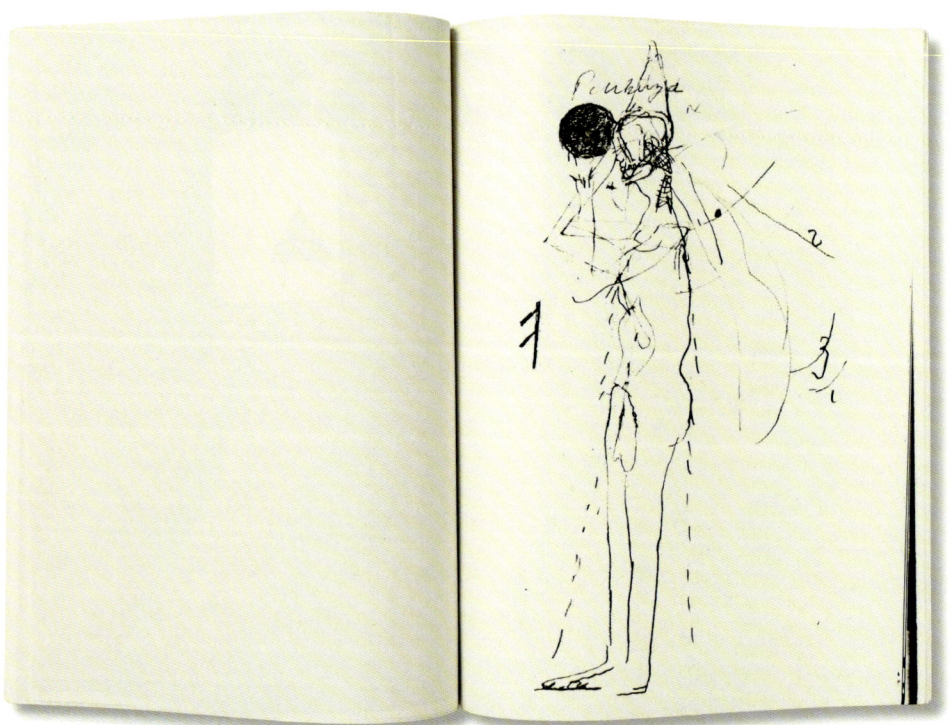

174 *STURTEVANT STUDIES DONE FOR BEUYS' ACTIONS OBJECTS and DRAWINGS*
NEW YORK, PARIS, GERMANY 1969–1971, 1971 (COPY)

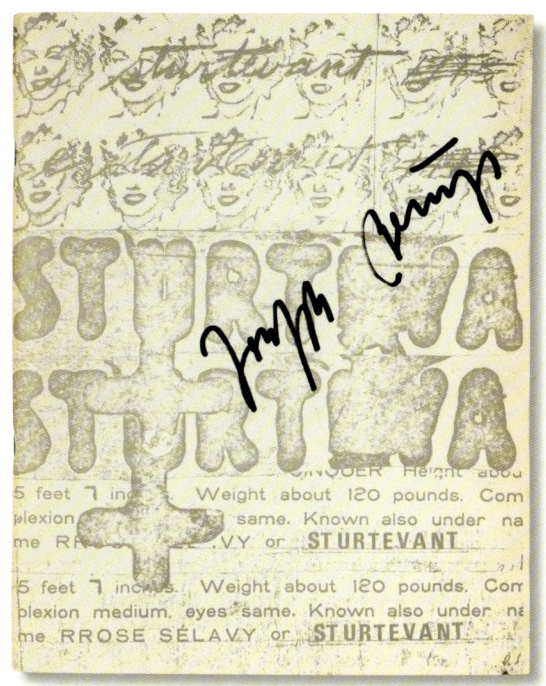

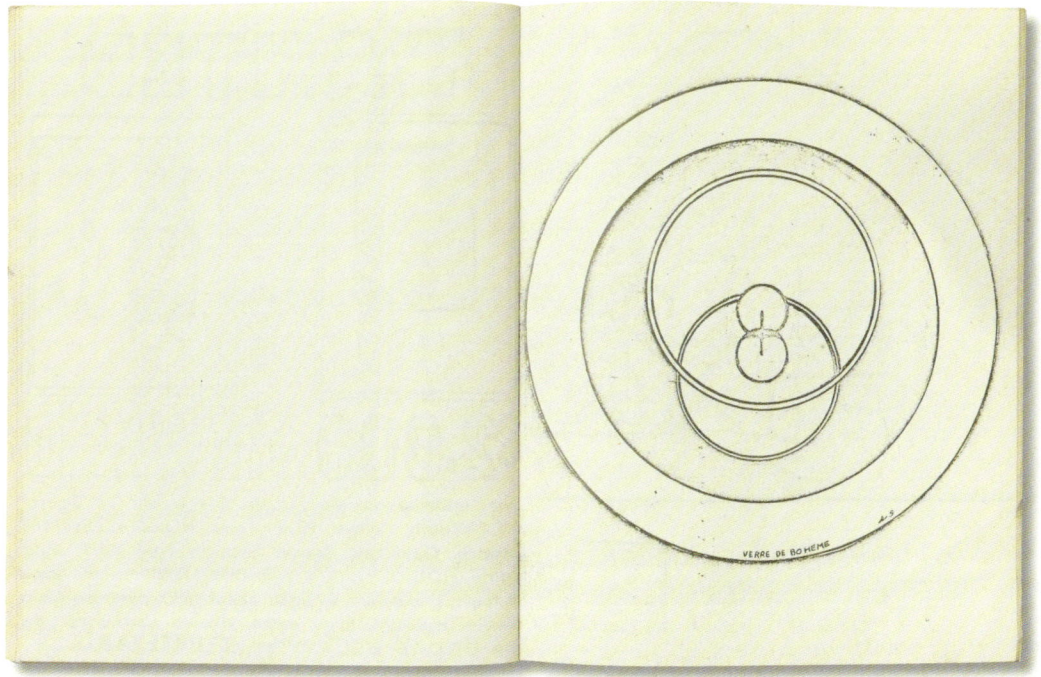

STURTEVANT STUDIES FOR WARHOLS' MARILYNS BEUYS' ACTIONS   **175**
AND OBJECTS DUCHAMPS' ETC. INCLUDING FILM, 1973

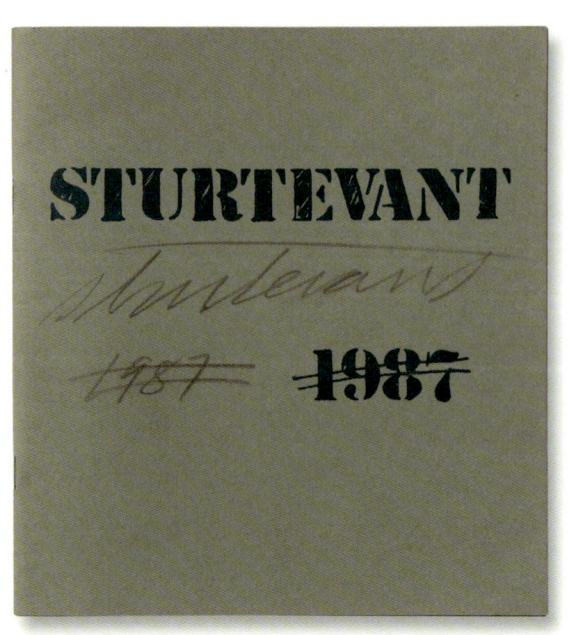

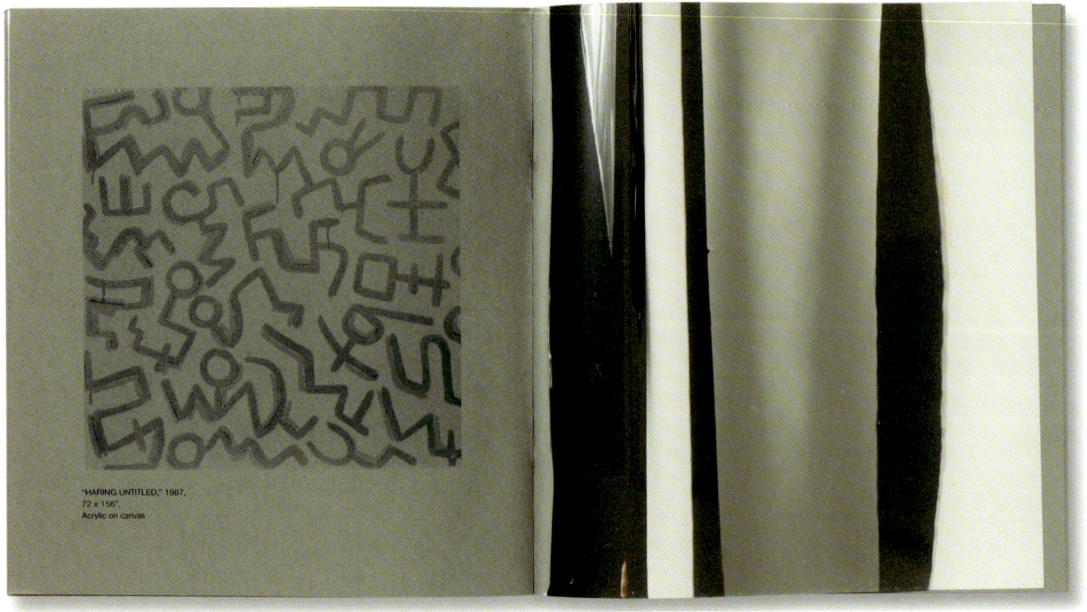

"HARING UNTITLED," 1987,
72 x 156",
Acrylic on canvas

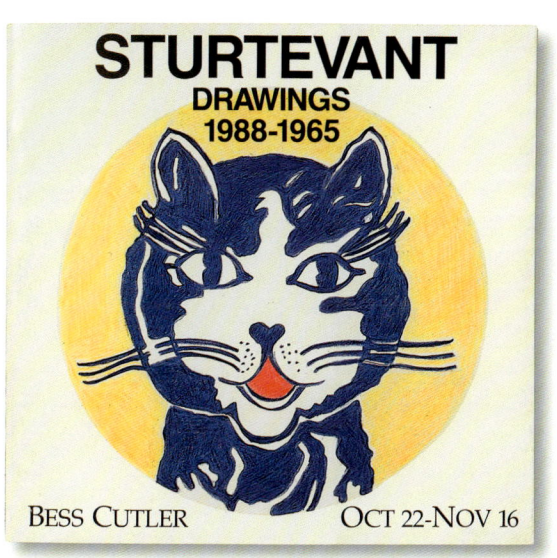

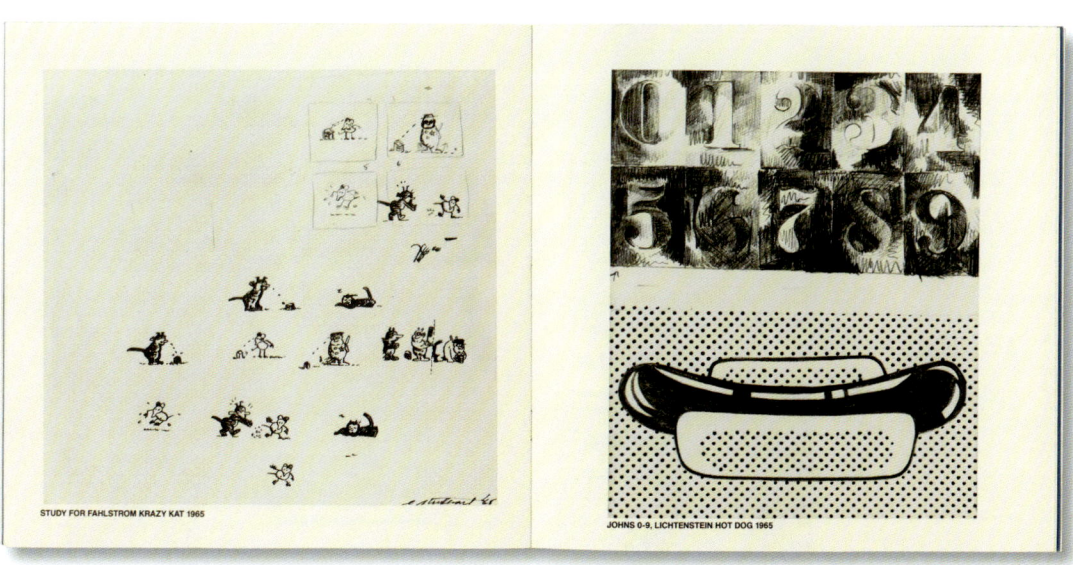

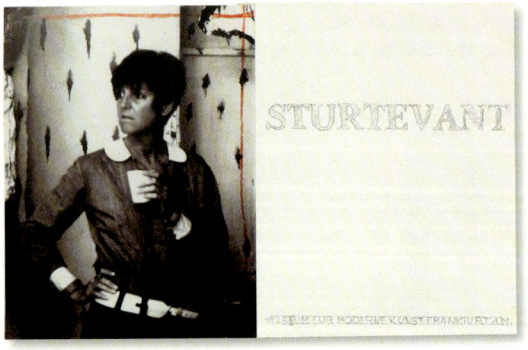
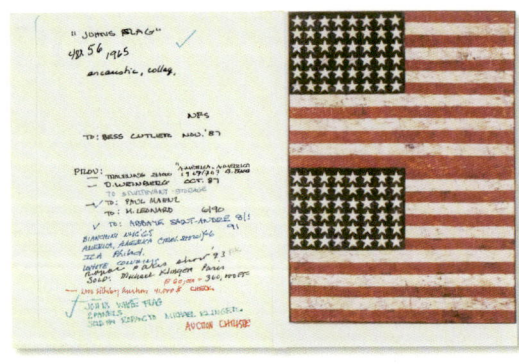
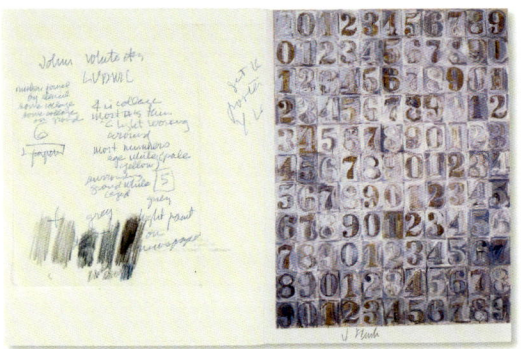
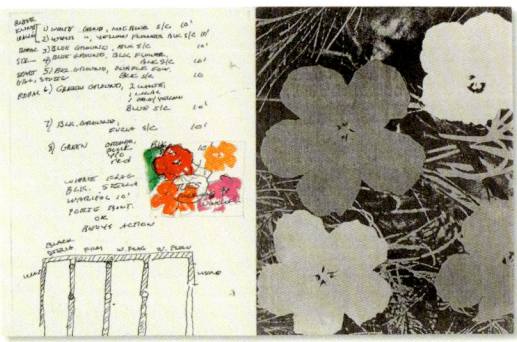
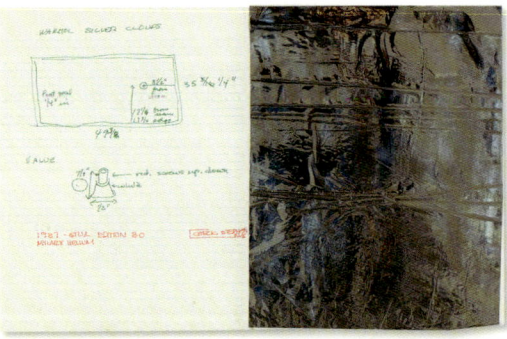
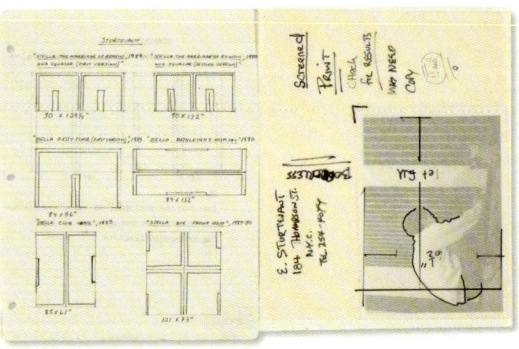
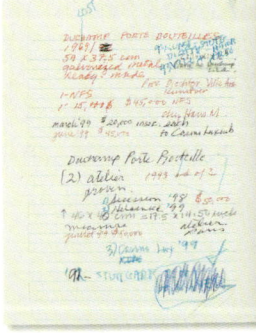
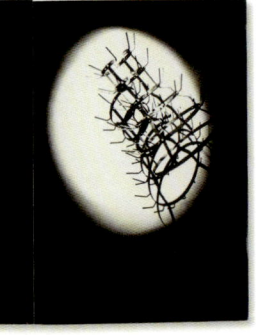
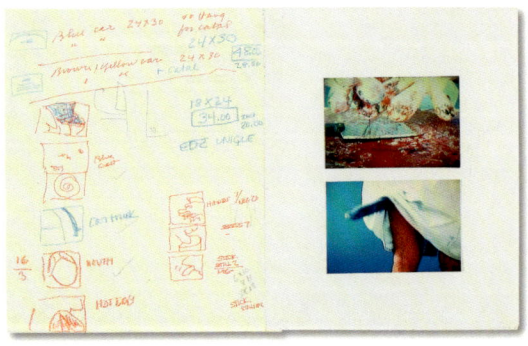

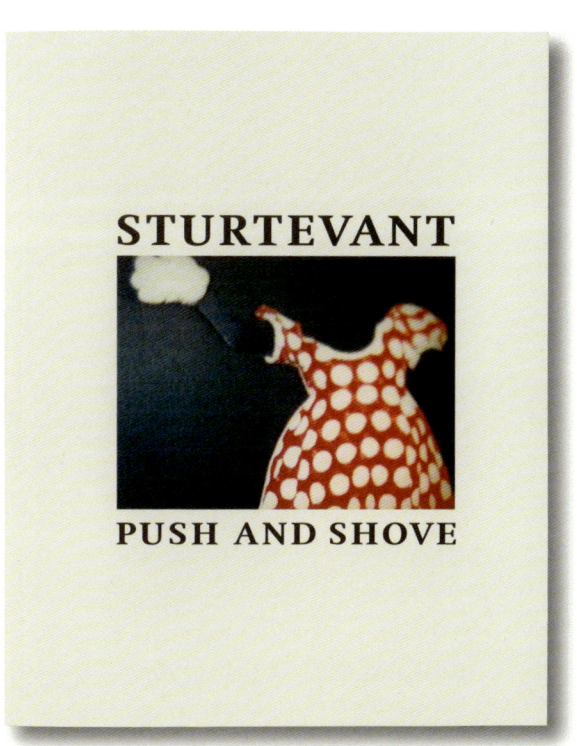

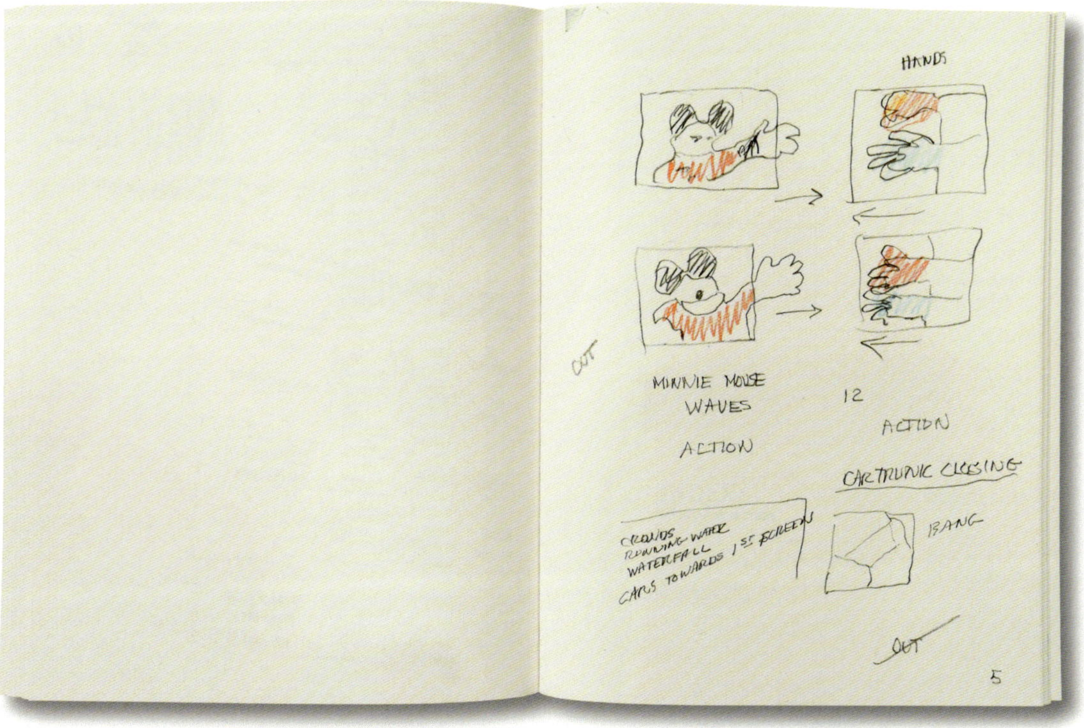

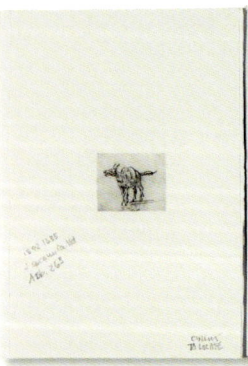

INCOMPLETE FRAGMENTS OF
THE DQUIXOTE

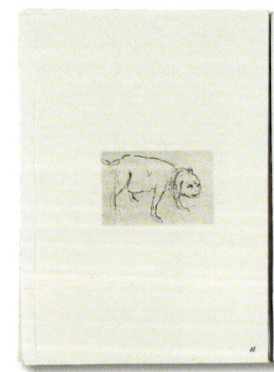

fallen short of the truth than to have
exaggerated so it seems to me, for when
he could and should have let himself go
in praise of so worthy a knight he
seems deliberately have passed on in
silence; an ill deed and malicious
since historians are bound by right to
be exact, truthful, and absolutely
unprejudiced, so that neither interest
nor fear, dislike nor affection, should
make them turn from the path of truth,
whose mother is history, rival of time,
depository of deeds, witness of the
past, exemplar and adviser to the
present, and the future's counselor. In
this history I know that you will find
all the entertainment you can desire;
and if any good quality is missing, I
am certain that is the fault of its dog
of an author rather than any default of
the subject. To conclude, the second
part, according to the translator,
commences in this manner:

The trenchant swords of the two
valorous and furious combatants,
brandished aloft, seemed to threaten
the heavens, the earth and the pit of
hell, such was their courageous aspect.

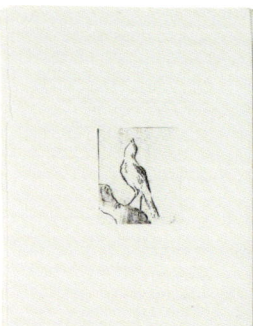

He was a lad of about twenty four and
came as he said from Piedrahita. Don
Quixote asked the same question of the
second man, who was too melancholy and
dejected to answer a word. But the
first man replied for him:

"This man is here for being a canary, I
mean a musician and a singer."

"How is that?" asked Don Quixote. "Do
men go to the galleys for being
musicians and singers."

"Yes sir," replied the galley slave,
"for there is nothing worse than
singing in anguish."

"I have always heard the opposite,"
said Don Quixote. "Singing away sorrow,
cast away care."

"Here it is the reverse," said the
galley slave. "If you sing once you
weep for a lifetime."

"I do not understand," said Don
Quixote.

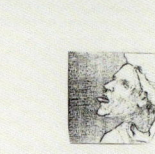

fifth convict lent him a tongue and
said:

"This honest fellow is going to the
galleys for four years after parading
the town in state and on horseback."

"I suppose you mean that he was exposed
to public shame," said Sancho Panza.

"That's right," replied the galley
slave, "and the offense for which he
got his sentence was trafficking in
ears, in fact in whole bodies. What I
mean is that this gentleman is here for
procuring, and also for having a touch
of a wizard about him."

"If it had not been for that touch,"
said Don Quixote, "and if it was merely
for procuring, he would deserve to go
and row in the galleys, but to be their
general and command them. For the
office of procurer is no easy one; it
requires persons of discretion and is
most essential office in a well ordered
state, only men of good birth should
exercise it, then, there ought to be an
overseer and controller of these

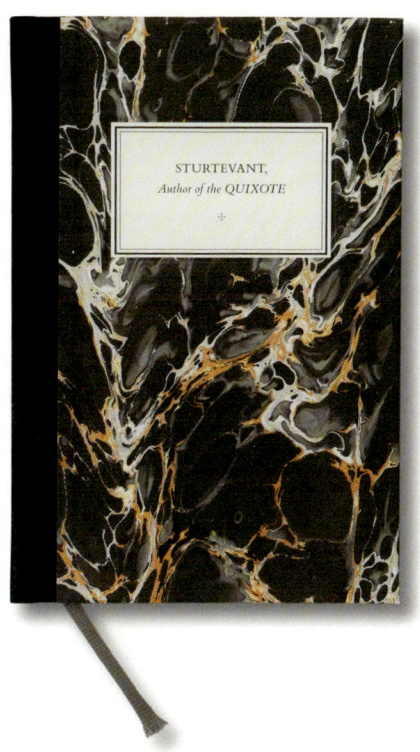

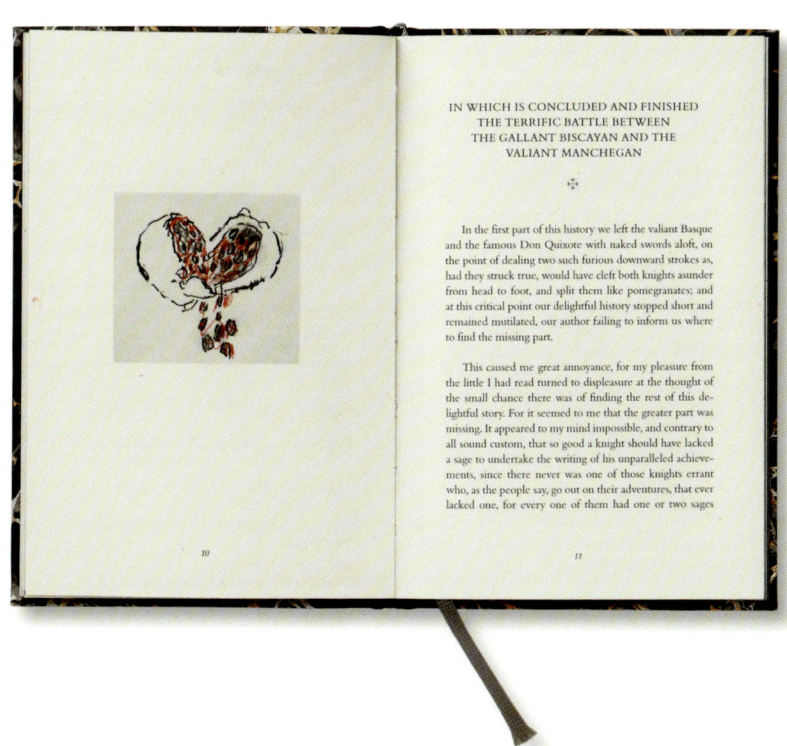

IN WHICH IS CONCLUDED AND FINISHED
THE TERRIFIC BATTLE BETWEEN
THE GALLANT BISCAYAN AND THE
VALIANT MANCHEGAN

⁜

In the first part of this history we left the valiant Basque
and the famous Don Quixote with naked swords aloft, on
the point of dealing two such furious downward strokes as,
had they struck true, would have cleft both knights asunder
from head to foot, and split them like pomegranates; and
at this critical point our delightful history stopped short and
remained mutilated, our author failing to inform us where
to find the missing part.

This caused me great annoyance, for my pleasure from
the little I had read turned to displeasure at the thought of
the small chance there was of finding the rest of this delightful story. For it seemed to me that the greater part was
missing. It appeared to my mind impossible, and contrary to
all sound custom, that so good a knight should have lacked
a sage to undertake the writing of his unparalleled achieve-
ments, since there never was one of those knights errant
who, as the people say, go out on their adventures, that ever
lacked one, for every one of them had one or two sages

LIST OF WORKS

Sturtevant was usually very precise in incorporating the artist's last name and the original title into the title of her own work. The titles in italics are Sturtevant's original titles. The non-italic titles are substitutes from the artist's studio or additions to improve identification.

41 Untitled (Oldenburg), 1964
Watercolor and graphite pencil on paper
35,8 × 31 cm
Estate Sturtevant, Paris, Courtesy Galerie
Thaddaeus Ropac, Paris/Salzburg

42 Untitled (Oldenburg), 1964
Watercolor, gouache and graphite pencil
on paper
21,5 × 28,5 cm
Estate Sturtevant, Paris, Courtesy Galerie
Thaddaeus Ropac, Paris/Salzburg

43 *Study for Oldenburg Hamburger*, 1964
Watercolor, acrylic and graphite pencil
on paper
19,6 × 22,8 cm
Estate Sturtevant, Paris, Courtesy Galerie
Thaddaeus Ropac, Paris/Salzburg

45 *Working Drawing Johns 0–9 Oldenburg
Hamburgers*, 1965
Graphite pencil on paper
60,1 × 47,6 cm
Collection of Virginia Dwan

46 *Johns 0 Through 9*, 1965
Encaustic on newspaper
27,5 × 36,5 cm
Collection de Bruin-Heijn*

47 *Johns 0 Through 9*, 1965
Encaustic on newspaper
10,5 × 17,7 cm (mat opening)
Estate Sturtevant, Paris, Courtesy Galerie
Thaddaeus Ropac, Paris/Salzburg

48 *Study Johns 0–9*, 1965
Watercolor, graphite pencil, gouache
and newspaper collage on paper
25,4 × 15,5 cm (mat opening)
Collection of Virginia Dwan

49 *Study Johns 0–9 Lichtenstein Hot Dog*,
1965
Graphite pencil and oil pastel on paper
33,5 × 27,8 cm (mat opening)
Collection Paul Maenz, Berlin

51 *Lichtenstein Hot Dog Magnifying Glass
Oldenburg Charms Hamburger*, 1965
Graphite pencil and felt pen on paper
55,5 × 35,2 cm
Estate Sturtevant, Paris, Courtesy Galerie
Thaddaeus Ropac, Paris/Salzburg

52 *Lichtenstein Hot Dog Magnifying Glass
Pointing Finger Oldenburg Charms Hamburger
Ice Cream*, 1965
Graphite pencil and felt pen on paper
55,5 × 35,2 cm
Estate Sturtevant, Paris, Courtesy Galerie
Thaddaeus Ropac, Paris/Salzburg

53 *Lichtenstein Hot Dog Magnifying Glass
Oldenburg Charms Hamburger*, 1965
Graphite pencil, felt pen and gouache on paper
55,5 × 35,2 cm
Estate Sturtevant, Paris, Courtesy Galerie
Thaddaeus Ropac, Paris/Salzburg

54 *Wesselmann Great American Nude Johns Flag*,
1965
Collage and graphite pencil on paper
40 × 30,1 cm (mat opening)
Galerie Thaddaeus Ropac, Paris/Salzburg

55 *Study for Johns Three Flags*, 1965
Graphite pencil on cardboard
29,5 × 42 cm
MMK Museum für Moderne Kunst
Frankfurt am Main
Acquired 2004 with generous support of the
3 × 8 Fund, an initiative of 12 companies in
Frankfurt plus the City of Frankfurt am Main

57 STURTEVANT
Invitation card, Bianchini Gallery,
New York, 1965
Offset print on paper
38,5 × 49 cm
MMK Museum für Moderne Kunst
Frankfurt am Main
Gift of Rolf Ricke, Cologne

58 *Study for Fahlström Krazy Kat*, 1965
Ink and graphite pencil on paper
33,8 × 35,1 cm
Estate Sturtevant, Paris, Courtesy Galerie
Thaddaeus Ropac, Paris/Salzburg

59 *Fahlström Elements*, 1966
Watercolor, ink and collage on paper
28 × 35,4 cm
Estate Sturtevant, Paris, Courtesy Galerie
Thaddaeus Ropac, Paris/Salzburg

60 *Working Drawing for Johns 0 Through 9
Fahlström Elements Rosenquist Spaghetti*,
1965
Watercolor and collage on paper
35,6 × 27,9 cm
(Present location unknown)**

61 *Study of Warhol Flowers with Rauschenberg
Drawing*, 1965
Serigraph, graphite pencil and watercolor
on paper
60.6 × 45.7 cm
(Present location unknown)***

62 *Working Drawing Warhol Flowers
Lichtenstein Pointed Finger*, 1966
Silkscreen ink and graphite pencil
on cardboard
55,5 × 35,1 cm
Collection Paul Maenz, Berlin

63 *Warhol Flowers Lichtenstein Pointed Hand*, 1966
Silkscreen ink and graphite pencil on paper
55,5 × 35,1 cm
Galerie Thaddaeus Ropac, Paris/Salzburg
(Former Collection Robert Rauschenberg, New York)

64 *Working Drawing Wesselmann Great American Nude Lichtenstein Hot Dog*, 1966
Graphite pencil, crayon and collage on paper
60 × 45 cm
Collection Lonti Ebers*

65 *Johns Graphite Flag Wesselmann Great American Nude*, 1966
Graphite pencil and collage on paper
43,4 × 35,5 cm
Private collection*

66 *Study Wesselmann Great American Nude Johns Target*, 1966
Graphite pencil and collage on paper
43 × 35 cm
Estate Sturtevant, Paris, Courtesy Galerie Thaddaeus Ropac, Paris/Salzburg

67 *Johns 0–9 Rosenquist Spaghetti*, 1966
Graphite pencil on paper
42,3 × 35,4 cm
Estate Sturtevant, Paris, Courtesy Galerie Thaddaeus Ropac, Paris/Salzburg

68 *Johns 0–9 Fahlström Elements Lichtenstein Hot Dog*, 1966
Ink, graphite pencil and collage on paper
43,1 × 35,5 cm
Estate Sturtevant, Paris, Courtesy Galerie Thaddaeus Ropac, Paris/Salzburg

69 *Johns Flag Lichtenstein Hot Dog*, 1966
Graphite pencil and collage on paper
42,2 × 27 cm
Estate Sturtevant, Paris, Courtesy Galerie Thaddaeus Ropac, Paris/Salzburg

70 *Lichtenstein Hot Dog Graphite Tire*, 1966
Graphite pencil and ink on paper
43 × 35,5 cm
Private collection

71 *Lichtenstein Tire*, 1966
Graphite pencil and ink on paper
21,8 × 24,3 cm (mat opening)
Galerie Thaddaeus Ropac, Paris/Salzburg

72 *Study for Johns 0 through 9*, 1966/67
Graphite pencil, ink and watercolor on two sheets of paper
34,5 × 17 cm
Estate Sturtevant, Paris, Courtesy Galerie Thaddaeus Ropac, Paris/Salzburg

73 *The Store of Claes Oldenburg*, 1967
Offset print and postal stamp (April 18, 1967) on cardboard
17,7 × 13,7 cm
Estate Sturtevant, Paris, Courtesy Galerie Thaddaeus Ropac, Paris/Salzburg

74 Musical Score (Duchamp Erratum Musical), 1967
Ballpoint on letterhead paper
27,7 × 21 cm
Estate Sturtevant, Paris, Courtesy Galerie Thaddaeus Ropac, Paris/Salzburg

75 Musical Score (Duchamp Erratum Musical), 1967
Ballpoint on paper
27 × 21 cm
Estate Sturtevant, Paris, Courtesy Galerie Thaddaeus Ropac, Paris/Salzburg

77 *Stella Lake City*, 1969
Ink and watercolor on graph paper
44,1 × 55,9 cm
Collection of Virginia Dwan

78 *Duchamp Rotary Disc* (LANTERNE CHINOISE), 1969
Watercolor, ink and graphite pencil on photocopy
35,5 × 21,5 cm
Estate Sturtevant, Paris, Courtesy Galerie Thaddaeus Ropac, Paris/Salzburg

79 *Duchamp Rotary Disc* (CAGE), 1969
Watercolor and ink on photocopy
28 × 21,9 cm (1/1)
Collection Mark Kelman, New York*

80 *Duchamp Rotary Disc* (VERRE DE BOHEME), 1969
Watercolor and ink on photocopy
28 × 21,9 cm (2/1)
Collection Mark Kelman, New York*

81 *Duchamp Rotary Disc* (POISSON JAPONAIS), 1969
Watercolor and ink on photocopy
28 × 21,9 cm (3/1)
Collection Mark Kelman, New York*

83 *Duchamp Rotary Disc* (ECLIPSE TOTALE), 1969
Watercolor and ink on photocopy
27,8 × 21,5 cm (1/2)
Estate Sturtevant, Paris, Courtesy Galerie Thaddaeus Ropac, Paris/Salzburg

84 *Duchamp Rotary Disc* (ESCARGOT), 1969
Watercolor and ink on photocopy
27,8 × 21,5 cm (2/2)
Estate Sturtevant, Paris, Courtesy Galerie Thaddaeus Ropac, Paris/Salzburg

85 *Duchamp Rotary Disc* (LAMPE), 1969
Watercolor and ink on photocopy
27,8 × 21,5 cm (3/2)
Estate Sturtevant, Paris, Courtesy Galerie Thaddaeus Ropac, Paris/Salzburg

86 *Duchamp Rotary Disc* (OEUF A LA COQUE), 1969
Watercolor and ink on photocopy
27,8 × 21,6 cm (1/3)
Estate Sturtevant, Paris, Courtesy Galerie Thaddaeus Ropac, Paris/Salzburg

87 *Duchamp Rotary Disc* (CERCEAUX), 1969
Watercolor and ink on photocopy
27,8 × 21,5 cm (2/3)
Estate Sturtevant, Paris, Courtesy Galerie Thaddaeus Ropac, Paris/Salzburg

88 *Duchamp Rotary Disc* (MONTGOLFIERE), 1969
Watercolor and ink on photocopy
27,8 × 21,5 cm (3/3)
Estate Sturtevant, Paris, Courtesy Galerie
Thaddaeus Ropac, Paris/Salzburg

89 *Duchamp Rotary Disc* (VERRE DE BOHEME),
1969
Watercolor, ink and collage on photocopy
30,5 × 23 cm
Estate Sturtevant, Paris, Courtesy Galerie
Thaddaeus Ropac, Paris/Salzburg

90 *Drawing for Duchamp Fountain*, 1969
Graphite pencil on paper
25,5 × 20,4 cm
Estate Sturtevant, Paris, Courtesy Galerie
Thaddaeus Ropac, Paris/Salzburg

91 *Duchamp Fountain*, 1969
Graphite pencil on paper
29,7 × 21 cm
Estate Sturtevant, Paris, Courtesy Galerie
Thaddaeus Ropac, Paris/Salzburg

95 *Duchamp Fountain*, 1970
Graphite pencil on paper
30,5 × 22,8 cm
Estate Sturtevant, Paris, Courtesy Galerie
Thaddaeus Ropac, Paris/Salzburg

96 *Drawing for Beuys Numbers*, 1971
Graphite pencil on paper
31,1 × 22,8 cm (mat opening)
Private collection, Los Angeles

97 *Drawing for Beuys Fettkugel*, 1971
Graphite pencil on paper
31,6 × 22,8 cm (mat opening)
Estate Sturtevant, Paris, Courtesy Galerie
Thaddaeus Ropac, Paris/Salzburg

98 *Drawing Beuys explodierender Schädel
mit Kristall*, 1971
Graphite pencil on paper
23,6 × 24,2 cm (mat opening)
Estate Sturtevant, Paris, Courtesy Galerie
Thaddaeus Ropac, Paris/Salzburg

99 *Drawing for Beuys Sonne Meer Steine
Himmel*, 1971
Graphite pencil on paper
16,7 × 17 cm
Private collection, Frankfurt am Main

100 *Drawing for Beuys Aktion Eurasienstab*,
1971
Graphite pencil on paper
47,6 × 34,9 cm (frame)
(Present location unknown)****

101 *Drawing for Beuys Aktion Manresa*, 1971
Graphite pencil on paper
33 × 21,7 cm (mat opening)
Collection L. Muzzey, Paris

105 *Haring Subway Drawing*, 1986
White chalk on black subway paper,
mounted on canvas
214,6 × 114,9 cm
Meredith Darrow, Venice, CA

106 *Krazy Kat*, 1986
Ink on paper
35,4 × 28 cm
Estate Sturtevant, Paris, Courtesy Galerie
Thaddaeus Ropac, Paris/Salzburg

107 *Krazy Kat*, 1986
Ink and graphite pencil on paper
28 × 35,4 cm
Estate Sturtevant, Paris, Courtesy Galerie
Thaddaeus Ropac, Paris/Salzburg

108 *Study for Krazy Kat*, 1986
Watercolor and ink on paper
35,5 × 28 cm
Estate Sturtevant, Paris, Courtesy Galerie
Thaddaeus Ropac, Paris/Salzburg

109 *Krazy Kat*, 1986
Watercolor and ink on paper
35,3 × 28 cm
Estate Sturtevant, Paris, Courtesy Galerie
Thaddaeus Ropac, Paris/Salzburg

110 *Krazy Kat*, 1987
Watercolor and ink on paper
7,1 × 7,7 cm
Estate Sturtevant, Paris, Courtesy Galerie
Thaddaeus Ropac, Paris/Salzburg

111 *Lichtenstein Laughing Cat*, 1987
Colored pencil on paper
29,6 × 27,4 cm (mat opening)
Estate Sturtevant, Paris, Courtesy Galerie
Thaddaeus Ropac, Paris/Salzburg

112 *Lichtenstein Laughing Cat*, 1988
Colored pencil and graphite pencil on paper
12 × 17,5 cm (mat opening)
Galerie Thaddaeus Ropac, Paris/Salzburg

113 *First Study for Lichtenstein Laughing Cat*,
1988
Graphite pencil on paper
15 × 21,2 cm
Estate Sturtevant, Paris, Courtesy Galerie
Thaddaeus Ropac, Paris/Salzburg

114 *Study for Lichtenstein Laughing Cat*, 1988
Graphite pencil on paper
22,1 × 14,5 cm (mat opening)
Estate Sturtevant, Paris, Courtesy Galerie
Thaddaeus Ropac, Paris/Salzburg

115 Untitled (Announcement Bess Cutler), 1988
Graphite pencil on paper and tracing paper,
tape
30,4 × 22,7 cm
Estate Sturtevant, Paris, Courtesy Galerie
Thaddaeus Ropac, Paris/Salzburg

116 *Study for Lichtenstein Girl with Ball*, 1988
Colored pencil and graphite pencil on paper
38,5 × 23,6 cm (mat opening)
Collection Maxime Guinnebault, Paris

117 *Lichtenstein Study*, 1988
Colored pencil and graphite pencil on paper
35,4 × 28 cm
Estate Sturtevant, Paris, Courtesy Galerie
Thaddaeus Ropac, Paris/Salzburg

118 *Study for Lichtenstein Girl with Hair Ribbon*,
1988
Colored pencil and graphite pencil on paper
35,4 × 28 cm
Estate Sturtevant, Paris, Courtesy Galerie
Thaddaeus Ropac, Paris/Salzburg

119 *Lichtenstein Study*, 1988
Colored pencil and graphite pencil on paper
35,4 × 28 cm
Estate Sturtevant, Paris, Courtesy Galerie
Thaddaeus Ropac, Paris/Salzburg

120 *Lichtenstein Study for Landscape with Figures*,
1988
Colored pencil and graphite pencil on paper
27,5 × 35 cm
Collection Ringier, Zurich

121 *Lichtenstein Final Study for Landscape with
Figures*, 1988
Colored pencil and graphite pencil on paper
41,7 × 60,8 cm
Estate Sturtevant, Paris, Courtesy Galerie
Thaddaeus Ropac, Paris/Salzburg

122 *Lichtenstein Study for Reclining Nude*, 1988
Colored pencil and graphite pencil on paper
10 × 13,6 cm (mat opening)
Estate Sturtevant, Paris, Courtesy Galerie
Thaddaeus Ropac, Paris/Salzburg

123 *Lichtenstein Final Study for Reclining Nude*,
1988
Colored pencil and graphite pencil on paper
42,5 × 58 cm
Collection Ringier, Zurich

124 *Lichtenstein Study for Still Life*, 1988
Colored pencil and graphite pencil on paper
10,5 × 8,3 cm
Collection of Virginia Dwan*

125 *Lichtenstein Study for Two Paintings, Folded
Sheets*, 1988
Colored pencil and graphite pencil on paper
9,5 × 13,3 cm (mat opening)
Collection of Robin Wright and Ian Reeves

126 *Lichtenstein Study for Female Head*, 1988
Colored pencil and graphite pencil on paper
35,1 × 27,3 cm
Private collection, Thaddaeus Ropac, Salzburg

127 *Lichtenstein Study for Woman with Flower*,
1988
Colored pencil and graphite pencil on paper
14,4 × 7 cm (mat opening)
Tilman and Gabriele Osterwold

128 *Lichtenstein Studies for Eclipse of the Sun I
and Eclipse of the Sun II*, 1988
Colored pencil and graphite pencil on paper
40 × 30 cm
Estate Sturtevant, Paris, Courtesy Galerie
Thaddaeus Ropac, Paris/Salzburg

129 *Lichtenstein Study for Red Horseman*, 1988
Colored pencil and graphite pencil on paper
44,9 × 56,3 cm
Galerie Thaddaeus Ropac, Paris/Salzburg

130 *Study for Lichtenstein Bull I and II*, 1988
Colored pencil and graphite pencil on paper
26,4 × 32,9 cm (mat opening)
Collection Aladin Guinnebault, Paris

133 *Johns Flag*, 1990
Pastel and collage on paper
27,1 × 36,4 cm (mat opening)
Collection Mark Kelman, New York

134 Untitled (Johns), 1990
Colored pencil, tape on paper
41 × 33 cm
Estate Sturtevant, Paris, Courtesy Galerie
Thaddaeus Ropac, Paris/Salzburg

135 Untitled (Johns), 1990
Colored pencil transfer on paper
27,9 × 20,3 cm
Estate Sturtevant, Paris, Courtesy Galerie
Thaddaeus Ropac, Paris/Salzburg*

137 *Working Drawing for Johns Figure 0*, 1990
Encaustic, graphite pencil, newspaper and
collage on paper
41 × 33 cm
Estate Sturtevant, Paris, Courtesy Galerie
Thaddaeus Ropac, Paris/Salzburg

138 *Drawing Study for Johns Figure 2*, 1991
Encaustic, watercolor and graphite pencil
on paper
19,9 × 20,5 cm
Estate Sturtevant, Paris, Courtesy Galerie
Thaddaeus Ropac, Paris/Salzburg

139 *Drawing Study for Johns Figure 3*, 1991
Graphite pencil and gouache on paper
32 × 23,9 cm
Estate Sturtevant, Paris, Courtesy Galerie
Thaddaeus Ropac, Paris/Salzburg

140 *Study for Johns 8*, 1991
Encaustic and graphite pencil on paper
40,5 × 33 cm
Estate Sturtevant, Paris, Courtesy Galerie
Thaddaeus Ropac, Paris/Salzburg

141 *Drawing Study for Johns White Numbers*, 1991
Encaustic, graphite pencil and collage on paper
32 × 23, 7 cm
Estate Sturtevant, Paris, Courtesy Galerie
Thaddaeus Ropac, Paris/Salzburg

142 Untitled (Johns), 1991
Graphite pencil on paper
30,4 × 22,8 cm
Estate Sturtevant, Paris, Courtesy Galerie
Thaddaeus Ropac, Paris/Salzburg

143 Untitled (Johns), 1991
Graphite pencil on paper
41 × 33 cm
Estate Sturtevant, Paris, Courtesy Galerie
Thaddaeus Ropac, Paris/Salzburg

144 *Johns Numbers*, 1991
Colored pencil and graphite pencil on paper
40 × 33,2 cm
Estate Sturtevant, Paris, Courtesy Galerie
Thaddaeus Ropac, Paris/Salzburg

145 *Johns Numbers*, 1991
Watercolor and graphite pencil on paper
41 × 33,1 cm
Estate Sturtevant, Paris, Courtesy Galerie
Thaddaeus Ropac, Paris/Salzburg

147 *1 of 3 Drawings for Johns 0–9*, 1991
Encaustic and graphite pencil on paper
29,2 × 21,8 cm (mat opening)
Collection Michael Loulakis, Frankfurt am Main

148 *2 of 3 Drawings for Johns 0–9*, 1991
Encaustic and graphite pencil on paper
30,7 × 22,2 cm (mat opening)
Collection Michael Loulakis, Frankfurt am Main

149 *3 of 3 Drawings for Johns 0–9*, 1991
Encaustic and graphite pencil on paper
30,8 × 22,1 cm (mat opening)
Collection Michael Loulakis, Frankfurt am Main

150 *Johns Target*, 1991
Gouache, pastel and graphite pencil on paper
32 × 23,7 cm
Estate Sturtevant, Paris, Courtesy Galerie
Thaddaeus Ropac, Paris/Salzburg

151 Untitled (Johns Target), 1991
Graphite pencil and colored pencil on colored
cardboard
29,5 × 20,8 cm
Estate Sturtevant, Paris, Courtesy Galerie
Thaddaeus Ropac, Paris/Salzburg

153 *Johns Green Target*, 1991
Encaustic, crayon and collage on paper
13 × 13 cm (mat opening)
Estate Sturtevant, Paris, Courtesy Galerie
Thaddaeus Ropac, Paris/Salzburg

154 *Johns White Flag*, 1991
Encaustic and graphite pencil on paper
36,8 × 57,1 cm
Estate Sturtevant, Paris, Courtesy Galerie
Thaddaeus Ropac, Paris/Salzburg

155 *Johns Flag*, 1991
Encaustic and graphite pencil on paper
38,6 × 58 cm
Estate Sturtevant, Paris, Courtesy Galerie
Thaddaeus Ropac, Paris/Salzburg

157 *Study for Johns Flag on Orange Ground*,
1991
Pastel, watercolor, graphite pencil and
newspaper collage on paper
30,3 × 22,8 cm
Collection Aladin Guinnebault, Paris

158 *Johns Green Flag*, 1991
Colored pencil and graphite pencil on paper
17 × 22,5 cm (mat opening)
Estate Sturtevant, Paris, Courtesy Galerie
Thaddaeus Ropac, Paris/Salzburg

159 *Johns Flag*, 1992
Colored pencil, graphite pencil, crayon
and collage on paper
18 × 23 cm
Estate Sturtevant, Paris, Courtesy Galerie
Thaddaeus Ropac, Paris/Salzburg

160 *Johns Flag*, 1991
Graphite pencil and lighter fluid on paper
34,3 × 37,2 cm
Estate Sturtevant, Paris, Courtesy Galerie
Thaddaeus Ropac, Paris/Salzburg

161 *Johns Flag*, 1991
Pastel, graphite pencil and newspaper collage
on paper
40,5 × 33,1 cm
Estate Sturtevant, Paris, Courtesy Galerie
Thaddaeus Ropac, Paris/Salzburg

162 *Johns Flag*, 1993
Gouache and graphite pencil on paper
30,8 × 41 cm
Estate Sturtevant, Paris, Courtesy Galerie
Thaddaeus Ropac, Paris/Salzburg

163 *Johns Flag*, 1993
Colored pencil, graphite pencil and newspaper
collage on cardboard
35,5 × 46,5 cm
Galerie Thaddaeus Ropac, Paris/Salzburg

165 *Johns Numbers*, 1994
Ink and graphite pencil on paper
67 × 52 cm (mat opening)
Estate Sturtevant, Paris, Courtesy Galerie
Thaddaeus Ropac, Paris/Salzburg

166 Untitled (Duchamp), 1992
Graphite pencil on paper
21 × 21 cm
Estate Sturtevant, Paris, Courtesy Galerie
Thaddaeus Ropac, Paris/Salzburg

168 *Dillinger Running Series*, 2000
Graphite pencil on paper
15,2 × 12 cm
Estate Sturtevant, Paris, Courtesy Galerie
Thaddaeus Ropac, Paris/Salzburg

169 *Dark Threat of Absence*, Storyboard,
Revealing, 2002
Graphite pencil, colored pencil and tape
on paper
14,8 × 17 cm
Estate Sturtevant, Paris, Courtesy Galerie
Thaddaeus Ropac, Paris/Salzburg

170 *Dark Threat of Absence*, Storyboard,
Immediacy Exterior, 2002
Graphite pencil, colored pencil and tape
on paper
15,1 × 19,1 cm
Estate Sturtevant, Paris, Courtesy Galerie
Thaddaeus Ropac, Paris/Salzburg

171 *Dark Threat of Absence*, Storyboard,
Same Difference, 2002
Graphite pencil, colored pencil and tape
on paper
14,8 × 16,9 cm
Estate Sturtevant, Paris, Courtesy Galerie
Thaddaeus Ropac, Paris/Salzburg

172 *Krazy Kat*, 2001
Ink and photo copy on paper
35,5 × 28 cm
Estate Sturtevant, Paris, Courtesy Galerie
Thaddaeus Ropac, Paris/Salzburg

ARTIST BOOKS

174 *STURTEVANT STUDIES DONE FOR BEUYS'
ACTIONS OBJECTS and DRAWINGS
NEW YORK, PARIS, GERMANY 1969–1971
(COPY)*
Reese Palley Gallery, New York, 1971
Photocopy, 46 pages
28,1 × 21,6 cm
Concept and design: STURTEVANT
Edition ca. 100
MMK Museum für Moderne Kunst
Frankfurt am Main

175 *STURTEVANT STUDIES FOR WARHOLS'
MARILYNS BEUYS' ACTIONS AND OBJECTS
DUCHAMPS' ETC. INCLUDING FILM*
Everson Museum, Syracuse, New York,
1973
Offset print on paper, 104 pages
27,8 × 21,6 cm
Concept and design: STURTEVANT
signed by Joseph Beuys with felt pen
on the cover
MMK Museum für Moderne Kunst
Frankfurt am Main

176 *STURTEVANT*
STUX Gallery, New York, 1987
Offset print on paper, 16 pages, two
of them reflecting Mylar foil
19,7 × 17,7 cm
Concept and design: STURTEVANT
MMK Museum für Moderne Kunst
Frankfurt am Main

177 *STURTEVANT Drawings 1988–1965*
Bess Cutler Gallery, New York, 1988
Offset print on paper, 20 pages
22,8 × 22,7 cm
Concept and design: STURTEVANT
Edition: 1000
MMK Museum für Moderne Kunst
Frankfurt am Main

178 *STURTEVANT THE BRUTAL TRUTH*
The complete artist catalog design
including the original drawings, sketches
and collages etc., 2003/2004
150 pages
27,2 × 41,6 cm
Concept and design: STURTEVANT
MMK Museum für Moderner Kunst
Frankfurt am Main
Gift of the artist

179 *STURTEVANT PUSH AND SHOVE*
Perry Rubenstein Gallery, New York, 2005
112 pages
27,9 × 21,6 cm
Concept and design: STURTEVANT
MMK Museum für Moderne Kunst
Frankfurt am Main

180 *STURTEVANT, Author of the QUIXOTE*
Original manuscript 1970
53 pages
20,1 × 15,1 cm
Concept and design: STURTEVANT
Private collection, Berlin

181 *STURTEVANT, Author of the QUIXOTE*
MMK Museum für Moderne Kunst, 2009
48 pages
17,5 × 11,6 cm
Concept and design: STURTEVANT
Hand colored by the artist
Koenig Books London
Private collection, Frankfurt am Main

*Not in the exhibition

**Reprint from the catalog: *STURTEVANT*,
Württembergischer Kunstverein Stuttgart, 1992,
publisher Tilman Osterwold, page 16.

***The Museum of Modern Art Archives, New York
Department of Circulating Exhibitions Album,
Art in the Mirror exhibition, circulated 1966–68;
Department of Circulating Exhibition Records,
IV.66–9 (condition photograph of Sturtevant's *Study
of Warhol Flowers with Rauschenberg Drawing*
[1965], January 27, 1967; gelatin silver print,
25.4 × 20.6 cm)

****Reprint from the catalog: *STURTEVANT
STUDIES FOR WARHOLS' MARILYNS BEUYS'
ACTIONS AND OBJECTS DUCHAMPS' ETC.
INCLUDING FILM,* Everson Museum of Art,
Syracuse, New York 1973, n.p.

BIOGRAPHY

STURTEVANT

Born in Lakewood, Ohio
Lived and worked in Paris

EDUCATION

Columbia University, NY (MA)
Art Students League of New York, NY
Chicago Art Institute, Chicago, IL
University of Zurich, Switzerland
University of Michigan, Ann Arbor, MI
Cleveland Art Institute, Cleveland, OH
Cleveland School of Art, Cleveland, OH
University of Iowa, Iowa City, IO (BA)

AWARDS

2013

Artist Award for Distinguished Body of Work for the exhibition *Rock & Rap/C Simulacra* at Gavin Brown's enterprise, College Art Association, New York
Kurt-Schwitters-Preis, Sprengel Museum and Niedersächsische Sparkassenstiftung, Hannover

2011

Golden Lion for Lifetime Achievement,
54th Venice Biennale

2008

Francis J. Greenburger Award, Omi International Arts Center, New York

2005

Beaux-Arts Magazine Art Award: Best International Exhibition for *Sturtevant: The Brutal Truth* at the MMK Museum für Moderne Kunst Frankfurt am Main, Beaux-Arts Magazine, Paris

2004

Best of 2004: *Sturtevant: The Brutal Truth*, MMK Museum für Moderne Kunst Frankfurt am Main, Artforum International, New York, Dec 2004

SOLO EXHIBITIONS

2015

Sturtevant Drawing Double Reversal, Nationalgalerie im Hamburger Bahnhof – Museum für Gegenwart – Berlin
Sturtevant: Double Trouble, Museum of Contemporary Art, Los Angeles
Sturtevant Drawing Double Reversal, Albertina, Vienna

2014

Sturtevant: Double Trouble, Museum of Modern Art, New York
Sturtevant Drawing Double Reversal, MMK Museum für Moderne Kunst, Frankfurt am Main
Number Eight: Sturtevant, Quadriennale Düsseldorf, Julia Stoschek Collection, Düsseldorf

2013

Leaps Jumps and Bumps, Serpentine Gallery, London
Sturtevant. The House of Horrors, Sprengel Museum, Hannover; traveling to: Musée d'Art moderne de la Ville de Paris
Finite / Infinite, Gavin Brown's enterprise, New York

2012

Image over Image, Moderna Museet, Stockholm
Rock & Rap/C Simulacra, Gavin Brown's enterprise, New York
L'Abécédaire de Deleuze, Galerie Thaddaeus Ropac, Paris
Image Over Image, Kunsthalle Zürich

2010

Sturtevant. The Razzle Dazzle of Thinking, Musée d'Art moderne de la Ville de Paris
Sturtevant: Vertical Monad, Galerie Neu, Berlin
Sturtevant: Elastic Tango, Anthony Reynolds Gallery, London
Sturtevant. Dillinger Running Series, Galerie Thaddaeus Ropac, Paris

2009

Sturtevant. Blow Job, Air de Paris, Paris

2008

Sturtevant: Vertical Monad, Anthony Reynolds Gallery, London
Sturtevant, Le Consortium, Dijon
Spinoza in Las Vegas (Performance), Tate Modern, London

2007

Sturtevant. Raw Power, Galerie Thaddaeus Ropac, Paris
Sturtevant. The Exterior of the Interior, Galerie Mezzanin, Vienna
Before (Plus Ou Moins), Palais du Tokio, Paris

2006

Cold Fear, Anthony Reynolds Gallery, London
Sturtevant. Dillinger Running Series, Site Galerie, Düsseldorf
Digital Click, Art Unlimited, Basel

2005

Sturtevant: The Brutal Truth, MIT List Visual Arts Center, Cambridge, MA
Push and Shove, Perry Rubenstein Gallery, New York

2004

Sturtevant: The Brutal Truth, MMK Museum
für Moderne Kunst, Frankfurt am Main
Perry Rubenstein Gallery, New York

2003

The Dark Threat of Absence/Fragmented and Sliced,
Galerie Thaddaeus Ropac, Paris
Sturtevant, Galerie Mezzanin, Vienna
*Sturtevant. The Sixties. Lichtenstein, Warhol,
Wesselmann, Rosenquist*, Galerie Daniel Blau,
Munich

2002

Sturtevant. Shifting Mental Structures,
Neuer Berliner Kunstverein, Berlin
I love Arlette, Galerie Thaddaeus Ropac, Paris
Sturtevant. Works on paper 1965/66/69,
Galerie Daniel Blau, Munich

2001

Sturtevant. Dillinger Running Series,
Galerie Thaddaeus Ropac, Paris
Ça va aller, Galerie Hans Mayer, Berlin

2000

Copy without Origins: Self as Disappearance,
École Régionale des Beaux-arts de Nantes

1999

Duchamp 1200 Coal Bags et autre pièces,
MAMCO, Geneva
Sturtevant 1225 Objects, Casino Luxembourg,
Forum d'Art Contemporain

1998

Int./Ext. Visibilities, Galerie Thaddaeus Ropac, Paris
Ça va aller, Air de Paris, Paris

1997

Galerie Six Friedrich, Munich

1996

Sturtevant, École Régionale des Beaux-Arts
Le Mans

1995

Powerful Reversals, Galerie Hans Mayer, Düsseldorf

1994

Galerie Thaddaeus Ropac, Paris

1993

STURTEVANT, Villa Arson, Musée d'Art
Contemporain, Nice
Stux Gallery, New York
Galerie Hans Mayer, Düsseldorf
Sturtevant. Arbeiten von 1964 bis 1992, Galerie Six
Friedrich, Munich

1992

STURTEVANT, Württembergischer Kunstverein,
Stuttgart; traveling to: Deichtorhallen, Hamburg

1991

Galerie Thaddaeus Ropac, Paris

1990

Sturtevant, Rhona Hoffman Gallery, Chicago

1989

Sturtevant. Werke aus 25 Jahren, Galerie Paul Maenz,
Cologne
Art Basel 89, Galerie Six Friedrich, Munich

1988

Sturtevant. Drawing 1988−1965, Bess Cutler
Gallery, New York

1987

Daniel Weinberg Gallery, Los Angeles
Sturtevant, Stux Gallery, New York

1986

White Columns, New York

1974

Onnasch Gallery, New York

1973

*Sturtevant. Studies for Warhols' Marilyns, Beuys'
Actions and Objects Duchamps' etc. Including Film*,
Everson Museum of Art, Syracuse, NY

1971

*Sturtevant. Studies done for Beuys' Action Objects
and Drawings*, Reese Palley Gallery, New York

1970

Sturtevant. Huit Tableaux et un Prototype,
Galerie Claude Givaudan, Paris

1969

Sturtevant. Huit Tableaux et un Prototype,
Galerie Claude Givaudan, Paris

1967

The Store of Claes Oldenburg, 623 East,
9th Street, New York
Relâche, School of Visual Arts, New York

1966

America America, Galerie J, Paris

1965

Bianchini Gallery, New York

Diese Publikation erscheint anlässlich der
Ausstellung /
This book is published on occasion of the exhibition

STURTEVANT DOUBLE
DRAWING REVERSAL

MMK Museum für Moderne Kunst Frankfurt am Main
1. November 2014–1. Februar 2015

Albertina Wien
14. Februar 2015–17. Mai 2015

Hamburger Bahnhof – Museum für Gegenwart –
Berlin
30. Mai 2015–23. August 2015

Eine Ausstellungskooperation von /
A Cooperation between MMK Museum für Moderne
Kunst Frankfurt am Main, Albertina Wien und /
and Nationalgalerie, Staatliche Museen zu Berlin

Ausstellungskurator / Exhibition Curator
Mario Kramer

MMK MUSEUM FÜR MODERNE KUNST

Direktorin / Director
Susanne Gaensheimer

Stellvertretender Direktor / Deputy Director
Peter Gorschlüter

Sammlungsleiter / Head of Collections
Mario Kramer

Kurator / Curator
Klaus Görner

Kuratorische Assistenten / Assistant Curators
Sabrina Franz, Anna Goetz, Christian Guth,
Marijana Schneider

Ausstellungsorganisation / Registrar
Bernd Reiß

Direktionsbüro / Director's Office
Christine Gemmer

Marketing und Kommunikation / Communication
Julia Haecker, Bianca Knall

Presse und Öffentlichkeitsarbeit /
Press and Public Relations
Annie Buenker, Daniela Denninger,
Julia Haecker, Christina Henneke

Bildung und Vermittlung /
Education and Interpretation
Janine Burnicki, Johanna Hildebrandt,
Katharina Mantel, Sonja Weidner

Verwaltung / Administration
Alexandra Zok, Melanie Petry

Restaurierung / Conservation
Annette Fritsch, Ulrich Lang, Ingrid Pradler

Depotverwaltung / Collection Maintenance
Uwe Glaser

Technik und Hausverwaltung / Technical Team
Axel Honer, Andreas Janik, Lothar Kant,
Hussein Mobark, Angelo Mule, Giancarlo Rossano,
Detlef Wagner-Walter, Oktay Yildiz

Archiv / Archive
Thomas Schröder

Aufbauteam / Art Handling
Stefan Bressel, Dierk Gessner, Philipp Göbel,
Marc Haub, Hannes Körkel, Mik Lüllwitz, Rahel Seitz,
Charlotte Malcolm-Smith, Markus Winkler

MMK Museum für Moderne Kunst Frankfurt am Main
Domstraße 10
60311 Frankfurt am Main
Germany
Tel +49 (0)69 212 30447

www.mmk-frankfurt.de

MMK MUSEUM FÜR MODERNE KUNST FRANKFURT AM MAIN

ALBERTINA, WIEN

Direktor / Director
Klaus Albecht Schröder

Kuratorinnen / Curators
Antonia Hoerschelmann, Elsy Lahner

Assistenzkuratorin / Curatorial Assistant
Maria-Christina Metzler

Projektkoordination / Project Manager
Susanne Berchtold

Kommunikation / Communication
Verena Dahlitz, Michaela Pachler, Barbara
Prikoszovits

Kunstvermittlung / Education
Ines Gross-Weikhart, Friederike Lassy-Beelitz

Konservatorische Betreuung /
Conservation Supervision
Elisabeth Thobois

Publikationen / Publications
Margarete Heck

www.albertina.at

ALBERTINA

HAMBURGER BAHNHOF – MUSEUM FÜR GEGENWART – BERLIN

Direktor / Director
Udo Kittelmann

Kurator / Curator
Udo Kittelmann

Projektkoordination / Project Manager
Melanie Roumiguière

Kommunikation / Communication
Mechthild Kronenberg, Anneliese Schäfer-Junker

Kunstvermittlung / Education
Daniela Bystron

Konservatorische Betreuung /
Conservation Supervision
Carolin Bohlmann, Johannes Noack

Registrarin / Registrar
Johanna Lemke

Depotverwalter / Storage Administration
Martin Baal, Thomas Seewald

Büroleitung / Office Management
Katherine Israel-Koedel, Janet Röder

www.smb.museum

Nationalgalerie
Staatliche Museen zu Berlin

PUBLICATION

EDITORS

Susanne Gaensheimer, Mario Kramer
(MMK Museum für Moderne Kunst Frankfurt
am Main); Klaus Albrecht Schröder, Antonia
Hoerschelmann (Albertina Wien); Udo Kittelmann
(Nationalgalerie, Staatliche Museen zu Berlin)

Editorial Coordination
Janine Burnicki, Sabrina Franz, Klaus Görner,
Mario Kramer, Helga Ostermeier

Translations
Judith Rosenthal, Ralf Schauff

Proofreading
Karin Prätorius

Design
Nicolas Eigenheer & Vera Kaspar

Typefaces
Theinhardt, Material (www.optimo.ch)

Photo Credits
Axel Schneider

Color Separation & Print
Musumeci S.p.A., Quart (Aosta)

© 2014, MMK Museum für Moderne Kunst Frankfurt
am Main, Albertina Wien, Staatliche Museen zu
Berlin – Preußischer Kulturbesitz, the authors,
the artist, the photographers, and JRP|Ringier
Kunstverlag AG

Printed in Europe

PUBLISHED BY

JRP|Ringier
Limmatstrasse 270
CH–8005 Zurich
T +41 (0) 43 311 27 50
F +41 (0) 43 311 27 51
E info@jrp-ringier.com
www.jrp-ringier.com

ISBN 978–3–03764–396–9

JRP|Ringier books are available internationally
at selected bookstores and from the following
distribution partners:

Switzerland
AVA Verlagsauslieferung AG,
verlagsservice@ava.ch,
www.ava.ch

France
Les presses du réel,
info@lespressesdureel.com
www.lespressesdureel.com

Germany and Austria
Vice Versa Distribution GmbH,
info@vice-versa-distribution.com
www.vice-versa-distribution.com

UK and other European countries
Cornerhouse Publications,
publications@cornerhouse.org,
www.cornerhouse.org/books

USA, Canada, Asia, and Australia
ARTBOOK|D.A.P.,
orders@dapinc.com,
www.artbook.com